The Wasted Years

American Youth, Race, and the Literacy Gap

James McCabe

A SCARECROWEDUCATION BOOK

The Scarecrow Press, Inc.
Lanham, Maryland, and Oxford
2003

A SCARECROWEDUCATION BOOK

Published in the United States of America
by Scarecrow Press, Inc.
A Member of the Rowman & Littlefield Publishing Group
4501 Forbes Boulevard, Suite 200, Lanham, Maryland 20706
www.scarecroweducation.com

PO Box 317
Oxford
OX2 9RU, UK

British Library Cataloguing in Publication Information Available

Library of Congress Cataloging-in-Publication Data
McCabe, James, 1948–
   The wasted years : American youth, race, and the literacy gap / James
McCabe
      p. cm.
   "A ScarecrowEducation Book."
   Includes bibliographical references (p.   ) and index.
   ISBN 0-8108-4714-0 (pbk. : alk. paper)
   1. Literacy—Government policy—United States. 2. Reading
(Secondary)—United States. 3. Minorities—Education (Secondary)—
United States. I. Title.
LC151.M274 2003
379.2'4'0973—dc21   2002154852

∞™ The paper used in this publication meets the minimum requirements of
American National Standard for Information Sciences—Permanence of
Paper for Printed Library Materials, ANSI/NISO Z39.48-1992.
Manufactured in the United States of America.

Contents

Part 2: What Are Best Practices in Literacy?

Part 3: Obstacles to Better Literacy Practices

Part 4: The Response of Clinton, Bush, and Congress

Preface

Many students in the classrooms where I worked made painful sacrifices to attend college. They were not dropped off at residence halls by their parents in minivans or Volvo station wagons piled high with their possessions at the beginning of the school year. They were not seventeen or eighteen; the median age in this community college in New York City is twenty-three. Many worked full-time during the day and used the evening classes in the City University of New York as a way to sample higher education. Some came determined to stay, but others were cautious. The American-born students were especially cautious. Even though this school was at the bottom rung of the ladder of American higher education, many of them hesitated. They were not sure college was a place where they belonged. The immigrants from China, Colombia, or Poland were tougher minded and determined to take advantage of a system where tuition for a course was in the hundreds, not thousands, of dollars.

The students in the classrooms where I worked for many years did not fare as well as the offspring from the Volvo station wagons. The dropout rates in the open admission community colleges of New York City remain enormous. Part of the failure can be attributed to a lack of preparation—a lack of mechanical skills in writing and computing—but another part is attitudinal. Too many students did not feel that their intellectual lives mattered or that they could have intellectual lives. They did not have a vision of themselves as readers or writers. Some remained at the edge of classes, reluctant to become involved.

This book is a response to the waste I saw for almost twenty years, first as a reading teacher and then as a writing teacher at LaGuardia Community

College in New York City. So many American students arrived unprepared for an environment where actually writing essays rather than filling in short answers or multiple-choice tests was the measure of success. They were not only unprepared but not sure about throwing themselves into the struggle for their own skills. It was hard so see so many talented American teenagers and young adults hold back—not giving this new school, this new level of education, their best. That experience has brought me to this book. I want to learn more about what in their earlier school backgrounds is contributing to this hesitancy, reserve, fear, and unwillingness to throw themselves whole-heartedly into print, into books, into reading the daily newspaper, into all the pleasures of an intellectual life.

Part of the reason for this book is to explore the factors in the backgrounds of American teenagers and young adults that make higher education such an unfriendly place for some young adults but a rather friendly place for others. The teenagers I came to know over many years of teaching were African American and Latino from Queens, Brooklyn, and Manhattan in New York City. They did not trust the school system. Many did not like print. Many did not have favorite writers. Most did not read the daily newspaper. In a writing class when I assigned a three-hundred-page biography of Thurgood Marshall that they had to read to complete the writing assignments, they told me it was the longest book they had ever been assigned. Some said they had never had a high school assignment to read a biography. But they liked reading about Thurgood Marshall. The biography of his life got nothing but good reviews. The immigrant students said it opened their eyes to the history of race relations in this country. For at least one African American student, this biography was the reason she stayed with the class. In the fall semester, when the readings were about education and the class was so packed with thirty-five students that there was no place to sit down, she had dropped my class. In the winter minisemester, when Thurgood Marshall was the first text and the class was much smaller, she stuck with the English composition course that I was teaching.

Investigating the quality of the reading assignments that school systems and teachers provide teenagers is a major part of this book. I contend that school systems that overlook the quality of what is being assigned influence teenagers in some extremely negative, unintended ways. Can a student who spent seven years of secondary schools—grades 6 through 12—laboring through dry textbooks that a commentator in chapter 8 calls "an overcrowded flea market of disconnected facts" be expected to suddenly become an avid reader in college? One major goal of this book is to challenge a major organizing principle of modern secondary schools, which is that all content in each subject area can be efficiently delivered through a single textbook. I will supply examples of schools where developing the habit of reading is a core function that is not dependent on a textbook.

In this search for information about reading assignments, I have spared the reader a rehash of the battles over the canon—the books on college reading lists—so common during the 1980s. Instead, I investigated what we assign and how much we assign. The debate in higher education was about which books belonged on English department reading lists; we now need a new national debate about how much reading to assign in secondary schools. Should trade books from best-seller lists and biographies and autobiographies, historical novels, and technical manuals for hands-on science become regular reading assignments in secondary schools, or is one textbook for the entire year going to continue as the main reading assignment in each subject area, as if all subject areas are the same? When will the canon in high schools and junior high schools move past one history book in social studies and one anthology in English class? Research tells us that the volume of reading accomplished matters and that practice, practice, and practice build fluency in reading, but this idea has been slow to arrive in classrooms. I am especially worried about what is assigned in social studies, which, if done right, could provide half of the opportunities to develop fluent reading and writing skills in high school.

When I taught social studies as a freshly minted teacher in the Cleveland Public Schools, evaluations were centered on one's ability to lead discussions. If you could engage your students in Socratic dialogues, lead them to conclusions, and keep them awake, you were successful. Creating an engaging Socratic dialogue around a theme five or six times a day in forty-five-minute blocks is a skill, and teachers who could engage students period after period deserve admiration, but what are students gaining from their participation? How does participating in debates and discussions make students better readers and writers? But an ability to develop fluent readers and writers was not required of history teachers in the early 1970s.

Are expectations for teachers different today? Interviews with teachers throughout the first nine chapters will help answer this question.

Teaching in Cleveland also showed me how little interest many public schools have in the actual books they hand out to teenagers. At John Hay High School on the east side of Cleveland, you could use any text you wanted as long as it was already in the book room. Ordering additional books was never discussed; it was not an option. Administrators at headquarters downtown had selected the book for the black history course I was teaching to seniors. *From Slavery to Freedom* by John Hope Franklin is a fine text, but it is written for college students, not high school students. More accessible books by Richard Wright and Julius Lester were not available.

A year in the Cleveland Public Schools showed me that many high school history teachers are powerless and that not much was expected in terms of the heavy work of developing the literacy of teenagers. Tests were short-answer or fill-in-the-blank; the weekly or biweekly essay at the heart of an effective writing program was not part of the job. Both of these ideas—the authority of teachers and what the school systems expect from them in terms of developing literacy of teenagers—remain core interests of mine, and I wonder whether school reform is giving teachers new freedom and new authority to obtain much needed resources of materials and time.

These are the topics of this book: how to engage teenagers in reading, how to increase the volume of reading, and the many institutional barriers to these changes. In the introduction, I talk more about the organization of the topics. But before I move on to the structure of the book, I would like to thank my colleagues in the City University of New York system who read earlier drafts of either this book or the articles that led up to it: Ernie Nieratka and Mary Fjeldstad of LaGuardia; John Garvey of City University headquarters on 80th Street; and Kenneth Peeples, the editor of the journal *Community Review,* who gave me great encouragement by publishing my articles on literacy. Alan Breznick, formerly of the *Prospect Press,* a neighborhood paper in Brooklyn that ran story after story on local politics and education, pushed me to write about the high schools in Brooklyn and to meet the paper's deadlines. I also appreciate the detailed criticism offered by Amy Herrick, a novelist and educator, at the beginning of the project, and by Cindy Skrzycki of the *Washington Post,* whose criticism and technical advice at the end of the project helped in a number of areas.

I gratefully acknowledge permission to use quotations from the following sources:

"Unwarranted Intrusion," by Richard F. Elmore, *Education Next* (Spring 2002). An excerpt from this article is reprinted by the permission of the author and *Education Next*.

"Doing the Decades," edited by James Brewbaker, a reading list from *The Assembly on Literature for Adolescents of the National Council of Teachers of English (ALAN)* 26, no. 3 (Spring 1999). Permission to reprint was granted by the National Council of Teachers of English.

"Afro-American and Latino Teenagers in New York City: Race and Language Development," by Jim McCabe, *Community Review* 14 (1996). Permission to reprint was granted by Transaction Publishers.

"Project Read," by Jim McCabe, *The Hill Rag* (Washington, D.C.), May 1983. Permission to reprint was granted by the Hill Rag.

"Summer Reading for St. Albans Upper School, Washington, D.C." Permission to reprint was granted by St. Albans.

I would like to thank Tom Koerner, editorial director of the Scarecrow Press, who encouraged me to move beyond New York City and examine how secondary schools deliver literacy elsewhere in the country. I am grateful also to the help of Cindy Tursman, Amos Guinan, Kellie Hagan, and Laura Larson for their work in the acquisition, editing, and production of this book.

Finally, I am grateful to my three daughters—Kate, Maggie, and Julie—for their patience with a project that lasted more than a few soccer, cross-country, and basketball seasons. And thanks to my wife, Joan Griffin McCabe. I learned a lot about New York City politics by working on both of her campaigns—both successful—for the New York City Council in 1991 and 1993. I learned even more about the politics of education as she worked to interest her colleagues on the City Council and other elected officials in New York City in literacy issues. Most of all, I have been blessed by her love, encouragement, and support for over twenty years.

Introduction

As President George W. Bush and Congress are about to embark on their journey to improve American classrooms, parents may ask what is in the toolbox of our politicians. Do the new president and the newly elected Congress have the tools needed to repair broken classrooms? And since President Bush has announced a special interest in ending the gap in reading skills between the races, parents might also want to know how his plan will close this gap that he mentioned so often during his campaign.

"It is a scandal of the first order when the average test scores of African American and Latino students at age seventeen are roughly the same as white thirteen-year-olds," said President Bush. "More and more, we are divided into two nations, separate and unequal. One that reads and one that can't. One that dreams and one that doesn't." I agree with him. This gap is an outrage. Even after years of local, federal, and state attempts to intervene, black and Latino teenagers lag far behind white teenagers.

According to a federal report in 1990, there was a four-year gap in the reading skills of American teenagers: "By grade 12, the average performance of Black and Hispanic students only reaches the level of eighth-grade white students."[1] In the most recent report on the reading skills of twelfth graders released in 1998, the gap was still four years.[2]

In other words, white thirteen-year-olds and black and Latino seventeen-year-olds have the same reading skills. Some years, the federal government actually has the courage to spell this out. It uses phrases such as "For example, the average proficiency of Black and Hispanic 17-year olds is only slightly higher than that of white 13-year olds."[3] In other years, the national assessments do not articulate the question of race. You have to read the tables to see the disparities.

We also know that high school—a period when many suburban teenagers hone their skills to compete for admission to selective colleges—does not improve the reading skills of African American and Latino teenagers relative to whites and Asians. High school doesn't matter, the federal government found. If a reading gap existed before high school, high school is not able to reduce this gap, as research from the federal government shows. "At the end of the twelfth grade, blacks are about three to four years of achievement growth behind whites, and Hispanics are about two to three years behind whites. Among students with the same eighth-grade achievement, however, the twelfth grade/ethnicity differences after four years of high school are a half a year or less and are statistically insignificant."[4] (See table A.1 in the appendix for a look at the reading scores of seventeen-year-olds from 1971 to the most recent assessment in 1998.)

Obviously, this gap in skills between the races is unacceptable. I want to examine the origins of this gap and how classroom practices and how national practices in education perpetuate it. I have three main goals in this book:

- To look at the reading and writing assignments given teenagers in city classrooms occupied by African American and Latino teenagers, and to see how the reading assignments they experienced may have shaped their attitudes toward print.
- To investigate whether the authority of teachers, especially their ability to order books, has improved during this age of school reform. As parents, we all want teachers with "high expectations" for reading and writing. As a society, are we supporting teachers with the high level of resources needed for teachers in classrooms with high expectations?
- Finally, I want to test the assumption in the current No Child Left Behind legislation passed by the 107th Congress that we can rely on state education departments to identify and then intervene in weak local schools. As the reader will see in the first six chapters, state intervention is not new. New York has been intervening in weak schools for over twenty years. As a nation, we need to see whether we can trust state agencies to reform failing local schools since this is what Congress has sent us in the name of school reform.

The first parts of this book look at classroom literacy practices — some that work and some that don't. Here the reader will see teachers, administrators, and students talking about the books that they have been assigned to read in high schools and the response of students to these books. The final sections look at the politics of how we as a nation arrived in such a condition, with such a literacy gap. Here I consider whether state interventions in weak schools have improved achievement in these weak schools, the barriers parents face who seek to compete in the politics of education, and how the way we as a nation treat teachers may still limit the opportunities for literacy in some classrooms. Finally, I look at No Child Left Behind and what improvements in classroom practices we may expect from this law.

It seems surprising that high school years cannot do more. In many urban systems, the troublemakers have dropped out by the end of ninth grade; those who attend city high schools after ninth grade are often ready to learn. What is it in the current literacy practices in our high schools that does not encourage reading and develop the intellectual lives in city teenagers?

This description of the literacy practices in secondary schools is much needed. Both states and the federal government have neglected secondary schools in the last decade. States have piled on new graduation requirements, but have they offered new resources to classroom teachers? The federal government is best known for its efforts in Title I compensatory education — a program that has always targeted its programs at elementary schools rather than secondary schools. And new federal initiatives have followed this pattern.

Much of the recent federal effort in education has been aimed at improving achievement in elementary schools through reduction in class size. In his State of the Union address in 1997, President Bill Clinton urged Congress to fund a classroom size reduction (CSR) program, and Congress agreed. The hope was that smaller class size in kindergarten through third grade would lead to major improvement in achievement, as it did in earlier pilot studies in Tennessee known in the literature as STAR, or student–teacher achievement ratio. What exactly was STAR, a program so influential that both the federal government and large states such as California have invested billions in efforts to replicate its successes?

With its smaller class size, STAR had some benefits, but those benefits did not come close to closing the achievement gap between the races that currently exists. "All students significantly benefited from participation in small classes, but the greatest advantages were found for minority, inner-city students from low SES [socioeconomic status] backgrounds."[5]

Unfortunately, the STAR results in Tennessee do not inspire much confidence that class size reduction in K–3 will be enough to close the gap in achievement between the races. As table A.2 in the appendix shows, changes in class size in K–3 did lead to real improvements later in secondary schools, but the changes do not look like they are of a magnitude that will close the achievement gap in the United States.

The many studies of STAR also mention improvement in grades, attendance rates, higher matriculation rates in college, and other positive results. Links to these STAR studies and other studies of class size are widely available on the web.

All of the studies of the STAR programs are all quantitative; the voices of the students, teachers, and administrators are absent. The researchers present only numbers. There is no information about the quality and quantity of the books teachers assigned, the number of reading and writing assignments, and other data closely tied to literacy in teenagers. My goal is to try to grab these details, to try to learn why the current practices of reading and writing assignments, and of developing literacy in general, are not working as well as Americans would like.

By comparing reading assignments in private schools, where money is not a constraint, with the offerings of public schools, parents may be able to see alternatives to the status quo in public school systems. (An example of an annotated reading list from a private school is in appendix C.)

An additional goal is to test the basic premise of American education: Planners in state education agencies know what local schools need and state intervention is enough to improve weak local schools. The recent education reform bill passed by Congress and signed by President Bush has further reinforced the power of planners at the state level. Now local schools that do not meet new federal standards will face even more scrutiny and intervention from state education officials. As a nation, we are about to take a huge gamble that state intervention works, that state officials can identify weak schools and then push these weak schools to better performance.

What is the history of state interventions in local schools? Did the students in these schools become much more literate by the time of graduation? Many state education agencies now have had the authority over the last two decades to take over weak local schools, fire local teachers, and reconstitute and reconstruct these failing schools. Are their efforts working? Are the terms that state education officials use such as *reconstituted schools, reconstructed schools,* and *schools under registration review* real terms to be trusted by parents? Congress and the president now trust that state sanctions are enough to reform weak local schools, but we don't know much about the successes and failures of state reform efforts in the past. Have state planners in Albany, Annapolis, Sacramento, and other state capitals been able to provide the tools teachers need to develop the literacy of teenagers?

I have included case studies of how state standards have influenced literacy in three states: New York, Maryland, and California. In both New York and Maryland, state intervention in failing schools has been the law for fifteen to twenty years depending on the state. Reports have been written. The results are in. In California, the current round of state intervention is only two years old; results are preliminary, but at least the models of reform offered by the state education agency in Sacramento can be analyzed.

The methodology here is qualitative: interviews and observations. The interview guides in the appendix show the questions asked of students, teachers, and administrators who work in both public and private schools. Interviews with teachers were taped and transcribed; notes were taken during interviews with students. Observations included planned visits to a high school social studies classroom over a period of three months and daily unannounced visits to junior high schools over a period of a year and a half as part of a technology job with the New York City Board of Education. My questions in the interviews concern the quality and the quantity of reading accomplished during the school year and to some extent teenagers' attitudes toward reading.

In the next chapter, the story begins. In one school, teachers require that students buy additional books, and the PTA is rich enough to supply each classroom with its own video camera and an extensive set of reading materials. In the second school, many miles away but in the same school district, resources are different, and reading opportunities are different. Was a new leader in the district, called a "schools chancellor" in New York City, able to bring reading opportunities to the second school? Was the intervention process in this state potent enough to intervene successfully in the second school?

NOTES

1. The National Assessment of Educational Progress, *Learning to Read in Our Nation's Schools: Instruction and Achievement in 1988 at Grades 4, 8, and 12* (Washington, D.C.: U.S. Department of Education, 1990), 14.

2. National Center for Educational Statistics, *NAEP 1994 Trends in Academic Progress* (Washington, D.C.: U.S. Department of Education, 1996), 111. Also see National Center for Educational Statistics, *NAEP 1992: Reading Report Card for the Nation and the States* (Washington, D.C.: U.S. Department of Education, 1993), 101, and National Center for Educational Statistics, *NAEP 1998: Reading Report Card for the Nation and the States* (Washington, D.C.: U.S. Department of Education, 1999), 44 and 45.

3. National Educational Assessment of Educational Progress, *The Reading Report Card: Progress toward Excellence in Our Schools: Trends in Reading over Four National Assessments, 1971–1984*, ETS Report, 15-R-01(Washington, D.C.: U.S. Department of Education, 1985).

4. John Ralph and James Crouse, *Reading and Mathematics Achievement: Growth in High School, Issue Brief* (Washington, D.C.: National Center for Education Statistics, 1997) (ERIC ED-415-275).

5. Helen Pate-Bain et al., *The Student/Teacher Achievement Ratio (STAR) Project, STAR Follow-up Studies, 1996–1997* (Lebanon, Tenn.: Health and Education Research Operative Services, September 1997). Accessed in 1999 at www.heros-inc. org/newstar.pdf, but no longer available online.

Chapter One

Photocopied Worksheets, Withheld Textbooks, Wealthy PTAs, and Classroom Libraries

Each of the three states in these case histories of literacy practices and school reform provides some new information. New York began its school reforms early. By 1981, a process was in place to identify and intervene in weak schools. Did school intervention in New York succeed and create schools where teenagers become fluent readers and writers?

Maryland's largest school district, Montgomery County, starting focusing on the achievement gap only in the late 1990s. These efforts may be of national importance. If they succeed, other suburban districts with more and more African American and Latino students can examine the policies in place in this county and at least have a starting place for their own changes.

The educational difficulties in California are well known. Over the past two decades, California has dropped to the bottom in national ranking of educational achievement. Will the new policies from the state capitol in Sacramento improve literacy in local schools? These issues comprise the content of the next seven chapters.

New York is a good place to look at how a state has attempted to reform its schools. The state has been a laboratory for three of President Bush's core proposals: regular testing, sanctions, and an emphasis on literacy.

- For over twenty years in New York, the state education department has used sanctions to force weak schools to file school improvement plans and then improve or close the school's doors and go out of business. Since this sanction of actually closing a school has occurred a few times, it is far more severe than what President Bush has proposed: merely ending federal funding in weak schools. What has been the result of this severe sanctions program?

- New York also began a new more rigorous state curriculum called the "Action Plan" in the mid-1980s to force more years of math and English on all students.
- For over twenty years, New York, like many other states, has used achievement tests to identify weak students and funnel them into remedial programs for special help.
- Finally, in the second half of the 1990s, the largest city in New York hired a new leader who made literacy the central project of his administration.

How did this mix of state sanctions, state curricula, state achievement tests, and a local emphasis on literacy play out? Did this experiment in New York City as a schools chancellor tried to implement a literacy centered curriculum lead to a set of "best practices" that President Bush can use in all of the nation's schools? We will see in the next six chapters.

BACKGROUND

As a supervisor in Project Smart, the rollout of four computers to every junior high classroom in New York City, I visited approximately two hundred junior high schools and middle schools during the 1998–1999 and 1999–2000 school years in all five boroughs. This chapter is based on informal interviews and observations conducted during those visits. Chapters 2 through 6 were based on formal interviews using detailed interview guides available in the appendix, which also were used to satisfy requirements for courses in a Ph.D. program in political science at the City University of New York Graduate Center.

Project Smart is itself an interesting story. Deliveries of classroom computers began during the 1997 reelection campaign of Mayor Rudolph Giuliani, and a number of teachers and administrators were not enthusiastic about the configuration of four computers in each class. While this arrangement made computers highly visible, many felt that the money would have been better spent on providing entire labs of computers to schools so that each child would work simultaneously on the same project. Some administrators felt that teachers would have difficulty assisting four students at computers while also teaching the rest of the class. Others felt that even six or eight computers in a class would not be enough for extensive hands-on practice with software applications and that with computer prices plummeting, the goal should have been to provide each student with a computer for home use, as the Edison Project is doing.

A TALE OF TWO SCHOOLS

Project Smart provided me with access to the full range of middle school classrooms in New York City. A few were the new parent-designed minischools. These were very small, with one hundred to three hundred students, and typically occupied a floor or two on the top of an elementary school. While their names often reflected a theme, the major differences were size and climate. When you walked the halls and entered the classrooms, you saw teenagers working with each other and with adults productively, not chasing each other or disrupting a teacher's attempts at instruction. This is how one of these small schools describes itself:

> The Clinton School for Writers and Artists is a District Two Middle School located in the Chelsea section of Manhattan. The school is small with a total of 210 students allowing everyone in the school community to know one another and to work together. We are also a small school physically. Clinton is housed on the fifth floor and part of the fourth floor of PS 11. This small environment is perfect for a child-centered education, tailored to the emerging adolescent student. Clinton's student population is diverse and reflects New York City's ethnic and social mix. Clinton is not a professional art school, but, rather, uses art and writing as a way of thinking, learning, and creating.[1]

Another small school known for order rather than the disorder so common in New York City's junior high schools is the East Side Middle School. Its principal's statement stresses the rigor of the curriculum:

> East Side Middle School is dedicated to serving those students who seek an atmosphere offering academic rigor through intensified instruction in literary, fine and theatre arts, as well as in science and mathematics. We are recognized

by City College and New York State Department of Education as a Professional Development School for science, mathematics, and technology. We recognize each student's individual mode of learning and believe that early adolescents learn best in a child-centered environment that builds self-esteem through accomplishments, and encourages individuals to explore new ideas, while developing new skills, interests, and abilities. Our dedicated staff of middle school specialists has created an exciting, differentiated, interdisciplinary curriculum, which goes far beyond the New York City and State curricula, and provides for both independent and collaborative group work. Problem solving and higher level thinking skills are its cornerstones.[2]

In this case, phrases such as "rigor" and "child centered" were accurate.

Located in the East Side Middle School on the Upper East Side in New York City, this classroom had bookshelves everywhere. They lined the walls, and they protruded in the open space of the room. They contained not only the official Prentice Hall textbook for eighth-grade social studies in New York City but also copies of *Night* by Elie Wiesel, *The Jungle* by Upton Sinclair, *Hiroshima* by John Hersey, *A Day of Pleasure: Stories of a Boy Growing Up in Warsaw* by Isaac Bashevis Singer, *The Great Gatsby* by F. Scott Fitzgerald, and *Animal Farm* by George Orwell.

"The books supplement the content," the teacher said. "We require kids to purchase some books, and we get help from the PTA and we use some of our own resources." In his humanities class, he said he would plug a book like *The Great Gatsby* into the social changes of the 1920s. "The novel gives the kids a way to see what was going on in the 1920s."

His classroom had other materials. The shelves had copies of several scholarly texts on American history, and each classroom I visited in his school also had a video camera setup.

This school obeyed the official state curriculum; it had a textbook needed to "cover" the New York state curriculum for eighth grade social studies—the United States since 1985—but it also had made fundamental changes:

- Resources were available. Located on the Upper East Side, New York's wealthiest area, the PTA gave East Side Middle School the resources needed to buy the class sets of novels and biographies for social studies, which the school called "humanities." As policy, the school demanded that students purchase additional books.

- The school decided that reading exciting books was at the heart of the curriculum.
- Teachers' schedules had been changed. By combining history and English into a single humanities class, this school allowed teachers to work with 75 or 80 students rather than the traditional schedule of five classes of 35 students each, or a total of 175 students, which still exists in many state secondary schools. This schedule helps avoid the common teenager complaint: "No one knows my name in school." Being one of 80 rather than one of 175 leads to more personal attention and to more writing assignments and more feedback on these assignments.
- The school was small. With 205 students, it felt much different than the usual New York City junior high school of up to 1,800 teenagers in a single building, where assistant principals patrol the halls with their walkie-talkies warning each other of disruptive students on the loose.

Unfortunately, this school is something of an anomaly in a city where junior high schools are still in crisis. In a year and a half of visiting New York City junior high schools, I saw few like it. Some of the new, much smaller junior high schools located on the top floors of old elementary schools in Manhattan have a similar feel: Teachers and teenagers are working together cooperatively, but few had the same number of books and the same emphasis on reading.

The second school visited that day was more typical. It was large, and the assistant principals roamed the halls trying to push the cutters back to class, but Middle School 27 in District 18 was far from the worst school on Staten Island. There were no students in the main office crying after being beaten by classmates—a frequent sight at a neighboring school. This school just was not paying much attention to what its teenagers were reading.

In this junior high school in a middle-class neighborhood near the Staten Island Zoo, the teacher said she did not have enough copies of the new eighth grade American history text to go around, so she made photocopies of pages from another history book for homework and used the old book in class. Did you select the books, I asked her. "No, I just started; the previous teacher left them." Her classroom had about twenty copies of the new Prentice Hall text, *The American Nation,* and more copies of the older history text. There was not a single biography or novel in the classroom.

In these two classrooms in New York City—one in Manhattan's East Side and one on Staten Island—state reforms of the last twenty years had not provided universal access to good books for teenagers to read. At least in these two classrooms, the state has not been able to provide books to all students. It looks like some children still take home photocopies; others take home six or eight different books to read each year.

DOES ATTENDANCE WARRANT A TEXT?

The situation in the high schools of New York City also varied from school to school.

As figure 1.1 shows, withholding books was an official policy in some schools at the end of the 1990s—in a city flush with tax revenue from the boom on Wall Street. In Aviation High School in Long Island City in Queens, the social studies chair exhorted her faculty not to waste books on students with attendance problems. Some might argue that weak students on the verge of dropping out should receive special attention, rather than be denied books.

Based on the sample of over two hundred secondary schools I visited in New York City, there does not seem to be one set of literacy practices but rather three distinct sets of practices: abundant books, as in the case of the East Side middle school; just the textbook in some classrooms, as in the case of the middle school in Staten Island; and no textbooks at all if students have poor attendance records, the policy in the Queens high school classroom.

As indicated, New York City had literacy practices that varied from school to school depending on leadership and the wealth of the local community. Obviously, the parent associations in the Upper East Side in Manhattan and Brownstone Brooklyn are far more capable of supplementing the budgets of local schools than in Tremont in the Bronx and East New York in Brooklyn.

Could this situation be changed at the local level? Could a new leader emerge to bring consistent practices designed at developing literacy to all classrooms? Could a strong leader insist that all classrooms in all schools develop the literacy of the city's children?

It was during this period in the late 1990s that a new chancellor, New York City's name for its superintendent of schools, arrived and soon decided

AVIATION HIGH SCHOOL   EILEEN TAYLOR, PRINCIPAL

TO: ALL TEACHERS OF SOCIAL STUDIES

FROM: C.J. GOMEZ, ASSISTANT PRINCIPAL

DATE: WEEK OF MARCH 2, 1998

RE: WEEKLY CONCERNS

Thank you for the.usual splendid job you did while I was
gone. Your warm and sincere good wishes for my mother are deeply appreciated.

1. FACULTY CONFERENCE IS DEPARTMENT CONFERENCE - TODAY SCHEDULE
    DISTRIBUTED

2. BOOKS -
    A. ALL TRANSFERRING STUDENTS - BOOKS WILL BE COLLECTED AND
    DISTRIBUTED THROUGH THE OFFICE. INSTRUCT TRANSFERRING
    STUDENTS TO REPORT TO THE OFFICE SO WE MAY ISSUE OR
    TRANSFER BOOK RECEIPTS.
    B.   STUDENTS WHO HAVE CLEARED THEIR BOOK ACCOUNT OR HAVE
    RETURNED FROM A LONG ABSENCE - TEACHERS ARE TO VERIFY, IN
    WRITING, THAT THE STUDENT'S RECORD IS CLEAR AND ATTENDANCE
    WARRANTS A TEXT.
    BOOK DISTRIBUTION HOURS - ONLY DURING STUDENT'S LUNCH
    PERIOD.

3. REVIEW BOOKS - S.O. STORE ONLY BRIEF - GLOBAL - $6
    KEYS - U.S.   -

4. TUTORING - IF A STUDENT REQUIRES REMEDIATION FOR
    REGENTS/RCT OR SOCIAL STUDIES FAILURES - INSTRUCT STUDENTS TO
    REPORT TO 296 ON THEIR LUNCH PERIOD.

5. MARCH IS WOMEN'S HISTORY MONTH
    Please incorporate incorporate relevant into your classes.

6. MARKING PERIOD ENDS - THURSDAY, MARCH 12. GRADES DUE - MONDAY,
    MARCH 16.

7. ABSENCE MATERIALS - WERE DUE.
    SEATING CHARTS DUE BY WEDNESDAY - MARCH 4.

S. MOCK TRIAL COMPETITION - CONGRATULATIONS TO MR. SIAS AND HSLW ON
    THE FIRST ROUND VICTORY - 2ND ROUND-THURSDAY,
    MARCH 5. GOOD LUCK!

SOCIAL: OUR BEST WISHES TO MARIA AND MIKE ON THE UPCOMING
ARRIVAL OF THEIR NEW TAX DEDUCTION. WE ARE ALL THRILLED
FOR THEM.

IA. you have any questions or problems please advise.

Figure 1.1.   Aviation High School sample, "Weekly Concerns."
Source: Aviation High School, New York City Board of Education.

that literacy was to be a central focus of his administration. What were his plans, and how did they connect with the existing literacy practices in the city's schools?

NOTES

1. New York City Public Schools, *2000–2001 Annual School Report: Clinton School for Writers and Artists, M.S. 260, Grade Levels 6 through 8, District 2*; available at www.nycenet.edu/daa/01asr/102260.pdf.

2. New York City Public Schools, *2000–2001 Annual School Report: East Side Middle School, M.S. 114, Grade Levels 6 through 8, District 2*; available at www.nycenet.edu/daa/01asr/102114.pdf.

Chapter Two

Chancellor Rudy Crew and a New Literacy Initiative

In the late 1990s, a new leader in New York City brought with him a new program to emphasize literacy. Schools Chancellor Rudolph Crew realized that increasing the volume of reading done by youngsters was a critical need and introduced a program called "New Standards" in 1997.

There is much of value in this attempt to emphasize reading. It is modern. It views reading as a skill that is learned through life-long practice, not a set of activities to be mastered by the end of third grade. It provides an emphasis on the volume of reading. In New Standards, as youngsters read, they write down information about their books and keep it in folders. By looking at these log sheets, teachers measure the amount of reading they have accomplished.

Chancellor Crew made the importance of this curriculum clear:

> I expect the New Standards to be used by everyone involved in teaching and learning in our school system. At the school level, teachers and administrators should use the standards to set goals, plan for effective instruction, and monitor and assess student performance. Districts and superintendencies should use the standards in all curricular initiatives and as one way of planning professional development activities.[1]

The standards for reading are made clear: Twenty-five books a year was the goal for each elementary and middle school student. Implementation in the high schools would come later.

> We have worked to make the expectations included in the performance standards as clear as possible. . . . For example, the reading standard includes

9

expectations for students to read widely and to read quality materials. And, instead of simply exhorting them to do this, we have given more explicit direction by specifying that students should be expected to read at least twenty-five books each year and that those books should be of the quality and complexity illustrated in the sample reading list provided for each grade level.[2]

Four years later, New Standards could be evaluated. According to the *New York Times,* results on city and state tests showed "little improvement" from Crew's arrival in 1995 to the fall of 1999, when his relationship with Mayor Giuliani began to sour.[3] Chancellor Crew was not rehired after a contract dispute with the Board of Education and a policy dispute with the mayor over school vouchers.

In an era when few school leaders even attempt to introduce a new emphasis on literacy to secondary schools, Chancellor Crew deserves some recognition for his efforts, however incomplete. In retrospect, he faced a number of obstacles in introducing an emphasis on literacy, and he did not confront them successfully in the fairly brief window when he enjoyed the support of both Mayor Giuliani and the public.

Obviously, Chancellor Crew inherited a school system that had not been encouraging literacy in its secondary schools. As chancellor, he did not challenge many of the literacy practices that had been damaging the intellectual lives of teenagers in the city's high schools. As interviews with administrators in the next two chapters show, the practice of withholding books from teenagers was not limited to the one high school in Queens mentioned in the previous chapter. Rather, book shortages were widespread, and this led to teachers and administrators hoarding scarce resources so that books would not be lost on trips home with students; these scarce resources would remain in classes. Chancellor Crew did not confront this fundamental literacy practice—the withholding of books—that seems to be shaping the classroom experiences of a significant number of students in New York City. He did not begin his administration by demanding new spending on books from the Board of Education or from the Office of Management and Budget, the mayoral agency that shapes spending on schools from behind the scenes. In fact, New York City began supplementing the New York State Textbook aid (then $36 per student per year) only in 1997, a mayoral election year. After all the literacy efforts of Chancellor Crew, total expenditure for all books was only $58 per high school student in the middle of the Crew administration;[4] this amount is a fraction of what was available for books in the city's private schools during the same time period.

Chancellor Crew also did not confront the state social studies curriculum with its rigid insistence on global history in ninth and tenth grade, American history in eleventh grade, and so forth. These state mandates force classroom teachers to cover topic after topic in six-hundred-page textbooks to prepare students for state exit exams, rather than read a series of biographies, autobiographies, and historical fiction, as private schools do. The problem with using one textbook as the only source of reading is that this strategy does not provide enough practice in reading.

According to a federal study, "the instructional strategy" of the single textbook leads to few pages of reading being completed each night for homework.[5] But increasing the volume of reading is not part of the state curriculum; preparing students for state exit exams is the heart of the curriculum. In many states today, students who do not pass multiple-choice exit exams do not receive high school diplomas. While social studies could provide a major path to literacy to secondary schools, this opportunity was missed during the Crew years in the late 1990s in New York City. The state official curriculum that states that ninth grade is the time for global history and eleventh grade is the time for American history was not challenged. After years of reading a single textbook containing literally hundreds of thinly explained topics, students then take exit exams on these topics.[6]

In his career in New York City, Chancellor Crew chose to stay with the one course, one textbook approach to literacy in the secondary schools. His New Standards program with its goal of twenty-five books was introduced as an extra program. It did not replace the state mandates to "cover" subjects such as American history in seventh grade or global history in ninth grade. The twenty-five books that children were required to choose were their individual selections, which could be completely unrelated to the daily curriculum. These books were not necessarily discussed in class, nor were they tied to writing assignments. They were individual reading activities.

While an examination of how this curriculum was implemented in over a thousand schools of New York City is beyond the scope of this book, some documentary evidence shows that the curriculum has been taken more seriously in the city's junior high schools and middle schools than at the high school level. Junior high school students were required to fill out reading logs documenting the amount of reading completed. In one high school I visited, the only evidence of New Standards was the letter from a principal at the end of the school year announcing a reading list and the list itself. The letter makes it clear that the books on the list had not been included in any aspect of the curriculum during the school year itself. And this letter was released an entire year and a half after the introduction of New Standards (see figure 2.1).

In a summary of Crew's tenure as chancellor, the *New York Times* said:

> His critics, who include many school officials, say that the other face of Dr. Crew's charisma and conviction is an autocratic and stubborn management style that has terrorized and demoralized principals and superintendents, without providing them with enough resources and support to meet his standards. They say he has led through pronouncements, promises and improvisation rather than through detailed management, with decisions involving thousands of students and millions of dollars made almost overnight and with little consultation outside his inner circle. Many parents, teachers and principals say Dr. Crew has failed to build the grassroots support he needs to move the system forward.[7]

Budget data seem to support this criticism. Chancellor Crew did not challenge the Board of Education's customary underspending on classroom materials. With total spending on books amounting to only $35 per student per year in the early years of his tenure, principals did not have the resources to implement his literacy-centered proposals. Simply handing out a reading list at the end of the summer is not making literacy the center of a school's curriculum. Chancellor Crew also never confronted the strict state curriculum that forces teachers to use review books filled with questions about ancient European, African, and Asian history to prepare students for state exit exams, rather than assigning the biographies and autobiographies, which might build the habit of reading.

More needs to be known about what was being done in the high schools of New York City in the 1990s. What were the day-to-day lives of students and teachers like in these high schools? Were resources and support missing, as the principals who complained to the *New York Times* and the budget numbers suggest? Or did principals find resources elsewhere, such as through the fund-raising of parents? What were the literacy practices in the high schools of the nation's largest school system?

GEORGE WESTINGHOUSE

VOCATIONAL AND TECHNICAL HIGH SCHOOL
105 Johnson Street, Brooklyn, NY 11201

FLOYD GREEN, PRINCIPAL

June 1998

Dear Student:

According to the New Standards issued by the New York State Department of
Education and the New York City Board of Education Chancellor we are
implementing a program to improve student reading and comprehension.

This program to improve the literacy skills of students will eventually require
that students read 25 books per year. This requirement will be phased in over
the next few years. At Westinghouse High School, our literacy program will
include a summer reading assignment. In addition to this letter, your English
teacher will give you a reading list, which will be arranged by grade level, and a
list of questions.

For this summer, students will be required to read two books. You may consult
the reading list for your current grade to choose a book to read. You will have
to do a report or analysis on the books that you read. Along with the reading
list you will receive a list of questions, which will be the basis of your report.
You should choose a separate question to answer in regard to the two books
that you would be reading this summer. Ninth graders will be required to write
an essay of 250 words or more, and 10th and 11th graders will be required to
write an essay of 350 words or more in answer to the questions. Your English
teacher will collect these reports during the first week of school when you
return in September. Reports will be due no later than September 10, 1998.
Your English teacher next term will give you specific instructions about
submitting the reports.

Your reports will be graded and will become part of your first marking period
grade. Failure to do the reports will result in a failing test grade being averaged
into your first marking period mark.

We hope you will choose a book that will be enjoyable and that you will profit
from this assignment designed to improve your literacy skills.

Yours truly,

Floyd Green
Principal

Figure 2.1. Letter from a principal at George Westinghouse Vocational and Technical
High School, Brooklyn, New York.

If the plans of President Bush and the Congress are to succeed, they need to look at how classroom teachers have decided to deal with books and teenagers and reading and writing. Today in the United States, the gap in reading skills is as large at the beginning of high school as it is at the end. The four years of high school—a time when many teenagers become more mature and more focused on schoolwork—are making no contribution to closing this reading gap.

The next four chapters will look at the literary practices of students, teachers, and administrators in the public schools of Brooklyn, New York. It is in the high schools of Brooklyn, the Bronx, Manhattan, and similar urban areas that the reading gap is not closing. In the next chapter, you will see what a veteran administrator recommends. Is an administrator with over twenty years of experience able to choose "the best practices" to develop the reading and writing skills of the teenagers he faces?

NOTES

1. New York City Board of Education, *Performance Standards—New York City—First Edition, English Language Arts, English as a Second Language, Spanish Language Arts* (New York: Author, 1997), 2.

2. New York City Board of Education, *Performance Standards*, 5.

3. Anemona Hartocolis, "After 4 Years of Crew, Still No Final Grade; He Champions Accountability, but Data Show Little Improvement," *New York Times*, October 14, 1999.

4. See New York City Board of Education, *School-Based Budget Reports: Fiscal Year 1997–98: System-wide Summary, June 1998* (New York: Author, 1998). See p. 76-#2 for Brooklyn amounts, p. 72-#2 for Manhattan amounts.

5. Mary Foertsch, *Reading In and Out of School—Factors Influencing the Literacy Achievement of American Students in Grades 4, 8, and 12 in 1988 and 1990* (Washington, D.C.: National Center for Education Statistics, 1992), 17.

6. More details about these state mandates are available at www.emsc.nysed.gov/ciai/socst/pub/sslearn.pdf and at the websites of other state education agencies; sample copies of the state multiple-choice examinations that shape education in New York City are available at www.emsc.nysed.gov/ciai/socst/pub/1samus.pdf.

7. Hartocolis, "After 4 Years of Crew."

Chapter Three

"Are They Worried I'm Going to Steal?"
Life in a Neighborhood High School

In his survey research on the lives of teachers, Samuel Bacharach, a professor of organizational behavior at the School of Industrial and Labor Relations at Cornell University, uses words like *scavengers, deprofessionalized,* and *makeshift* to describe the work experiences of teachers. He states that "before a job can be performed effectively, it must be properly designed" and concludes that schools are not providing the resources needed for teachers to be effective. He states that "no matter how well-motivated people may be, a lack of resources will prevent them from accomplishing their job responsibilities. In fact, a lack of resources often results in frustration and ultimately de-motivates job holders."[1] Do Bacharach's conclusions apply to New York City, with its traditions of progressive politics? Is the job of teacher with the New York City Board of Education designed so that teachers can be effective?

Each of the teachers and principals in the next three chapters has at least fifteen years' experience. They are not new to the job. They did not drop in from a college campus last year. While they were not scientifically selected on the basis of age, race, gender, and income as in a survey of voters, I believe their experiences do illustrate the lives of teachers in New York City's public schools today.

The first two teachers worked at John Jay, a neighborhood high school in the well-to-do area of Park Slope in Brooklyn, but in New York City the "neighborhood high school" is often a place to avoid. Built very large, with an average capacity of 2,500 and some as large as 4,000, neighborhood high schools are designed as places for the students who do not have the grades in middle school to be admitted to the city's elite science high schools or the city's magnet high schools, called *ed-op* or *educational option* schools. The total size of the student body is the only obstacle to success in these neighborhood high schools. They also tend to stay with the traditional factory schedule of short forty-five- to fifty-minute periods, with each teacher seeing at least 165 students a day.

The third teacher lived in Park Slope but bypassed John Jay to commute all the way into Manhattan to work in a school built on an entirely different model. Supported by the Annenberg Foundation, the New York City Board of Education created fifty New Vision schools in the late 1990s as alternatives to its massive, impersonal neighborhood high schools. With much smaller enrollments, and each teacher facing fewer than eighty students a day and in some cases as few as fifty, the New Vision schools were a new model. Did this model work? Would teenagers become more literate in alternative environments? Chapter 5 will look at some of these questions.

The names of the educators interviewed in this chapter and in the next two chapters have not been changed. When asked at several different times about privacy, they decided to use their real names. Pseudonyms have been used for the names of all students.

THE YEAR BEGINS AT JOHN JAY HIGH SCHOOL IN BROOKLYN

The first high school in the sample, John Jay, is locally famous because none of the children in the immediate neighborhood go there. They shun John Jay and attend other public schools in Brooklyn or Manhattan or leave the public school system entirely and attend Catholic and private schools.

Visitors to Brooklyn can find John Jay easily. The building is massive. It is the largest structure on a busy commercial street, and it dwarfs the one- and two-story restaurants, bookstores, barbershops, and other stores that line the street. The high school covers the entire width of the block and about one-third of the length of the block.

There is not a blade of grass or a playing field in sight. There are no playing fields or running tracks or green spaces around this high school. The site consists entirely of the five-story brick building that sits right on the concrete sidewalk. There are no setbacks or empty spaces around the building on the east, west, or south sides. There is the building, a short stretch of sidewalk, and then the street in these directions. On the north side of the school is a small faculty parking lot, completely filled with cars.

Dr. William J. Hunter, the assistant principal of John Jay and the chairperson of the English department, who is the focus of this chapter, is the administrator with the longest service in the school. He served as a teacher from 1969 and as a supervisor from 1981. He recalls when John Jay used to receive student teachers from the schools of education in Manhattan—Teachers College, Bank Street, New York University—but now the professors in these schools feel Jay is too rough. It sits alone on 7th Avenue with only the attention of two or three police patrol cars at dismissal.

Its neighborhood, Park Slope, is full of three-story Victorian brownstones on tree-lined streets. Park Slope is now sought after by those priced out of apartments and townhouses in Manhattan. But the children of the lawyers, stockbrokers, television producers, and journalists of Park Slope do not attend John Jay. With college boards scores around 400, Jay does not attract the middle class, Hunter said. "You see, this is a strange school—you know the school. It's an inner-city school in an upper-middle-income neighborhood. But the people from the neighborhood do not send their kids to this school. They bus around them; they train under them. They would fly, I suppose if they could do that."

Its reputation is not for violence, as in the case of Thomas Jefferson High in Brooklyn (with two murders in the building in one year), nor is it for student walkouts, as in the case of Eastern District High School. Rather, John Jay's reputation is simply for low achievement. In 1999–2000, only 26 percent of the school's seniors took the SATs, with an average verbal score of 383 and mathematics score of 406. The school did not achieve the state standard for the passing rate for the state exit exam in English or in mathematics, and its dropout rate also violated the state standard in this area.[2] It was very overcrowded in the 1999–2000 school year, operating at 147 percent of capacity.[3] Its students are primarily Afro-American and Latino, and they arrive with poor academic skills. What is this school and others like it doing to improve the intellectual skills and the intellectual lives of the teenagers who attend each day?

Hunter said the year began with problems. "The halls started out with a sense of disrespect and violence; the principal suspended people left and right. Ironically, we were very fortunate. There was a massive gang retribution on the Avenue [7th Avenue] and 9th Street, and most of the kids who were the worst offenders in our school transferred out for safety reasons.

Now we just have left students who are disrespectful, and it amazes us how little they have been socialized before they came to high school.

"They act as if they were in the streets. I talk about that to a large extent because it affects one in the classroom sometimes. It affects teachers at meetings where they should be discussing academics; the first thing you want to do is complain about student behavior. Student lack of control. Student lack of respect. And I think it's a carryover from a society that does not respect teachers, does not respect education—at least in New York City and probably out of it."

Hunter also had opinions about students' reading habits and their language skills: "The kids do not have a great working vocabulary. I supervise the after-school program, and there is a little core of kids who just recently entered the Lincoln–Douglas debates. They competed with the Midwood [a high school in a different section of Brooklyn] kids, and they got killed. And they got killed on cross-examination. They had difficulty with the vocabulary the kids were using in asking them questions. It was an interesting recognition on their part as well as the fact that these [Midwood] kids read all of the books that they didn't read.

"They said, 'They read the whole book?' It was a great discovery for them. They're juniors. I don't think they are going to be demoralized. The problem is that the teacher is leaving, and one of us has to find a debate teacher, and that's not so easy to find. A tremendous amount of time involved, and very little money is provided. So you moan for them; you sigh for them. Kathy Roberts, a social studies teacher, has been working four days a week with them, four days a week, an hour and a half, two hours a day, every single day. There's no way she's getting paid for what she's doing. So, you know, you moan for them. . . .

"My son is an inveterate reader. Our students are not. My son is an inveterate television watcher also, but he reads. He also has two English teachers for parents. Unless the parents are willing to make the commitment to their children, the schools are going to find it very difficult to repair the damage that's already been done. See, the myth is that there was some golden age of schools. There probably was not a golden age but a better age of parenting. When the divorce rate was infinitely lower. When one parent worked and there was much more control over the children.

"I read or my wife reads to our daughter now every night. We have always done that since birth. This is part of what builds that kind of tradition of valuing the page, the written page. I don't know if the SATs are going to ever go up. I don't know whether there was some kind of mythical golden age. The average when I was going to school was a mere hundred points higher, fifty points higher. Unless there is a commitment by the society and the parents, the schools are going to be able to do something but not everything. The schools are being asked to do everything now, which I find kind of bizarre. They try to train us to do everything."

Attendance Rate

Hunter had much to say about the obstacles to literacy in the home and in the school.

"You can't separate home and school," he said. "We have a high failure rate. One of the major causes of the failure rate is the attendance rate. Students who come here from junior high school, for example — over 40 percent come with more than twenty days absent a year. When you have that kind of absence rate, it is very difficult to have continuity in the classroom. It is very difficult to do group work. It is very difficult to develop projects. Some of our better classes, our Law and Justice Program, has approximately a 95 percent attendance rate, which would match with any school in the city. Their passing rate is over 90 percent. We had an Acorn program for the brighter students — well over 90 percent rate and attendance rate." (John Jay's overall attendance rate is 75.6 percent.[4])

"When you take students who come from troubled homes, or they tell you they have been out and their mother knows they have been out, or they had to go to wherever they had to go because of a death in the family, or because there was a vacation, these are obstacles."

Skill Deficiencies

"Another obstacle is that the students come here with enormous skill deficiencies," Hunter continued. "The tendency, of course, is for the high schools to blame the junior high schools. The junior high schools blame the elementary schools. We have social promotion. To a certain extent, social promotion is an obstacle. You could argue, 'Well, we don't know how to teach them.' But students come into the first grade with deficiencies.

They come into the second grade with deficiencies. And over the summer, the deficiencies are extended.

"I would argue that if you see no books in the house, if the sole means of entertainment is television, that's an obstacle. I'm not going to blame the parents totally for this, but I'm not going to say that schools are totally responsible. I think that's an inane proposition held forth only by business people who say, 'Well, if you didn't sell the shoe, you are a lousy shoe salesman.' If you didn't sell the shoe to someone who doesn't have enough money to buy shoes, I don't know whether you are a lousy shoe salesman or not."

Hurry to the Pace (of the State Curriculum)

Silent reading programs are sometimes used as a way to increase the amount of reading done inside secondary schools, and Hunter had clear opinions about the value of silent reading. He said his high school didn't have a schoolwide silent reading program in which everyone in the school reads for thirty minutes a day.

"No, it's one that I brought up many, many, many years ago, but we are constrained. A large number of principals—and I have worked under a large number of principals [laughing]—feel that because of the state mandates to achieve a series of calendar lessons, that we hurry to their pace. You have a statewide curriculum in math, in biology, in social studies. Social studies I know has a calendar of lessons. . . . I feel that it's largely because of the responsibilities they feel they must meet, the pressures they feel they must meet in terms of achieving this calendar of lessons. . . . The only department which can go its own way to a certain extent is the English department. And if I have a very low passing rate, no, I get looked at, askance.

"I think [silent reading] is a fairly decent idea. I think that writing across the curriculum is a good idea. I am aware of the research by Fader in *Hooked on Books* on what people should be doing. Implementing it is another ball game.

"And I'll go a step further. It's hard to find a principal who has an academic vision. And understands that in order for the academic vision to succeed you have to have a schoolwide disciplinary policy. They have to work hand in hand. And then get the cooperation of the students and the teachers. It's a complex juggling act."

Hunter believes that state-mandated curriculum may not be what the students need.

"I would say to hell with the curriculum. It's moronic. . . .

"[The school] could junk the entire state-mandated curriculum and say to everybody that we are going to accept the fact that kids are here not on the four-year plan. Which many of our kids are not. We acknowledge that they are not here on the four-year plan. You are here on a five- or six-year plan. And you are going to spend the first part of your year reading and writing. That's all you are going to do. We can decorate the rooms. And make the doors very secure. Yesterday one of the loveliest people in this building who is not a teacher, who is a counselor of kids in need, literally had her door kicked off its hinges and her pocketbook ripped off. And so it goes."

Focus on Reading

"I'd focus on reading. But I'd diagnose the entire school—there are three thousand students—and say, 'OK, the entering class is about eight hundred or nine hundred. Your reading skills are poor. This is what you are going to do. You are going to read books and then you are going to write about them. You are going to do that. And then you are going to talk about them with your teachers. That's what you are going to do for a long time. Until you show that you have some skills.

"'The rest of you, yes, we are going to move ahead. Forget age. We will just do phasing.'"

Hunter said that he had introduced new programs into his high school, but obstacles to learning continue year after year.

"We have had things come into this school. I brought the Writing Consortium into this school. It originally comes out of the San Francisco Bay area. To a certain extent, it is [used] districtwide in 15 [i.e., School District 15 in central Brooklyn]. It is a methodology which talks about how to enter the student's world with reading and writing and get him or her interested in what [he or she is] doing—different approaches. It is so far removed from when I went to high school—and they said write three hundred words on this particular topic—as landing on the moon is from the Wright Brothers. It's not as if we've remained backward. The English department specifically was the first to develop collaborative learning in the school. It does an enormous amount of group work and project work. People have used us as a model for how you do certain things and how you change your department around."

TEENAGERS READING FAR BELOW GRADE LEVEL

"But it doesn't help our passing rate much," Hunter added. "We just start with a lot of kids who don't do the reading. They are not going to do the reading. They resist it every inch of the way. They don't and can't write. They come to us barely literate. I went to the Annex, and we had three discipline problems. The dean was perceptive enough to say, 'I thought that you should see this, Bill. These kids have reading problems.' She had pulled out from the computer—which is a very nice little tool—their whole history, their whole academic history. Reading problems? These kids read on DRP [degrees of reading power] levels of 0 to 10. The average is 50. Fifty is the average; 0 to 10 is where they read. Yes, there has been a programming problem. One kid was special ed. One kid was resource room. And the other kid was just damaged.

"We have a lot of kids who are like that. Twenty-five percent of our population comes in reading like that. Now New York state says they must, and New York City in its brilliance says, 'Everybody is going to college and everybody is taking four years of this, three years of this.' This is one of the stupidest educational philosophies that I have ever heard in my entire life. It is contrary to every other school system in the world. Forget this country—the world, where they say, 'You don't seem to be interested in academics. You really seem to be interested in acquiring a trade. Let's get you into that kind of school.'

"We do not link high schools and junior colleges. We do not link high schools and junior colleges with the world of work. We separate things. We compartmentalize things. We make these moronic rulings that antagonize and alienate students and frustrate teachers. People say, 'Well, you are not in the real world. You are not in the world of work.' The real world is right in this school. This is not a microcosm of the real world. The real world is a microcosm of what goes on in this school, even if we are smaller than they are. This school is what is going to nourish this economy and make this economy survive, make this world survive culturally. This is not going to happen given this world's power and this society's power and its incredible stupidity."

Hunter said that the lack of reading skills and the resistance to reading that his students bring to high school makes learning difficult. He feels that this resistance to reading begins early if students fail to become fluent readers in elementary school.

An Insidious Disease

"My first training, interestingly enough, was as a reading coordinator," Hunter said, "and one of the things that I learned when I was taking reading courses is that when you can't read, it becomes an insidious disease which feeds on itself emotionally. You feel incompetent, and you feel an absolute lack of self-esteem and ability to function. When you can read, you feel better about yourself. It's behavioral rather than attitudinal, but the attitude becomes part of the behavior. And you don't change that so quickly. That's why small classes, I think, work so well because you can help people who have serious problems and knew they had serious problems, and knew that the only reason they were there was to get help from someone who wanted to give them help. It's not so easy when you have thirty or forty kids in the class."

Someplace to Send the Latinos and African Americans

"I think [resistance] starts very early. Most of the evidence shows that if the kid does not learn how to read by the third grade, the kid is going to have troubles the rest of his life. And I think that we have a lot of kids who have troubles by the third grade. I think that the love of reading or the joy of it, or the fun of it, starts when you are one year old, or two years old, or three years old. When your mother or father reads to you. If it doesn't happen, I don't think that it starts. I think that you have to come into school ready. I'm sorry to keep harping back to early ages, but I think that it starts there. And I think that the negativity starts there also. 'Johnny, would you read? Ah, ahh. . . .' He doesn't want to. Kids laugh. The kid feels like garbage. The kid doesn't want to read. The kid doesn't want to see books. He doesn't want to see anything associated with letters. It ain't easy to change that.

"We get them in high school—they're already fourteen or fifteen or sixteen. By the time we get them in high school, the kid's reading habits are firmly entrenched. The kid's attendance habits are firmly entrenched. The kid's behavioral habits are firmly entrenched. This school, as much as I love it—I've been here a long time—should be broken up into little pieces. Just broken up into little pieces, or sealed off one floor at a time, or redesigned totally. The community doesn't want that. It has to have someplace to send its Latinos and African Americans. This is it."

Federal Aid

As students continue to arrive with poor reading skills and a resistance to reading, there is no longer any federal help to intervene. Hunter explained that his high school no longer received federal Chapter I funds and this change limited the school's ability to help below-grade-level readers.

"I have to laugh. Until two years ago, we had five extra teachers, and they were funded specifically to do remediation. The federal government—in its brilliance—decided that rather than reading scores, we should depend on lunch forms which indicate their financial need. We were not able to do this. We have a large number of students who will not turn in any kind of federal form. I think that they are probably here sub rosa and don't want to reveal it, or they are cheating or whatever. All I know is that I've lost those teachers.

"I had zero remediation in the English department in the main building. I have one class of remediation in the Annex. I have it only because the superintendency has a congruence teacher there teaching one class. That's it. If you want to talk to me about the rest of the borough, I don't have a clue as to what is going on. . . . I have very little money [from the state program—Pupils with Special Educational Needs (PSEN)]; I think most of the money may be in the math department."

Hunter said that the students in the one remedial program did not seem to feel any stigma from their participation in remedial reading. "It's been my experience, contrary to some of the research which shows that children feel negatively about being in the program, that they had no feelings one way or the other. Kids who were cutters cut eighth period or first period anyway. The kids who wanted to succeed did so. For example, the kids who failed the Regents Competency Exam, who were students that we would put into many of our Chapter I classes—we had an extraordinarily high passing percentage from those kids. I did the research because I was curious to see whether the money was being spent wisely. I mean, we would have 97 out of 106 pass. When we had cut down a class, we had

27 out of 31 pass. That's a rather high passing percentage for kids who don't read very well or who don't write very well to start with. So I was impressed with that.

"The teacher [in the remedial reading program] was generally supportive. We worked only with small groups. There was a paraprofessional in there so that you had seventeen, sixteen students coming. But again, attendance would mar what was going on. If you were scheduled for twenty students, it was possible that you were only seeing twelve. If you were scheduled for fifteen students, it was possible that you were only seeing five. Those five did very well, almost invariably. Even kids who started out with zero scores. I think we did remarkable work with those kids. We don't do anything now."

What did Hunter do with those students who entered high school reading far below grade level?

"First of all, every one of those students was diagnosed. We used whatever tools we had to find out whether he just was totally illiterate, had no vocabulary, had no alphabet to start with, or whether he was having specific problems trying to find details to support main ideas. Whether in general he couldn't find what a main idea was and didn't understand the concept of what a main idea was. Whether he couldn't understand sequence. We would assess the child. Then everything would be based on that. Within that construct, students had independent reading. We had full libraries in there. Kids read freely minimally once a week. Talk about silent reading—they did that.

"They did book reports as well—not low-level reading; they chose their own books. Many liked to read Danielle Steele, and why not? She's a very popular writer. . . .

"They read those books. If we found three kids who had one problem, they would be grouped together. They would be working either with the teacher or under the guidance of the teacher-paraprofessional. They would be working on those skills maybe two times a week so that the week was broken up; it wasn't drill, drill, drill. We obtained computers to do CAI [computer-assisted instruction], which is not my favorite type of instruction, but we found the kids liked it as a motivator so they went to the room where these special computers were and they did some drill work there. Everything reinforced. Everything picked up. Because the numbers were very small, the teacher kept track of everybody.

"We did the same thing in writing. We did a pretest and posttest right along the way. And the kids evaluated themselves. The kids saw how they were going. How they were making progress. It just happened to be a highly effective program. The rooms were small. They were what we called our labs. They were always decorated. The teacher was there. It was her home so she put up stuff. The kids' work was all over the place. When I went in to evaluate, that was one of the criteria. 'Yeah, this room looks like a morgue. Let's make it a little livelier.'

"All the teachers were certified in reading. They were trained in it. And this is in addition to their starting out as English teachers and moving over. But that was when we had the funds."

New York City's List of Approved Books

In addition to a lack of federal funds for remedial education, Hunter also faced a New York City book list that he said limited his freedom to buy books.

He talked about the city book list as an obstacle. "Several years ago I wished to teach *Maus, Maus 1, Maus 2,* rather well-known books by Art Spiegelman. They are comic novels with Jews being mice and Germans being cats and the Polish being pigs. It is the pre-Holocaust, Holocaust literature. Last summer I had a grant, an NEH [National Endowment for the Humanities] grant. I studied Holocaust literature. It was one of the books that was on there. It wasn't on the New York City approved list at the time. I also wrote a letter to the chancellor telling him that he should cut that junk out. He slammed me down pretty good through the chain of command, of course. This year it's still not on the approved list. But there is a book company who will get it on the approved book list, quote unquote.

"It's listed for $14. I can get a 25 [percent] discount from the company which is not on the approved list. I just bought from this other company. I paid $14. You figure how many of us are going to get around these stupid rules imposed on us and just get killed with money? But I don't know an English chairman worth his salt who doesn't see a book which is a classic or a book which just came out and say, 'Wow, this is a really dynamite book. This should be taught,' and not find a way to get it taught.

"I'll come back to Stuyvesant—if you will. [His son attends Stuyvesant, New York City's elite science high school.] Stuyvesant's PTA gathers almost $200,000 a year through its radio phonations. The English chairman there a couple of years ago was given $7,000. He did not have to account for a nickel of that money. Now, there's a book company called Dover Books Publishers. Through Dover Publishers, I could get books for a dollar, for $2 a book—not brilliantly bound and certainly not hardcover, but with the best price. I have to spend $6 and $7 a book because I have to follow Board of Ed rules.

"Are they worried I am going to steal? If I buy a VCR, I have the same problem. I can't go out and buy it—'Look! Sale, Sharp twenty-seven-inch, four-head VCR thing for Nick who does our video classes.' Follow Board of Ed rules and spend $300 or $400 more. Everywhere down the line, the Board of Ed is an obstacle probably because it doesn't trust us."

In addition to the barrier of a list of approved books and approved vendors, Hunter also faced another obstacle. He said that the budget provided by the principal and Board of Education provided funds for few new books for the year.

"One of the teachers wants to teach *Maus*," he said, "so I just ordered it for her. We are in an awkward situation, I think, in this school to a certain extent; that is, we have an incredible amount of book loss. So this is almost a filling in of a book loss of 20 to 25 percent a semester. We are not unusual, I think. So we are filling in a lot." Hunter said that he asked a teacher in the office, "Nick, you know any new books we bought this year, new titles?" "Nothing exciting," the teacher answered.

"I ordered Kate Chopin's book, *The Awakening*, and *Billy Budd* will be taught in our AP [advanced placement] class next year," Hunter continued. "But nothing comes to my mind, either. I'd have to look in the book room. *How the Garcia Girls Lost Their Accent*, I bought. I bought *Miguel Street*. *Annie John*, I bought."

Juggling Books

But Hunter said the number of books he purchased often wasn't a full class set—that is, enough for a teacher to distribute a copy of each to 165 students.

"It depends. We had a teacher once who wanted to teach—this I remember rather vividly—*As I Lay Dying*. I advised against it. It won't work. We argued back and forth. He said, 'Let me give it a shot,' so I bought thirty copies for one class. Unfortunately, I was right. Those books are now someplace in the dust in our bookroom.

"But ordinarily if you have three classes, I will try to get three class sets. The problem, of course, is that you have to revolve those among other teachers. So you have to depend on the teachers finishing the books, collecting, giving them out to the students, the other students returning the book. It's a lovely little game you play when you may have 150 or 170 students in your five classes."

And at Hunter's high school, unlike the junior high on the Upper East Side, teachers did not ask students to buy paperbacks on their own.

"At many schools, they do ask the kids to buy them. At our school, they do not come well endowed with funds. So it would be preposterous to ask. You have to understand that our student population is (a) poor, (b) needy. Deficient in skills, deficient in funds. Not everybody, but a chunk of them. "I have stood up in my temple and suggested that maybe the temple was a little racist. I did that on Yom Kippur when it was members' day. It was an interesting speech and an interesting reception. You want the best for your kid. My kid's going to Stuyvesant. It is probably the best or one of the best schools in the city. I also would be reluctant to send him here because I go out in the halls, and I don't want my kid being beaten up because his father is the chairman of the English department. That's the only way to get to me.

"But it prevents you from doing things you want to do. We do have an AP English class. We have an AP math class. We have an AP foreign language class. And they are for very small numbers. We find a way to carry them.

"But there's things we can't do. And that's one of them: buy books. . . .

"As far as supplies go, I would be a moron if I didn't order what my teachers needed because they would be pounding me on the head. 'I don't have paper; I don't have pencils; I don't have chalk.' So I look at my supplies once a week and I say, 'I need this; I need this; I need this.' And as much as I can get, I get from the supply man who I am friendly with. So we have composition paper; we have chalk; we have pencils. We have whatever we need. If they say, 'I need this and it's not here,' I'll get it.

"A supervisor, as far as I can see, a supervisor's role is to make the lives of his teachers as easy as possible. Maybe that's his first job. I don't know."

Teachers as Professionals?

When Hunter and I talked about whether teachers were treated as professionals in his school, he asked me to define a professional. I said private school teachers who could point to a best-seller list and pretty much get what they want three days later were professionals.

"You can't do that [here]," Hunter said. "Flat-out, we can't do that. (a) We don't have the money, and (b) the Board of Ed is too stupid to let us do with it as we think we need. It's an elephant out there. It just doesn't want to change as far as I can see. I think most people in the field hold the Board of Ed, the whole downtown, pretty much in contempt. Very restrictive. Not very supportive. I would say that once upon a time, maybe twenty-five years ago, twenty years ago, they put out some fairly good curriculum materials. I haven't had stuff coming out of them for years. I would sell 130 Livingston Street. I don't know why they have 65 and 110 [Board of Education addresses]. There are a series of redundant layers of bureaucracy. If they were managed the way corporations were managed, they would be delayered themselves: sending them out to the schools or just firing them."

He added that the PTA "is very small, is very poor, is very inactive," and it is not able to provide books for classes.

Finally, Hunter did not expect that changes in leadership at the school would lead to improvement in the academic lives of students. Talking about the leadership of John Jay High School over the years, he laughed.

"I'm sorry I'm laughing," he said. And then he began to count the number of principals he had worked with over twenty-five years. "Let me see . . . I think this is my tenth. In the past six years, I think that I have had four. That's been a spectacular run." How effective have they been in improving the reading skills of students in this building? "Not particularly."

The Unions

In his years in the school, Hunter said that the teachers' union—the United Federation of Teachers, the local affiliate of the American Federation of Teachers—had done "nothing" to improve the school. The principals' union, called the Council of Supervisors and Administrators (CSA), had also done "nothing" for the school.

"Ask me how we survive," he said. "We're tough. We're better than most teachers. I mean that very seriously. We are goddamn good at what we do. First of all, in order to deal with our kids, you have to be tough. And yet it's amazing how much warmth teachers can give. Oh, yeah, we can bitch about them. We can say that piece of garbage and probably mean it, too. In this school, maybe 5 percent of three thousand—is what, 150 kids?—can drive you crazy. And we don't have the legal power to get rid of them. But we've been given a job that is almost undoable given the strictures that society places on us. Given the problems you have with society that are mirrored in here. If you have people running around with guns, you'd be a jerk not to think that you are not going to find knives and guns in here. When you have violence out there, you'd be stupid not to think that you're not going to find violence in here.

"Why do we have a city university four-year system, a city university two-year system? It's a statement of the failure of the schools. We have social promotion. OK, so this high school inherits every social misfit who comes from the public school system through the junior high schools to here, and I know that the junior high school in the neighborhood (and I know it because my kids went there) channels the better kids away from this school. And the whiter, wealthier ones and the blacker, wealthier ones and the browner, wealthier ones probably go to private school. They go to Packer [a private school]. There are about four private schools in the area. So you have that loss. That creaming right off the top.

"This system provides alternative schools, which I think it should—magnet schools. Additional creaming, so we are left with kids who know themselves that they are not brilliant, and they are not successful, and we try to drill into them that they can do it. And you get frustrated. We are human, but we do it. So I think that we are better than most people in the system. I think that if you put those kids there, those schools would be fine. On the other hand, I don't think they do as well because they are used to asking one question and running with one question, instead of saying, 'What's plan B, what's plan C, what's plan D?' You have to think that way in this school.

"I think we're goddamn good at what we do, notwithstanding the data, which are horrible. And I admit it, they are not very good. But we don't have a country that values education. For all its baloney about what it says and its goals and this and that, and the other thing, we are putting billions and billions of dollars into starships, warship systems, and we don't want to put anything into education. That's nonsense. That's absurd. It doesn't compare with any, any Western country.

"But come back to the four-year, two-year. Why don't we have a system that . . . some people are going to be tracked into a six-year system, a high school, a university. . . . We have brilliantly hit upon the notion that everyone is going to college. Have you ever heard of anything so stupid in your entire life? Everyone is going to college.

"What if you don't want to go to college? What if they are just not apt?" Hunter said that there is no link to the world of work. "None, and that's a society problem. Not just a school problem. Unions have to make that happen. Industry has to make that happen. Corporate leadership has to make that happen. And the leadership which we don't have—political leadership—has to be willing to do that. We don't have that in this country. That's sad. Really sad."

CONCLUSION

Hunter shows how the superstructure of the city and state educational bureaucracies hangs over local classrooms and shapes literacy practices:

- City funding is not sufficient for book purchases.
- City purchasing rules limit his ability to use his existing funds correctly.
- State curriculum laws herd teenagers into standard English and social studies classes that they are not prepared for and may have little interest in. Spending a year working on reading and writing skills at the beginning of high school is not possible regardless of a teenager's skill level. The state's tests must be passed.
- State curriculum laws may not offer full credit for remedial reading and writing classes.
- Federal record keeping, which depends on teenagers to fill out low-income lunch forms, reduces the funds available for reading and writing classes.

We will see in the final chapters which of Hunter's complaints will be addressed by the new literacy initiatives of President Bush and the 107th Congress. Will the new literacy initiatives on the way from Washington change the literacy practices now in place in Brooklyn that so limit intellectual development in schools such as John Jay?

Hunter's complaints—state mandates that have become obstacles, a curriculum further shaped by shortages of materials, the absence of help from either the teachers' union or the principals' union, cuts in federal programs that had helped the students furthest behind, and the idiocy of the city's approved vendor list, which raises prices—also exist for teachers in departments at John Jay.

Of course, Hunter and the English department are only part of the opportunity to learn one's native language at John Jay High School. History classes are another. In some high schools, teenagers can read biographies of George Washington, Frederick Douglas, and Susan B. Anthony and social histories of the labor movement, the suffrage movement, and the civil rights movement. In other high schools, the only reading is from guidebooks using outlines to prepare for state-mandated minimum competency tests.

What kind of reading is going on at John Jay High School, and what are the results in history classes through New York City?

NOTES

1. Samuel B. Bacharach, Scott C. Bauer, and Joseph B. Shedd, *The Learning Workplace: The Conditions and Resources of Teaching* (Ithaca, N.Y.: OAP, 1986), 5 (ERIC ED 279-614).

2. New York City Board of Education, *1999–2000 High School Annual School Report, B.A.S.I.S Superintendency, John Jay High School* (New York City: Division of Assessment and Accountability, New York City Board of Education, 2000), 9.

3. New York City Board of Education, *1999–2000 High School Annual School Report,* 2.

4. New York City Board of Education, *School Profile: John Jay High School, 1990–2000* (New York: Author, 2000).

Chapter Four

What Drives Current Literacy Practices in High Schools?

The results of substandard texts are far-reaching. Simply put, poorly written books educate poorly; there is a lack of depth, a lack of analysis, and a lack of excitement in our classrooms. Because textbooks drive the curriculum, mediocre texts can lead to mediocre teaching. Finally, dull, uninteresting textbooks give reading a bad name and encourage students to flee to the flashier world of video.

—(National Association of State Boards of Education, 1988)

The opening quotation summarizes several key details about how some school systems present books to teenagers. According to the National Association of State Boards of Education, these are the current literacy practices in many American schools:

- "There is a lack of depth, a lack of analysis, and a lack of excitement in our classrooms" because of poorly written textbooks prepared to cover thousands and thousands of facts for survey courses.
- Since these books are mediocre, and since "textbooks drive the curriculum, mediocre texts can lead to mediocre teaching."
- Finally, the poor quality of books assigned in high schools and earlier in youngsters' intellectual lives drives them away from reading and toward "the flashier world of video."[1]

Is this analysis correct? Is the curriculum in high school driven by poorly written, dull textbooks? To learn more about how teachers present books to teenagers, I interviewed a social studies teacher, who, like Dr. Bill Hunter in the previous chapter, worked at John Jay, the neighborhood high school in Park Slope in Brooklyn. I had met Paul Feingold years before when we both served on a committee trying to improve John Jay. He was not a rookie in the classroom. He had "about fifteen or sixteen years of teaching experience," he said, and thirty hours of graduate credit beyond his master's degree. His only administrative duty was to work in the cutting room—"recording the names of students caught in the halls for cutting." This responsibility rotated and was his every third term. He had no specific responsibility for staff development of new teachers but was "often asked to have teachers observe my lessons by a supervisor who thinks that I do some things well."

In social science terms, he was a "persister." He stuck with the local school year after year and went to the fund-raiser for the local assemblyman and city council member, trying to meet the people he needed to improve his school.

"The school year's been fair by John Jay standards," Feingold said. "There's been nothing terrible, but there's still a certain level of disorder that they seem to be trying to deal with. Still, kids in the hall, kids not getting to class promptly, things of that sort.

"We have a broad range of average and below-average students. Very many of our incoming students are below average [in] reading based on standardized exams. Overall in the school, we get a tremendous number of students with deficiencies—overage, low achievement. We also get a number of good students, particularly in our law and justice ed option program.

"We lost our Chapter I funding several years ago because the school did not have a sufficient number of lunch forms filled out. That's how the government determines eligibility. So we don't have those remedial programs. Really, there's very little done as far as I can tell to deal with the situation. The teachers struggle with it. I assume there's still a PCEN [a state-funded remedial program].

"At this point, there is virtually no choice of classes by students; they are assigned," Feingold said. "This year one big change was in February when the state mandated that all students be given a full program, so at the last minute they added many classes and hired additional teachers [laughs].

"I teach three classes of Global History 4 and two classes of criminology. In the school we have tried to annualize classes to some extent, but it depends on how the programs break," he said. "So it's not annualized. I have some kids I had last term and others I did not.

"The global history kids I give daily homework to based on information which they find in their textbook. I write the questions, and they hand it in. I get pretty good results with the homework. I follow up on that.

"The criminology kids I prefer to do a project basis. I give them a project for each marking period in lieu of homework, a major project. Either a journal on certain topics or a research paper. This term I'm doing a career-oriented one—a certain career in criminal justice, which could be anything from social work and psychiatry on to being a police officer or whatever."

PREPARING FOR THE STATE TESTS

"The tests are based on what I've covered. A combination of the textbook, the notes in class, the do-nows that I've done, and class discussions. The Global 4 kids take the Regents and a RCT [Regents Competency Test] in June, so it's a lot of test preparation, and it will also include a lot of review of what they are supposed to have learned in the previous globals." The RCT, a minimum competency test developed in the 1980s, has since been replaced by a state mandate forcing all students to take the more rigorous Regents examinations. Feingold said the Regents exam for global history covered all four semesters of global history, "which is why the passing rate is usually very low, but I've had pretty good success particularly in having the kids pass the RCT. The Regents is much more difficult. My goal is building almost a cultural literacy with the kids." The global history classes look at different world cultures, he said.

"The assistant principal for supervision makes the decisions about which books to buy," Feingold said. "She sometimes consults with the teachers as to which books they prefer. She makes the decisions. As I said, sometimes she will consult with the teachers."

REVIEW GUIDES ARE THE ONLY
BOOKS IN GLOBAL STUDIES

"I haven't ordered any new books this year. We just have the latest edition of a review book, which is the fourth edition of a Regents and RCT review book. That's the book which the kids take home and leave home for homework. I have another textbook which I use for do-nows [in class], so I don't have to do reprints of stuff. The review book (which they take home) gives outlines and highlights of things. It doesn't go into depth. The depth we try to do in class discussion. I have enough copies for each kid to take the review book and keep it at home," he said.

"This term started out very badly. In all of my classes I have at least thirty [students], but in one class I have nearly fifty, about forty-seven or forty-eight. I grieved it, of course, but the procedure is rather delayed. So I'm told now that it will be resolved by March 10, which is the end of the first marking period."

NOT ENOUGH DESKS

"I actually have a situation in my fourth-period global class where I don't have enough seats or even enough room to put the chairs. The kids are sitting literally all over the room because they do show up, but I'm still teaching them. We get single chairs; they don't have desks you know. We just get single chairs to squeeze all over the place.

"Each student was given a textbook. We especially make sure that each kid about to take a Regents or RCT has a book to take home." (The global studies review book is *The Key to Understanding Global Studies,* 4th ed., by James Killoran, Stuart Zimmer, and Mark Jarrett, Jarrett Publishing.) "The classroom set I have [for global studies] is published by Amsco and is written by our former principal, Henry Brun."

NO BOOK FOR ELEVENTH-GRADE CLASS

"The criminology students do not have a book to take home. Criminology has traditionally been given to juniors, although they sometimes put kids from other levels into it. This book *Crime and Justice in America* is a classroom set for criminology, which I use sometimes. It's basically a college text." A classroom set refers to the practice of city teachers keeping thirty or thirty-five textbooks in a classroom to be used by several different classes during the day. In this way, a small number of books can be used by up to 160 students a day—five classes of up to 32 students each when the contract is being enforced.

Feingold said the kids read in class both out loud and silently.

"I usually have a do-now prepared for the kids which takes about ten minutes, which they can do individually or in some cases they do in groups, they do collectively. That sometimes gives the information base with which we can pursue the lesson. That involves reading. Sometimes I will have students read passages out loud as well. With the criminology kids, I usually use current events topics, which I reproduce from newspapers and magazines, and they form the basis of our class discussions."

Feingold said these courses did not have a booklist or syllabus with reading assignments for the semester.

"The books are adequate. I found the criminology text book tough. . . . When we used to have overall a higher caliber of student, it was easier to use that book; now the vocabulary is too difficult for most of the students so I rarely use the criminology text.

"Between the do-nows and the homeworks, they read about twenty-five pages or so a week [for global studies]," Feingold said. "The kids accept the books they have. The kids are basically uncritical.

"With the criminology kids, I have much more latitude since there is no formalized exam at the end. I have a curriculum which was developed by myself and other teachers, but I don't stick to that. I look for high-interest articles on current topics that have broader implications. I always look for high-interest things.

"The other students, the global [history] kids, we talk about wars and revolutions and immigration and other topics. I try to make it as relevant and interesting as possible. There are more Hispanic students than black, and there are also some Arabic, Bangladeshi, Indian students as well, a few white kids, but most of the white population is Arabic.

"We also supplement the books sometimes. We have bulk subscriptions to *Scholastic Update*. We use that sometimes as a change of pace. I have no real complaints about it. Our big problem at John Jay is that with so many kids mobile . . . moving . . . with kids with erratic behavior, we lose a lot of books so we have to spend an awful lot of our budget replenishing our supply to have adequate classroom sets. That's why there was an effort not to give kids books to take home in classes where they did not have a Regents or an RCT. That was last year. I'm a senior teacher. I have keys to the bookroom. I make sure my kids get books. Whether everybody does, I really don't know."

Feingold added his high school was not effective in building the habit of reading in students.

"I don't think that there is enough reading or writing done. I'm always surprised at how our even clearly smarter students do not do well on the SATs or the PSATs. I think that we do not push them to read and write enough overall."

DISRUPT THE POPULAR CULTURE OF THE KIDS

"I think the obstacles are the habits which have been established, the patterns which have been established," Feingold said. "So much has been talked about the effects of television. Kids preoccupied with their current social lives. A tradition has to be developed of reading, of the practice of reading and writing, and I don't think that the school has managed to disrupt the popular culture of the kids. I doubt if many schools have done that.

"I don't have any personal favorite writers," Feingold said. "I'm an inveterate newspaper and magazine reader, so it's more in that genre than literature."

Feingold said he did not know how much money his school spent on books for each student that year. He said the New York state textbook allowance did provide funds a couple of times a year, but he did not know if the school spent beyond the amount of the state funding: $35 per pupil a year.

He did suggest some changes in the materials available to his students. He said that he would prefer if "we could use more topical materials, more newspapers, magazines. I don't mind having a textbook to use because it's easy for the kids to refer to it. But it would be nice if there were a variety of materials available.

"I understand, and it's not my area, that it's not always easy to order these materials because there are lists of approved materials. The reality is that we commonly break copyright laws and just photocopy whatever materials that we think will cover a topic well with the kids. We do that all the time. So if we have one good book or set of materials, we will reproduce it."

WITH 180 STUDENTS, LOGGING IN THE HOMEWORK

One strategy that worked well last term was journals, Feingold said. "Instead of book reviews, having them review a variety of TV shows and movies. Also to review books. I tried to incorporate what they look at anyway with a writing exercise. Kids like homework. Surprisingly, they like it. It's very tangible to them."

How do you grade them? You must have 150 or 160 students?

"This term it's closer to 180 students. But as I said, the criminology kids have a term project, so I don't have a daily thing with them. The globals, I try to correct as much as I can but certainly check off that they've done it so that I can tell them immediately if they are missing any homework. They always have a chance to make it up. . . . I mark them on Delaney cards. Each homework is numbered. It's very quick to write if a kid has homework number 4, homework number 8. You write those numbers on Delaney cards which are boxes. So it's very quick and easy to do, really." (Delaney cards provide a space for marking the receipt of a homework or test score on a card with a student's name.)

"What's harder is if you want to correct the work, particularly for the kids who don't do it well." Going through sentence structure and grammar? "That would take forever if you did it in detail."

PRINCIPALS AS DIRECTORS OF SECURITY

Feingold said that he had worked with four different principals at John Jay, and none had been effective in improving the reading skills of students in this high school.

"I haven't really seen any academic initiatives from any of the principals. A tremendous amount of their time is taken up with security matters. For example, when a student is suspended by a principal's suspension, the principal actually has to have a hearing with the parents and so forth. Those things can be very, very time-consuming. Principals have to be in the halls; they have to check personnel; they have to do observations of teachers as well. I think the bulk of their time is taken up with that. Rather than being educational leaders, in terms of initiatives, in terms of curriculum, in terms of whatever. I think they leave those things to the assistant principals for supervision, the department supervisors.

"We don't have the college system of department chairs who rotate. We have assistant principals who are appointed. Assistant principals are not elected. They go through the C-30 process principals and assistant principals have to go through now. All applicants are screened by a committee of parents, teachers, and administrators. And interviewed. And five names are recommended to the superintendent, who then makes his recommendations to the high school division, and ultimately someone is selected.

"I think that position is archaic at this point: assistant principals of supervision. I think the system has basically accepted a type of middle management that is probably superfluous, and I would prefer to see the college model instituted which some schools have with rotating elected chairmen."

Feingold laughed out loud when asked about the efforts of the union to improve the school.

"As you well know, when I was [union] chapter leader, I certainly played an active role working with the community to secure additional funding for the school, which was $3 million that we got from the federal government. We had for several years something called the school based option where on one day of the week, we shortened periods by a couple of minutes so that there was an extra period, and that period was used for meetings, conferences, and staff development. But the staff felt that after several years that period was not being used well. The time was not being used well, so we stopped it. That was a union initiative.

"It gave us time to talk about schoolwide programs, staff development, case conferencing on the kids. The potential was great, but it was never realized, I think, due to poor administration."

He then explained how the teachers' choice program was contributing to his classes. "In social studies, one of our main concerns is having functioning copy machines because we generate so much of the material and try to tailor-make it to our students' needs, so we usually turn over a good portion of our teachers' choice funds collectively to use for supplies and service contracts for the machines."

TRAINING

At John Jay, training was limited to presentations in monthly departmental meetings.

"Sometimes at our department meetings which are monthly, the assistant principal will have teachers present different methods, different things they are doing," Feingold explained. "One of my lessons was videotaped and shown, and I explained what was going on—just to try different approaches. There is also a lot of informal sharing of information and approaches at least within our department." He said that all the training was inside the school, and there were not opportunities to observe what teachers in other schools were doing.

"Occasionally there is a staff developer from the district who comes by to our department meetings. We had one program that we participated in. I forget the name of it—interdisciplinary with English and social studies. It's a citywide program, so folks from that program came and presented together with the teachers from our school who were involved showing their approach. That was real staff development.

"The assistant principals for supervision are really responsible for training, but I have not observed that they really train people as much as act like foremen over them. My experience has been, particularly as chapter leader, they very quickly make up their minds whether a teacher is good or not good. And then observe them accordingly rather than really try to train them and work with them. I think that is the pattern in the city, which is why so many teachers resent supervisors—because they are not seen as resources which they should be, but they are seen as foremen looking over the back of a factory worker, which is how they view teachers."

THE TREATMENT OF TEACHERS

Feingold laughed when asked whether teachers are treated as professionals in his school.

"Sometimes yes and sometimes no. If I have to sweep my classroom in the morning because it wasn't swept properly, if I have to clean graffiti off the desks, which I do, wash my blackboards, which I do—these are not professional duties, but it helps to maintain order. Many teachers complain that they put too much of their energy into discipline, which is necessary, but it takes so much out of you to wind up being like a cop, a disciplinarian, rather than a teacher. When teaching works well, it's a great feeling, but all too often teachers don't get that feeling of satisfaction. It's too much of a daily struggle.

"I don't have that huge a problem with the kids. Others do, and sometimes I do as well. It depends on personalities. Some kids come in with an awful lot of problems. I had a couple of kids last term who were very pleased. It was the first time they had ever passed a course at John Jay High School. They were smart boys but discipline problems. I was able to relate to them somehow. One of them I have again this term, and he's doing fine.

"I think that there is so much cynicism and apathy, which has been so well earned in the system, that most teachers feel that nothing fundamental is going to change. And I think that fundamental change is needed because too many of the kids are failing. Too many of the kids are not succeeding. Our success stories are more anecdotal than widespread. I think that even though most teachers will agree with that, they don't have any faith that things will change, or that it's really worth the effort to try to change things."

"RESOURCES, ATTENTION, PRAISE"

"I think that supervision has to be much more supportive. Our current supervisor in social studies has tried to be supportive and has encouraged peer observations and things of that sort. She refers teachers to other people for help. That kind of collegiality is good. Overall, though, I think there needs to be an educational vision, and I think that has to come up and down the line. I think that it would be great for the entire leadership, for every pedagogue at the Board of Ed and the UFT to teach occasionally because I think that teachers by and large view them as being totally out of touch.

"I think that priority has to be in teaching. It has to get back to that. The resources, the attention, the praise has to go back to that teaching. Leadership has to set an example with that. I think that absolutely everybody who is supposed to be a teacher ought to come into contact with students. That's not the case now.

"At least in the high school, assistant principals [for] supervision do teach one class. Frankly, I think they should teach more than that. I think the principal should teach. I think that the assistant principals [for] administration should teach. I think guidance counselors should be programmed to meet with the kids on a regular basis in a group situation as well as individual counseling. As I said, I think the superintendent and all the folks at the district offices should teach as well as the union leadership. And that should be the emphasis."

"IT'S NO WAY TO LIVE"

"I think that it's a wartime situation," Feingold said, "and the slogan is 'All resources to the front, and the front is the classroom.' Then if they are going to show what they are doing, not in the abstract but in reality, with students, that will set an example. They will experience the difficulties; they will experience the successes. I think that would help to galvanize the system. Because right now, we are being hit with one cut after another. The struggle becomes harder and harder, and a lot of folks are just counting the time until they can get out.

"The biggest topic for teachers is whether there will be a retirement incentive. It's no way to live. It's no way to live because unless you are accomplishing things with the kids, it a god-awful hard job. While we do achieve some success with the kids, it's not enough. That needs to change but the way to change it first is to face reality. Not by just having high-falutin new standards, new arbitrary standards. The only standard should be for the kid to move ahead in the time you have him, not to achieve some absurd level. Yeah, all kids should learn calculus. Of course, all kids should kids learn calculus—what are the prerequisites? Have they passed that?

"Yet we hear the nonsense spouted time and again at the highest levels from chancellor after chancellor, from our own union as well—arbitrary high standards. I think there need to be standards, but they need to be reasonable, achievable standards."

LIFE IN A NEW VISIONS HIGH SCHOOL

The teacher in the next chapter decided to avoid the well-known frustrations of life in a neighborhood high school with its rigid curriculum, lack of authority for teachers and principals, factory schedule of 160 students a day, shortages of resources, and a variety of other problems. Instead, she chose a long commute to a new model of school being built as an alternative to the large, impersonal high schools of New York City. We will see the literacy practices in this new type of school in the next chapter.

NOTE

1. National Association of State Boards of Education, *Rethinking Curriculum: A Call for Fundamental Reform* (Washington, D.C.: Author, 1988).

Chapter Five

Can New Experimental High Schools Socialize Teenagers?

RESISTANCE TO READING

New York City's neighborhood high schools are well known for a number of features: Large size—average 2,500, about twice the national average. Violence. Weapons. Enough knives, guns, and box cutters show up in school to justify all the methods to reduce violence: security guards, stationary metal detectors, hand scanners for metal, locked doors, and so forth. But the city is trying new ways to offer safer schooling. It has long had a number of alternative schools for students unable to adjust to life as one of 2,500 in a neighborhood high school. In the mid-1990s, it added fifty new small high schools of no more than five hundred students in an attempt to provide safer, smaller-scale education for students who had not yet failed in larger schools. Since the beginning of these schools, their number is continuing to expand.

What are the results? Are these new schools—some of which are part of Ted Sizer's Coalition for Essential Schools—successful in developing youngsters into readers? As many readers know, the Coalition for Essential Schools is probably the nation's premier school reform effort. Its goals, such as using a single humanities teacher rather than separate history and English teachers, would radically change the number of students teachers face each day. With no more than 80 students rather than the traditional 160, Sizer, Deborah Meier, and other reformers believe than teachers can accomplish much more. And students who now see fewer teachers will no longer feel as anonymous.

Linda Brown is a veteran teacher who lives adjacent to John Jay High School in Brooklyn, but rather than walk three blocks to Jay, she endures a long commute to Manhattan to teach at Vanguard, a New Visions high school. Her school is small: fewer than five hundred students. Her schedule is reasonable: only thirty-three students a day. Her school is not adrift but rather connected to national school reform efforts through Sizer and Meier and the Coalition for Essential Schools in Manhattan and at Brown University in Rhode Island.

What is life like in this New Visions school? Is school reform possible in New York City? Can new models of education improve the reading and writing skills of teenagers in an age of headphones, television, and other distractions? Or is age fourteen, at the beginning of high school, too late to build the habit of reading?

I had known Brown for a number of years. She was the reading specialist at the school for dropouts where we had both worked in the early 1990s. As one of the most technical people in the building, she took on the responsibility of working with adults with reading levels below fourth grade.

Having watched her teach day after day, I knew we shared beliefs about reading. We both had regular silent reading periods. We both sought out exciting books. And we both believed that assigning a large number of books was one of our main responsibilities as teachers.

After we left the Young Adult Learning Academy (YALA), the school for dropouts, I wondered about Brown's new job in one of the city's experimental high schools. Her response shows that reforming high schools may not be enough. Students who spent years in the city's chaotic, low-expectation, low-print, low-technology junior high schools, surrounded by adults who go home at 2:30, may resist classrooms where expectations for reading are much higher.[1]

But, as this interview also shows, it is the job of a teacher not to back down when students resist. It is the job of the teacher to push teenagers to read even as they complain and resist. While I may have chosen different books to use than the titles Brown selected, she shows that teachers need to do much more than follow state curricula. They need to be determined that the youngsters in their classrooms develop as readers and writers.

Brown said that most of the kids in the school are Latino. Her humanities classes are a mix of ninth, tenth, and eleventh graders. The school was first located near the projects by FDR Drive on the Lower East Side of Manhattan and still recruits from that area, although the school is now located on the Upper East Side.

What is life like in a new small high school?

"On the one hand, great; on the other hand, complicated," Brown replied. "What's great is that in the middle of New York City, there are these wonderful people, many of whom came to this school in the middle of their careers, and they have built this quite extraordinary small school. And it has to be extraordinary because the kids are really tough, and it's run by two directors who are both exceptional people and whose exceptional qualities complement each other. There's no jockeying for position. There's no one person trying to be the boss. They work together wonderfully.

"And the teachers are exceptional. It's just an amazing place. I can't believe how lucky I am because I know about two other alternative schools which are under the same umbrella we are under—actually I know of about three others—and they sound much more problematic. I'm thankful all the time.

"On the other hand, it turns out that I am not yet a good teacher in this place, so I have to say to myself like a little mantra, 'I have been a good teacher before; I have been a good teacher before; I've even been a great teacher before.' But I'm not yet in this place because it's teenagers who are a very particular group of folk these days, and they are very different from what I was as a teenager, very different from what I might have expected. I'm really glad I had the YALA experience [a school for dropouts in Manhattan] because that helped me get a bit prepared for the incredibly free-floating hostility not just to me but to each other and to adults.

"Breaking that down and getting kids to actually work is really tough. Plus, we are planning all of our curriculum at the same time, and madly looking for materials and deciding what we are going to do and what the kids are going to do and photocopying millions of things, so that's hard, too.

"I'm too new at the school [to know who decides about the buying new books,]" she said. "But I assume that we do it collaboratively. Most of the books that I am using are books I find myself and buy. I'll buy a copy and photocopy. I love looking for different things for kids to read, and I'm really good at it. It's probably my best shot as a teacher. This term we have done Native Americans—a whole bunch of different tribes—and African Americans. If I'd had two sets of textbooks, they might not have contained the information which I wanted. They might have been either way too easy or way too difficult or way too boring."

A TEACHER'S SCHEDULE AT A NEW VISION SCHOOL

"This year is turning out to be 'Peoples of American History' chronologically. We are going to get to immigrants next. In each humanities class, I have about seventeen students; in the literature class, I have about twenty-two. Basically I'm responsible for thirty-three kids—incredible. The literature class with twenty-two students only meets twice a week.

"For my class—remember each teacher uses different things—students read selections from *My Indian Boyhood*. Students also went to the library and got their own books on different tribes. That was a requirement. I had another great Indian book, a book of Indian folktales. One of the favorite things I did with them was Ian Frazier, *The Great Plains*. I first read it in the *New Yorker*, and it has this extraordinary chapter on Crazy Horse that is thrilling. So I photocopied that for them. Also, an easy reading book by Ann McGovern called *If You Lived with the Sioux* for people at the low reading level, and various other things that I can't remember."

Brown said that she has her students read both silently and out loud in class.

"Always. Students hate it. They hate me, but it's fascinating. Well, here's the deal. Our classes are ninth, tenth, eleventh graders mixed. All different reading levels. And the great majority of kids are reading-phobic, even the ones who can read. So I had suggested to some colleagues that what I have done in the past with people who have great difficulty reading is to split them into small groups of three and have them each read half a page because they are not reading in front of the whole class. But it is more likely to keep you awake because you are listening to someone else reading and so on. Other teachers said that worked really well for them. In my class, that was a disaster. It did not work. And it took me about four months. Now when we read, people pretty much settle down and read. They read silently, and I usually go around and sit and read with individual kids. Some kid will read me a page, and I will read the kid a page, and then I will go to another kid, starting with the kids who are having the most difficulty settling down, which is a bunch. And they will read to me."

"IT'S THE MOST IMPORTANT THING"

"I think one of the biggest difficulties in high school is to get kids to read," Brown said. "What happens all the time if kids are sitting for more than five minutes and they're supposed to read, they're like asleep. They'll go wild. Or they'll start twitching and fidgeting and going to the bathroom and talking to each other and whatever. To get them to just sit and read is amazing. But I realize that's the most important thing I can do all year, so no matter what else I do, if I can get them so that they can sit and read for forty-five minutes, that will be great. So I don't do it now for forty-five minutes. I started out having them read for about twenty minutes. Now we are up to about thirty or thirty-five per class.

"I found some wonderful books. A student just brought in this wonderful Virginia Hamilton book about African American history which I had never seen before. I loved the book about Indian boyhood. Terrific book. And there were a couple of other books about African American history which I really loved a lot.

"They read forty pages [of photocopies] each week for homework, and then they read in class. Classes meet four times a week, and each day they read for about half an hour, so they read for about two hours a week in class.

"They hated *A Light in the Forest,* which was the one I didn't pick. We all decided to do it together because the school had copies of it. Now this was fascinating to me because I remember reading *Light* in high school and not liking it especially. I look back now and realize that at the time I was fourteen or fifteen, and it was all about a guy. There aren't any girls in it at all. The reason that I was surprised that my kids didn't get into it more is the whole feel of the book that the kid does not want to act white, which is so incredibly relevant. He hates white people. He feels they have hurt his people and massacred some of them and killed children. And there's a very strong feeling among a lot of the kids in my school. We brought the kids together for the O. J. Simpson verdict, and the kids cheered. So there's this very strong feeling of not wanting to act white and the whole teenage cool ethos. So I would have thought that would translate. But just as it says in *The Gutenberg Elegies*, it's the language. He wrote it in the 1950s or something. The language, the literariness of it, is so foreign to them that they just can't get through that. So having the theme being close to home is not enough. Absolutely not enough.

"A book they loved was *The Outsiders*. We did *The Outsiders* as a whole school. We took a week's break and all read *The Outsiders*. And they loved that because the language was accessible. The theme was accessible."

A BOOK'S APPEARANCE

"I pick very carefully, and it looks kind of easy. . . . It's very interesting when they type their papers on computers. They always do it in large print—some of them do it in the outline letters. It should be big print. So if I find them something with wide white borders, and the print is kind of big, and it's not too long, and it's relatively interesting, they will read it.

"On their own, the only books that I have heard the kids talk about a lot are the *Goosebump* series. And for some kids that seems to be the only thing they will read. And some kids read *The Source,* the rap magazine. A couple kids will read Stephen King. A couple kids read romances."

READING-RESISTANT TEACHERS

Not all the teachers in this new school were committed to building the habit of reading in their students, Brown said. "It varies incredibly from class to class, and here's what's interesting: On the humanities team, there are six teachers. Of the six teachers, three—the three men, interestingly— I would say are reading-resistant themselves. So whenever we get together for a humanities meeting and we are talking about things for the kids to read, the women say we could read this, or then there's this, or then there's this, and at the next meeting we all come in with arms full of books and reprints and so on, and the guys sort of look at what we have brought because they don't like to read very much, either, I think. I'm sure that's true not just in our school. I like these men. These are good men and good teachers; one of them at least is a wonderful teacher—an amazing teacher, but he's not a reader. I mean, he has read in the past and still does read some, but not a 'reader-reader.' And probably a lot of teachers are not reader-readers."

RESISTANCE TO READING

Even with schoolwide reading assignments and with time to read during the school day, teenagers still resisted the amount of reading she assigned, Brown said.

"This is where teaching is today. You almost don't need that question. It's not some kids—it's most kids except if you are at Stuyvesant [New York City's elite science high school]. It's most kids. I don't know when you became a reader. We didn't get a TV until I was eight. And I learned to read in school at the age of six. In that two year period when you are a little kid and you wake up at six o'clock and your parents won't let you run around or be crazy, I had to do something so I read, so I already had a reading habit by the time I was eight and then went into that voracious reading thing. Also, my parents limited television. But no kid or hardly any kid has that experience anymore. It's a very, very, very rare experience.

"It's one of those times when I am so pleased that I am an experienced teacher because I remember reading things and hearing things from teachers at YALA, and they would say the classes are really alive when we have class discussions and would go all-out for class discussions. I think that class discussions are fine for part of the time, but when do we think kids are going to read?"

"I HAVE TO KEEP PUSHING THEM"

"If they are resisting it like crazy with us, do we think that they are going to go home and read? Please! When I started teaching, I thought if something didn't work, I should change it. Now that I've taught for a while, I realize that if some things don't work, I should change them. But there are a few things that are so important that even if they absolutely don't work, I have to keep pushing them because it's what the game is.

"And if these kids want to do anything, if they want to become auto mechanics, and they want to be able to read the manuals to tell how to fix the computerized parts of every single car these days, they've got to be able to read. And they have to not look at anything that's longer than a damn paragraph and say, 'Oh, my God, I have to read this. I have to read this much. I have to read three pages.' It just has to be a kind of natural activity for them. It's very deep.

"I just kept doing a silent reading period every day until my students have gotten to know that there is no use groaning or complaining or carrying on or doing what you do because we are just going to do it. That's it.

"I don't blame them for this. My kids are bouncing around. I don't think it's their fault. It's an experience they haven't had. It's sitting in one place not watching TV or whatever. They haven't had that experience. They have to learn how to do that."

She blames electronics for much of the resistance to reading that teenagers bring to school. "A lot of this is theory. Maybe all of it is theory. Surely three big things: television, headphones, and video games. So that you never have to be not hooked up somehow or other. You can always have something going on if you are bored. You don't have to read."

"HAVE NEVER HAD A GOOD EXPERIENCE WITH READING"

"I think a lot of kids have never had a good experience with reading. Not many kids are read to when they are children. There's a certain stratum of the middle class which does that, but even there, a lot don't. A lot of middle-class parents don't read to their kids much. They'll get them books on tape or something like that. Some kids haven't had the feeling 'Oh, wow, isn't this great?' 'Oh, wow, isn't this great?' is *The Little Mermaid* or something else, but it's not reading. Also, it's not what challenges them intellectually. Something else must. I'm not quite sure what it is. But that's not where they get that challenge. Plus they don't want to work. Reading is work, right? The same way I don't want to do housework, they don't want to read."

Brown cites the chaos in junior high schools as one factor in the attitudes toward reading that teenagers bring to high school.

"I hate to condemn people's previous schools because I think reading in schools—a lot of the city schools—is going to be almost an ancillary thing. What you are trying to do to keep things from being almost totally crazy. I just think that in so many schools, people are not in control of what is going on. And there is just so much craziness going on that you are trying to keep things from being bizarre. And too, classes are too big and periods change too much. I would assume that reading is not a big thing. You must know that Allington study where [researchers] went around—this was done maybe ten or fifteen years ago—and the average grade school class kids read for less than fifteen minutes a day."

"TALKING TO A FRIEND OF YOUR BROTHER'S"

Brown believes that reluctant readers need to begin with books close to home.

"If the books are so close to them that it's like talking to a friend of your brother's, then, yes, they will read it. They will love it. If it's a friend of your father's, then it's a generation removed; already you have problems. And if it's a friend of your grandfather's, forget it."

Isn't that what we should be doing, is finding books that speak to their experiences?

"I try to find books that speak to their experiences all the time," Brown said. "I would have my students in this school read *Disappearing Acts* [by Terry McMillan], but I'm scared in the same way that we say to students all the time 'Who are you? What do you want?' There's this incredible self-referential stuff . . . but the thing is, will we ever get beyond that?

"It's also very tricky in a high school even though there is a lot of latitude. For example, you couldn't teach *Makes Me Wanna Holler* in a high school. I couldn't teach *Disappearing Acts*. *Disappearing Acts* is sex and the swearing. There are some parents who would freak. . . . In high school you are not going to have them read *Disappearing Acts*, where they go to bed together on the second date. That's not going to do it.

"And the kids are going to object if you don't because they want the stuff with the swearing. There was a movie [a student] had seen, *Jersey Ride* or something like that. And I said, 'What did you like about it?' She said the cursing. That was the best thing about the movie—the cursing? They have cursing everyday right around here. Why do you have to go the movies? She laughed and said it makes it seem real. So if people aren't saying, 'Fuck you, mother fucker,' it doesn't seem real.

"I think what I could try is this guy who taught at YALA for a year named Paul Beatty (he's really well known these days as a rap poet), and I'm going to get one of his books.

"*Black Boy* might also work," Brown said. "It's hard to think of books that are hot and real which don't have sex and violence. That's right. But they're so into sex and violence that part of you says I don't want to be up to my neck in entrails. . . . One of my favorite students had loved this book *Monster,* which is by some guy who is incarcerated probably for life in a California penitentiary. And I had read somewhere about this book, and he details his life of crime. Lord knows what all he did.

"I'm scared for the kids. I'm scared at the furniture which we put into their minds which is unbelievable: violence. I heard this great commentary on [National] Public Radio, and the woman said it's so terrible that kids grow up and their culture heroes are Beavis and Butthead. It's really cool to be selfish and to be a goof-off. To get over all the time and to laugh at violence. . . . So many kids are so unconnected to what they could get out of school."

SCHOOLS AND READERS IN A VIDEO AGE

Can schools in a video age still develop readers?

"School in a video age can still develop readers, but they have to be incredibly self-conscious about it, and they have to feel it's one of their major tasks," Brown said. "It's not so much to give people specific information—although that, too. I actually do not think that [E. D.] Hirsch was a terrible human being when he talked about cultural literacy. But that more that they should be really good readers and pretty good writers. And pretty good computer users by the time they leave. Then they'll be OK. They should have some specific information, but mostly they should be able to do those three things well.

"Private schools are probably the best at developing readers," she said. "They have reading lists; they have reading lists over the summer. They have books and also have the self-consciousness on the part of the kids of wanting to be sophisticated in a certain way. And I know that this is one of the reasons that I kept reading after that first rapture, after the first six or seven years—because there were interesting people in the world, and they were sophisticated and they knew things, and I wanted to be like that. And because there was a glamour attached to it, and a glamour attached to the life of the mind. I don't see that now. Kids have an idea of glamour, but it's real different. It has to do more with money and cars.

"One of the things I'd like to introduce our kids to is the idea of the romance of college, and I mean all kinds of romance. They are seeing it as job related, and that's the way we sell it: how are you going to manage in your life rather than this amazing time. I don't think that it's sold to city kids that way. It's a time out of time, but I don't think they have that view of it at all, and they don't have that view of reading at all. It's not who they want to be—readers are not connected to who they want to be. But in private schools, a lot of kids do have that self-image. Their family culture is closer, and they see themselves as inheriting the Earth in some way . . . and going to Paris. Ask which of my kids wants to visit Paris. I could take a poll—maybe two. Ask at Fieldston [a private school], and 'In order to do that [go to Paris], I should know these things, and how am I going to know that stuff? I need to read about it.'

"I think you see it a lot in black autobiographies. Somebody like Henry Louis Gates. If you want to be a certain kind of person, if you want to know certain kinds of things, you read. I like him a lot, and I love his essays. I didn't like the autobiography as much as I like his essays . . . there were parts that were interesting. I love his essays in the *New Yorker*. I devour them."

Brown mentions many factors that are shaping teenagers' attitudes toward books, basically their entire previous socialization to books: parents not reading to them; a lack of previous good experiences with books before high school; the whole electronic world with *Monday Night Football,* thousands of hours of televised sports, video games, headphones, and so forth.

She believes that schools can develop readers only if these schools become "incredibly self-conscious about it and have to feel it is one of their main tasks. But in New York City, and in many other cities, controlled by state education laws, the abilities of teachers to engage children and teenagers in language development are still limited."

VIEWS AND RECOMMENDATIONS

While I agree in most places with Brown's discussion of why teenagers resist reading, I would want to expand the choice of books available at the Vanguard School.

Brown began this school year in the fall of 1995. She talked about the students' reaction to the verdict in the O. J. Simpson trial. The "case of the century" had been on television all fall. Of course, junior high and senior high teachers in the regular high schools cannot respond to this trial and use it in their classes to motivate reading. They cannot browse the shelves of Borders or Barnes and Noble and search the very popular genre of crime and justice, and order books for their classes. This genre fills literally shelf after shelf in large bookstores. Teachers in the city's regular high schools must follow the state curriculum, but in the alternative schools, and in the New Visions schools, teachers have more freedom. They could have used books about our criminal justice system. I don't know why the staff of the Vanguard School didn't use the public fascination with the O. J. Simpson case to build courses full of popular books about the case.

Where were the books about crime and justice and other popular topics in this experimental high school? I have had students love books like Michael McAlary's description of police corruption in *Buddy Boys* and his description of police heroism in *Cop Shot*. McAlary's writing is accessible. It is dramatic. I remember young men right back from city jails and upstate prisons who did not like to read but were willing to read *Buddy Boys* about police corruption. (It ended up that their complaints about police corruption in Harlem were justified, when officer after officer at the Thirtieth Precinct in Harlem was arrested.)

I have also used Robert Sam Ansom's book *Best Intentions: The Education and Killing of Edmund Perry* several times. The book works with teenagers and young adults. This is a nonfiction account of a teenager from Harlem who mugs a cop the summer before he is to attend Stanford University on a scholarship. I have had students ask, Why did the police officer shoot, and why did the teenager try to mug the undercover police officer in the first place?

These conflicts between police and community are real. They exist. Schools that want to be taken seriously by teenagers need to look at these conflicts. Too often adults want to hide them, even adults who work in education. I have had professors in graduate school say, "Poor people don't want to read about city life and violence; they see enough of it." How do we know what city teenagers want to read? Schools never ask them. There is no choice in their literary lives and intellectual lives inside schools. As noted in chapter 9, in some private schools, teenagers' interests are taken more seriously. Students are allowed to choose their courses and the books that they will read. But in high schools run by the state, the literature is sanitized and homogenized. Police are never corrupt; criminals are never bestial. These topics are real and might engage teenagers more than stories about Sioux Indians (although Ian Frazier is a very engaging writer).

The rich literature about crime and punishment in the United States could be used in the first year of high school. This literature offers opportunities to learn about the Constitution, the ebb and flow of the debate over the death penalty, and the many damaged lives that Sister Helen Prejean presents in *Dead Man Walking*. Teenagers could learn how the courts tried to extend the rights of the poor in Anthony Lewis's *Gideon's Trumpet*. I wouldn't start with *Gideon's Trumpet*. It is the past. It is not today. It is not as dramatic as McAlary or Ansom. But a teacher could work up to Lewis and beyond. "Start with the dramatic and the accessible, and then move to the more abstract and more difficult" is the advice I have received. In other words, make the curriculum developmental. At some point, have teenagers decide in writing if crime and urban poverty is the result of a lack of jobs, as William Julius Wilson believes, or the result of a culture of poverty, as Charles Murray believes. A teacher who starts with the dramatic and the accessible can win students' confidence and then move to the more difficult reading and writing assignments.

I think that teenagers should have the right to choose literature that speaks about their lives. For example, Luis J. Rodriguez's autobiography, *Always Running*, is a hard-edged book. There are some ugly scenes in it, but these events took place and still take place. Schools that deny teenagers the chance to read about these realities contribute to teenagers' indifference to school and hostility to school. Teenagers should be allowed and even encouraged to speculate on why Luis Rodriguez and Nathan McCall were able to move away from danger. Why did they survive and prosper and transform themselves, while Edmund Perry put himself in a situation where he was shot to death? Why did Brent Staples succeed in his education in *Parallel Time: Growing Up in Black and White*, while so many from his neighborhood did not even finish high school? If teenagers begin high school interested in what the world may hold for them, isn't this coming-of-age literature a place for them? Should they have the right to choose six or seven books from this genre, rather than Global History I and II as the reading material for ninth grade?

Even private school students complain about reading assignments that are too far away. In the case of this New Vision school, I would offer alternatives to assignments in books such as *My Indian Boyhood* or *The Great Plains* or *If You Lived with the Sioux*. While short reading assignments about Native Americans seem to be very popular in New York City schools — at all levels — this the only place to start a school year. Reading assignments could begin much closer to home with books about the lives of teenagers in cities like New York, Los Angeles, and Norfolk, Virginia. Let's see whether teenagers will respond to this coming-of-age literature early in high school. My college students love reading and writing about these books. They love books that acknowledge that there are obstacles out there. Yes, people are incarcerated in the United States. People do die from drug overdoses. People do commit armed robberies. Yes, people are transformed in prison. Yes, finding the money to attend college is an obstacle.

I wonder whether providing teenagers with a choice of courses and books, as some private schools do, might have reduced some of the resistance to reading that Linda Brown reported.

I think the New Vision schools and the other alternatives to the large factory high schools in New York City should encourage students' commitment to what they are reading. Construct a number of courses each semester in the humanities. Make the reading list public. Invite parents in to discuss book choices. Have students actually see what they are going to be expected to. Or go even further: Have them help construct the reading lists before the semester actually begins. Do everything possible to force this issue of commitment to developing one's reading and writing skills.

The teenagers in the next chapter did what we asked. They have stayed in school, and they continue to complete the lessons their teachers assign. I did not interview these teenagers at one of the two high schools on Rikers Island, New York City's large complex of jails, but rather in a school program where they were receiving extra tutoring and support. These are the teenagers who believe in education. But even by completing these lessons, high school is not preparing them for success in higher education or the world of work. The high school years do not help bridge the racial gap in achievement according to a recent federal report. What is being asked of these teenagers in high schools in cities such as New York?

NOTE

1. Jim McCabe, "Afro-American and Latino Teenagers in New York City: Race and Language Development," *Community Review* 14 (1996): 13–26 (ERIC EJ532978).

Chapter Six

What Are Teenagers Being Asked to Read?

At the heart of President Bush's education plan, No Child Left Behind, is the assumption that once states have identified weak schools based on their test results, the states can intervene and repair these schools, or that local alternatives to these weak school exist. The teenagers in this chapter attend high schools in an educational environment that looks very much like what Bush has proposed for the nation. They were students in a state school system that had the key elements of the Bush plan in place since 1981.

- They have been subject to regular testing since they began school. State tests at third and eighth grades are mandated. City achievements tests, also mandated, occur annually. This combination of city and state tests currently already surpasses the annual testing mandated in President Bush's education plan.
- These test scores are then used to identify weak schools.
- A state intervention process exists to restructure weak schools based on test scores. (This is the subject of chapter 15.) In the state in question, the intervention process was almost fifteen years old by the time students entered high school in the mid-1990s.

Each of these three pillars of test, intervene, and restructure is now common nationally. I have collected dozens of documents on this process in New York state. Each visit from a state inspection team generates a school registration report, and many schools in Brooklyn have been revisited time after time. The New York State Department of Education in

Albany will release these reports to researchers upon request but does not provide them to parents. Maryland, Virginia, and California are among other states that are now basing their entire school improvement effort on this premise that identify, intervene, restructure is effective.

Many teenagers, however, continue to fail a state's exit tests. At some high schools in New York City, passing rates on state exit tests are in the single digits (see table 6.1 to see results in Brooklyn). What is happening in our classrooms after a state intervention process that began in 1981? Did this state intervention lead to a new emphasis on literacy? What books are our teenagers being asked to read? Why are they failing current state college prep tests in such large numbers? And remember that the numbers presented here were compiled after a significant number of an entering class had already dropped out. The figures show the percentage of the students still enrolled at the end of high school who passed the test showing they are prepared for college, not the percentage of the entering class who started high school together in ninth grade who passed the tests.

I have included excerpts from earlier state inspection reports so the reader can begin to judge whether the state inspection/intervention process has influenced the opportunities for literacy in the high schools being discussed.

To learn more about what teenagers are reading in Brooklyn's schools, I interviewed thirty public high school students in the mid-1990s, starting with my neighborhood high school, John Jay in Park Slope.[1] The questions I asked are in an interview guide in the appendix.

BENNY VASQUEZ—A LATINO TENTH GRADER AT JOHN JAY HIGH SCHOOL IN BROOKLYN

Benny's schedule was unique. He was the only student in this group to be enrolled in two English classes simultaneously—a standard English 4 and a special class, English 4 Workshop, to prepare him for New York's minimum competency tests, still in place in the 1990s. Benny said that he was enrolled in the college-bound program at this high school and that this workshop was only for students in the college-bound program.

Table 6.1. Brooklyn Rates on New York State Exit Examinations (Regents) to Measure High School Students' Preparation for College

School Name	1994–1995 Regents Passing Rate	1995–1996 Regents Passing Rate	1996–1997 Regents Passing Rate
George Washington Vocational & Technical High School	2.8%	2.2%	N/A
William H. Maxwell Vocational High School	N/A	2.2%	N/A
El Puente Academy for Peace & Justice	N/A	N/A	N/A
Campus Academy of Business and Technology	N/A	2.0%	N/A
Campus Academy of Humanities	N/A	1.8%	N/A
Harry Van Arsdale High School	1.7%	N/A	1.4%
Bushwick High School	4.3%	5.1%	1.5%
Paul Robeson School of Business & Technology	6.7%	4.2%	1.5%
Prospect Heights High School	4.8%	1.8%	1.9%
Samuel J. Tilden High School	1.5%	4.0%	2.6%
George W. Wingate High School	5.3%	4.1%	3.2%
East New York Vocational & Technical High School	1.7%	0.7%	3.8%
Sarah J. Hale High School	0.6%	2.0%	5.0%
Franklin K. Lane High School	3.3%	2.8%	5.4%
Automotive High School	4.1%	2.4%	5.7%
Thomas Jeffferson High School	3.1%	0.6%	6.0%
William E. Grady High School	3.4%	10.1%	6.5%
Clara Barton High School	13.9%	12.6%	8.0%

John Jay High School	4.8%	2.4%	8.0%
Middle College High School at Medgar Evers	N/A	N/A	8.1%
Canarsie High School	13.4%	10.1%	8.9%
Campus Academy of Science and Math	8.0%	8.2%	11.0%
South Shore High School	22.0%	12.9%	11.2%
Lafayette High School	7.6%	12.4%	12.5%
Sheepshead Bay High School	13.5%	12.0%	12.8%
High School of Telecommunications	12.8%	11.5%	12.8%
New Utrecht High School	14.8%	10.6%	14.1%
Boys & Girls High School	11.3%	16.0%	14.6%
John Dewey High School	17.4%	15.1%	16.0%
Abraham Lincoln High School	23.3%	20.9%	19.5%
Franklin D. Roosevelt High School	18.0%	19.0%	20.8%
James Madison High School	26.6%	24.8%	23.8%
Fort Hamilton High School	18.7%	15.4%	24.2%
Science Skills Center High School	N/A	N/A	25.5%
Edward R. Murrow High School	45.7%	45.4%	49.2%
Kingsborough Academy for the Sciences High School	N/A	60.0%	55.8%
Midwood High School	62.9%	62.3%	61.0%
Brooklyn Technical High School	74.6%	79.3%	83.9%
Median	8.0%	10.1%	11.0%
Average	11.3%	14.5%	11.5%

Source: New York State Department of Education, *New York State School Report Card* (Albany: Author, June 10, 1998); available at www.nysed.gov.

What opportunities to read did these two English classes provide?

In his regular English class, Benny said that "we read out loud, [do] folder work, read by yourself—that's it." What's the folder work? "Conclusions, stuff like that."

For English Workshop, Benny said that there was no textbook but that he read plays such as *Romeo and Juliet*, which was presented in a magazine. "*Romeo and Juliet* was a magazine she gave us. We read it in class." On other days, he read books in the class. "Today we were reading a book. *The Man with the Red Badge.*"

In the English class itself, Benny said, "We read the language book; we don't read any stories."

For both of his English classes, Benny said that he had read three books so far this year—up to the end of April. He mentioned two books read during the first semester, *Jackie Robinson* and *Wilt Chamberlain*. For second semester, he said that he read a book about Hank Aaron and that the class hadn't "started another book."

Benny said that he had selected each of these books and read them for book reports. He said he preferred to choose what he read. "If a teacher picks a book for all of us, I might not like it. If I pick a book, I'll like it more and get into it."

Like many other students, his reading in social studies was just the textbook. "We leave the textbook home, and we have a textbook in school. He gives us a sheet of paper with questions, and we look at the book to get the answers." Benny said that he had homework in social studies three times a week. "He gives us three questions, and we have to read the chapter to get the answers."

As to his personal reading habits outside school, Benny was one of the few public school students to report a daily newspaper—*Newsday*—in his home. How long he read *Newsday* depended on "if they have good articles. I'd say an hour and a half." Benny said that he liked to read when he was bored. The one book that he had read on his own was *Jaws* from the public library.

Magazines were not a part of his reading at home. "My mother gets magazines, but I don't remember the names."

He had not bought any books on his own, nor had he received any books as gifts.

Finally, Benny reported major problems with noise when studying at home. "It's really bad, you can't concentrate, you can't focus. I'll lose my spot. I could probably read on, but I won't get the information in my head." What's the problem? "Dogs, music, fighting," he said.

ARIEL MIRANDA—A LATINO NINTH GRADER IN A COLLEGE-BOUND PROGRAM AT JOHN JAY HIGH SCHOOL

The next teenager whom I interviewed at Project Reach Youth, a neighborhood center in Park Slope, also attended John Jay High School.

Last semester in English I, Ariel remembered reading "a playbook with a lot of plays in it, and *The Outsiders* by S. E. Hinton, and *The Pig Man* by Hinton—that's it."

In addition to his regular class, Ariel also took English Workshop, for students reading below grade level, which provided more opportunities to read.

"In English Workshop, we read autobiographies. We work on cloze [reading out loud]; we read to ourselves. We discuss things. That's it.

"We get to pick whatever we want but it has to be on a famous world leader. First, we did research on the person. Then read the autobiography. Then do a book report. I'm reading *J.F.K.*, his autobiography.

"First semester, we read novels. Just Kennedy this semester."

Ariel's interest in world leaders and their stories about them carried into his global history class. "In this class," he said, "We learn about Indians, world leaders. We read about Egyptians and their tribes. Now we are reading about a Spanish tribe in Latin America.

"Some of the stories don't interest me. I like some of the stories about world leaders."

His opinion about what had been assigned in English class was about the same: "Some of [the reading] was good. Some of the stories were boring. Some were good. It was fair."

He said that he had read all of the assigned short stories (mysteries in a book by Isaac Asimov) that semester, "because we read it in class, but if you give it to me to take home and read, I wouldn't read it; I'll just leave it there."

Reading for homework was not even a question in Ariel's global history class. He was not allowed to take either of his softcover textbooks home.

For homework in this class, he said, there were "sheets with the questions on them, questions on world leaders or your opinions."

ANOTHER BROWNSTONE BROOKLYN HIGH SCHOOL

The next school is at the eastern edge of prosperous Brownstone Brooklyn. It is close to three of Brooklyn's most splendid cultural institutions: the Botanical Gardens, the Brooklyn Art Museum, and the main branch of the Brooklyn Public Library. With acres of lawns, rose gardens, ponds, and greenhouses, the Botanical Gardens may be Brooklyn's single most beautiful spot. But the monies raised at black-tie fund-raisers there are not shared with Prospect Heights High across the street. As the well to do attend fund-raisers for the Chamber of Commerce or other worthy causes, many may not know what the state is saying about the school across the street.

When a state inspection team visited Prospect Heights High School, they found teachers with low expectations who did not want to be there. Here is an excerpt from their 1989 findings:

> The Team's informal conversations reveal that there is some number (variously and subjectively estimated as from between ten (10) and sixty (60) percent) of the teaching staff who either do not wish to be at Prospect Heights High School, or who believe that nothing they do can make a difference. In either case, these individuals do not hold high expectations for Prospect Heights High School's students, and their attitude, though subjective, is a formidable barrier to the full realization of the school's mission statement and motto. A staff development program would provide the opportunity to change defeatist attitudes, and to inculcate positive expectations and beliefs.[2]

During this visit, the state inspection team also found a school building with seventy-five broken windows and one functioning bathroom for all the male students in a high school of 2,200.

> The physical plant is in deplorable condition. For example, at least 75 windows have been boarded up instead of being replaced with glass; the

playground is littered; and, there are no rings on the basketball back-boards. Once inside the building, physical conditions do *not* improve. The floors are dirty; halls and stairwells are poorly lit; some stairwells are permeated by the stench of urine; broken clocks in the halls have not been replaced; broken doorknobs *remain* unrepaired or unreplaced; and, at least three (3) broken drinking fountains that have been removed from the walls, still have not been replaced. Seventeen (17) years after it be-came a co-ed school, this five (5) story *building* still has only one (1) bathroom with urinals for males, and students do not have lockers in which to store their books and coats. Indeed, Principal Cioffi was pre-sented with a petition by a student leader on this very issue on the second day of the Team's visit. By allowing this, the State and the City convey a powerful message: Prospect Heights students and staff do not deserve, and should not expect, an attractive environment in which teaching and learning may proceed.

Defeatist attitudes, low expectations, a pitiful physical plant, teachers who did not want to be in the building. Did the state visit and this subse-quent report change this high school? Did teachers' expectations change? Did achievement improve?

It has not.

In fact, in the years after the state visit, the number of students who passed the state's college prep exams, the Regents, declined to only 1 per-cent (see table 6.2).

Students' results in the individual tests in English, global history, and American history and government are also very low. What are students being expected to read at Prospect Heights High? What curriculum did they face in the mid-1990s after fifteen years of state intervention in the high schools of New York state?

Table 6.2. Percentage of Graduates Earning Regents Diplomas at Prospect Heigths High School, Brooklyn, New York

1993–1994	1994–1995	1995–1996
2	4	1

Source: www.NYSED.gov.

TONYA BLAIR—AN AFRICAN AMERICAN ELEVENTH GRADER AT PROSPECT HEIGHTS HIGH SCHOOL

In English class, Tonya said that "we read poetry . . . he'll tell us how to decide what's important, the point of what the poet is saying to the readers. That's it. Basically we read the poetry and stuff."

Tonya had clear memories of the reading that had been required during the year—both for her first-semester class, English 5, and her current class, English 6.

"The book we're reading now is *Mice and Men*. That's the first book we started this semester [English 6]. . . . The book for English 5 had all different types of stories, a variety of stories. We'd read them and talk about them, just one big book of stories.

"For English 6 now, there is no textbook; he gives us [photocopied] sheets of poems. Then we go over the beat and the lines. We go over stress, and accent, which syllables are stressed. That's my major, English."

Pointing to *Mice and Men*, her first book of the spring semester, Tonya said, "To me, it's OK. So far it's OK."

Books were much less a part of her social studies courses during the current semester. During this semester, she was enrolled in two Regents social studies classes: global history and U.S. history and government; she also was taking an elective in social studies, African American history. She described the activities and reading in her African American history course.

"She [the teacher] talked about segregation and the fight for rights for blacks. We watch a lot of movies; that's basically what we do in that class, watch movies. We don't use any books. She just gives us a whole bunch of [photocopies]. She don't really tell you to read them. She just gives them out."

Tonya's two other social studies courses did not involve traditional textbooks or supplementary reading in biographies; instead, Tonya had review texts of facts and figures to prepare her for the Regents exam in each course. For example, she showed me her copy of the review text for U.S. history: *U.S. History Review Text* (2d ed., Amsco Publications). According to Tonya, these review texts were the only reading assigned this semester in these two social studies courses, and she was allowed to take these books home. (See table 6.3 for a list of all the books assigned to Tonya in her eleventh-grade classes.)

Table 6.3. Tonya Blair's Reading for the Eleventh Grade at Prospect Heights High School, Brooklyn, New York

Subject	Title
English	A short story book
English	*Of Mice and Men*
English	Photocopies of poems
Global history	A review textbook
U.S. history	A review textbook called *U.S. History Review Text*
African American history	Photocopies—no textbook

A HIGH SCHOOL PROMISES TO IMPROVE

The next school in this sample, Eastern District High School, enrolls Latino and African American students from the Bushwick and Willliamsburg neighborhoods in Brooklyn. Eastern District, built in the late 1970s, is considered new rather than old. It sprawls over an entire city block and has its own AstroTurf playing field, a luxury in Brooklyn.

Eastern District is famous in Brooklyn, at least in my mind, because it has continued in operation for more than fifteen years without ever meeting the minimum state standards. Teenagers in this school never passed the state's minimum competency tests, the RCTs, in sufficient numbers for the school to remain registered or accredited. But year after year, through the twelve years of Governor Mario Cuomo, and now Governor George Pataki, Eastern District has stayed open. Year after year, the state accepted *promises* to improve rather than actual improvement. (New York allows its failing schools to file plans for improvement rather than actually improve.)

Here are samples of what state inspectors have written about Eastern District in past school registration reports:

Eastern District: 1984—Missing Textbooks and a Meager Overall Program

The English classes were observed to lack literature textbooks. An insufficient amount of materials is provided for pupils. . . . The school has a meager and unappealing overall program. Many subjects and courses such as printing, carpentry, and other industrial arts courses cannot be scheduled. They are unavailable because no teachers for these subjects are on staff, although well-equipped shops are in the building.

Eastern District: 1989—Low Expectations for Students and a Lack of Textbooks

In teachers' desire to teach students content material, many seem to have taken over the responsibility for student learning, thus giving the impression that the students are not capable of performing at a higher level of expectation, e.g., teachers dominating lessons, majority of time in classes devoted to teachers talking, outlines done for students on the chalkboard, lack of utilization of textbooks, and reliance on worksheets.

Eastern District: 1989—Little Staff Development

The total faculty is not involved in continuous staff development toward school improvement. We saw no evidence that any staff development activities were particularly focused on assisting teachers in developing strategies that would improve communication with students of varied backgrounds. The absence of such a program is acknowledged by the principal.

Today, nearly twenty years after state inspectors first found a "meager" program at Eastern District, not much has changed. The Board of Education decided to divide the one large school into four minischools, but achievement is still weak.

Eastern District is unusual also for its parents. Most parents in Brooklyn are silent about the borough's weak secondary schools. Eastern District's parents, mostly Latino from the Williamsburg section of Brooklyn, have taken to the streets and protested violence in the school's lunchroom and a racist comment by a teacher some years ago.

What are students experiencing at Eastern District?

Robert Holmes—An African American Ninth Grader at Eastern District High School

Robert was the only public high school student to report a silent reading period during his English class. "In English class at certain times during the week, we read short stories silently for almost half the period—we have forty-five-minute periods." He said that sometimes the students choose what they read; sometimes the teacher gives them an assigned story.

Robert said that he was taking Regents or college prep classes in his major subject areas. He did have a textbook for English, but no novels to read. All of his books that involved literature were "collections of short stories, no novels." He said that his class worked on grammar skills, punctuation, and letter-writing skills in English class.

For his social studies class, which was Global History II, he had a textbook and handouts to read. Robert said that he was allowed to take his social studies textbook home and that he took it home almost everyday. Beyond the textbook, he said that he had done no other reading for social studies that year.

There had been no book reports to write that year, Robert said. He remembered reading one book for the year and a number of short stories. He said the book was called *Jed*, about a frontiersman, Jediah Smith. He added that he would recommend this book and his short story book.

VIEW AND RECOMMENDATIONS

Reading Experiences of Minority Students in This Sample

1. *Volume of reading not a part of the curriculum.* The New York City Board of Education does not seem to make a connection between the number of books assigned in high school and the development of fluency in reading. Many educators assume that reading is a skill completely developed by early elementary school, which does not need attention after this period in the regular curriculum. Reading teachers reject this view. They believe that reading is a developmental process that never ends, and they would like to see a constant effort at assigning books and encouraging reading.

All of the public school students in this sample report a limited number of books assigned to be read during the school year. For these public school students, an average number of books assigned for the entire year in both English and social studies was six. In many cases, this was two novels or plays in English each semester. Sometimes an English textbook was available to be taken home. In social studies classes in most cases, the only reading was a textbook or a review guide for the Regents Competency Tests, the state's set of minimum tests, or a review book for the state's college prep tests, the Regents.[3]

2. *Old titles.* The titles assigned in English classes are old; it seems teachers are stuck with the classics of the past such as *Wuthering Heights*

and the work of S. E. Hinton and have little access to more contemporary fiction. Students complain about these titles. "I did not like any of them. They were, like, obsolete because they don't speak the same way anymore so it was kind of pointless," one student told me. As classroom teachers know, the ability of schools to coerce reading is limited. Starting with titles that students enjoy and actually read may be a crucial first step in improving students' reading skills.

3. *Heavy use of photocopies and short stories.* Also, these English classes seem to emphasize short stories with short-length reading assignments rather than the longer reading experiences available in novels. The use of photocopies and short stories reduces students' reading experiences and probably contributes to the very weak performance of New York City high school students on the SATs and the state Regents exams. Longer reading assignments would build students' vocabularies and, in general, better prepare them for college or the workplace.

4. *Little multicultural literature.* Does New York City have a multicultural curriculum in its high school social studies classes? The controversial New York State Department of Education social studies syllabus, "One Nation, Many Peoples: A Declaration of Cultural Independence," which urged the adoption of more diverse texts,[4] seems to have had little impact on the classrooms the Brooklyn youngsters in this sample attend. While the small sample presented here cannot offer any conclusions, it does at least show the need to examine how difficult it may be for a new "official" state curriculum to improve the reading experiences offered in local schools.

Although world history textbooks have included many more topics about Africans and Asians, are these textbooks what teenagers should be reading? As readers will see in the next chapters, some private schools don't think so.

5. *Just the textbook or review book in social studies.* In terms of developing youngsters into readers, social studies assignments look like a wasteland in this sample. Very little reading is assigned in social studies courses beyond the textbook or review book, and the textbooks are not available to be taken home in each case. It looks like the state's use of minimum competency courses and Regents Examinations in Global Studies and American History has pushed local schools toward using review books to prepare for these tests. Private schools in New York City have re-

jected the state's crippling of history. "We spend a lot of time on the French Revolution and the Industrial Revolution, but not all the dates, battles, and wars in between. But if they give you tests, you have to teach all those things. You can't have any creative teaching," said one private school official in explaining his opposition to the state tests.[5]

6. *Little socialization to read in school.* The students whom I interviewed reported that there is very little use of activities such as sustained silent reading periods (SSR) in their schools. Silent reading periods are designed to build the habit of reading in youngsters who otherwise may not be reading much. Other activities that might also influence socialization toward reading, such as participation in a Reading Is Fundamental program, were also not reported.

7. *Socialization activities outside school.* The public school students in this survey also report limited family involvement in their reading experiences. They did not report receiving books as gifts, and few public school students bought books on their own. Magazine reading varied; many students read no magazines at home, but only one student did mention reading four magazines: *Young and Modern, Movieline, Fashion Magazine,* and *GQ.* There was little reading of a daily newspaper. Unfortunately, this survey did not contain direct questions about summer reading.

Conclusion

The big five cities in New York—Buffalo, Rochester, Syracuse, Albany, and New York City—are not the only school districts in the United States with literacy problems. As the suburbs become economically and racially diverse, closing the achievement gap between the races has become the announced goal, the top priority, of suburban superintendents also.

In chapter 2, we saw time run out on Chancellor Crew and his literacy initiatives in New York City before substantial progress was made. He pushed a plan for reading twenty-five books a year into the junior high schools but made little effort at providing new training and new dollars for books to actually give teachers in these schools the ability to energize their reading and writing assignments. His efforts at the high school level did not make it past announcements on memos. Of course, the obstacles were immense when he started. He began with a system that was not paying much attention to reading and writing.

As we saw in chapter 1, simply providing each student with a textbook was not always a practice in the school system Crew inherited. Some administrators in New York City schools feared losing a book more than providing a teenager with opportunities for homework.

Is progress easier in smaller suburban systems, often with larger tax bases from the property taxes of their affluent residents? Presumably the fear that students might take books home and lose them is not crippling education in these districts. We will look in the next four chapters at literacy practices in the public schools of Maryland and California. The school district in the next chapter is a prototype of a wealthy suburb. Its well-educated parents manage the laboratories at the National Institute of Health and direct the nation's business at the State Department and other federal agencies. What has happened so far to the efforts to close the achievement gap in this suburb?

NOTES

Most of this chapter is reprinted from a journal article I published in 1996 and is used here with permission of Transaction Publishers.

1. Jim McCabe, "Afro-American and Latino Teenagers in New York City: Race and Language Development," *Community Review* 14 (1996): 13–26 (ERIC EJ532978).

2. New York State Education Department, *Registration Review Report for Prospect Heights High School,* November 14, 15, and 16, 1989, 6–10.

3. In a letter to parents in January 1997, the commissioner of education in New York state, Richard P. Mills, announced that the students would be taking Regents or college preparatory tests in the future to graduate, rather than the state's minimum competency examinations. This announcement had been made to the press and reported in the media some months earlier.

4. New York State Social Studies Review and Development Committee, *One Nation, Many Peoples: A Declaration of Cultural Independence* (Albany: New York State Education Department, 1991).

5. Neil S. Rosenfeld, "Private Schools Spurn NY Course Plan," *Newsday*, November 9, 1985, p. 11.

Chapter Seven

Are Suburban Schools
Closing the Reading Gap?

The Experiences of Montgomery County in Maryland

In the late 1990s, a new leader, Dr. Jerry D. Weast, arrived at work in the Maryland suburbs outside Washington, D.C. At the hiring ceremonies, he announced that closing the achievement gap between the races was his top priority. In this district, money was not going to be an obstacle. It was not Baltimore, or Jersey City, or Newark, or Camden, jurisdictions that would close in a week without state aid. Instead, in this county, money had never severely limited the quality of the schools. With neighborhood after neighborhood of half-million to million-dollar-plus houses, the tax base was more than adequate. This county can generate much of what it needs through local property taxes; state aid is important here but not the basis of the school economy. With spending per pupil at close to $9,000, the story of schools in Montgomery County should not be one of shortages. (See figure 7.1 for spending data.)

Even with this funding, Weast faced some challenges. Enrollment was growing rapidly as farmland in the northern sections of the county turned into townhouses, condominiums, and single-family houses. Portables were being added to older schools. Some high schools received large additions, moving their total size well over two thousand. New schools were being built. And enrollment was changing. Once an almost all-white district, now it was less than half white—with large enrollments of Asian, Latino, and African American students (see figure 7.2).

Weast's investments are clear. A recent report outlines where the new superintendent decided to take this suburban school system. Closing the achievement gap was the core goal.

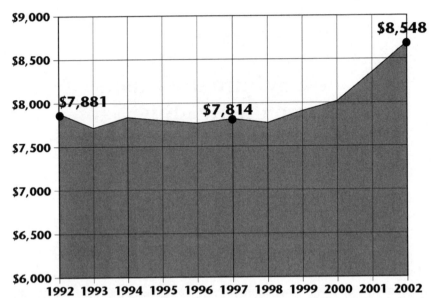

Figure 7.1. Cost-per-pupil amounts in Montgomery County Public Schools (Maryland), fiscal years 1992–2002.
Source: Citizens Budget, 2002, Maryland County Public Schools.

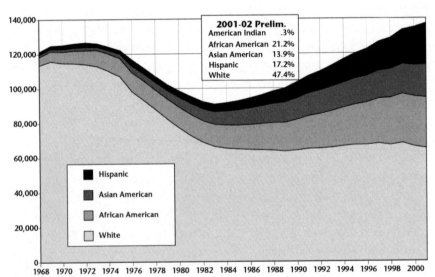

Figure 7.2. Montgomery County Public Schools, enrollment by race/ethnic group, 1968–2000.
Source: Citizens Budget, fiscal year 2002, Maryland County Public Schools.

In 1999, the Montgomery County Public Schools (MCPS) began to make fundamental reforms in the way the school system works. The goal is to raise the bar of expectations for all students and to close the achievement gap between groups. The Board of Education adopted a set of five academic priorities to which it committed itself and the entire school system for at least four years. These priorities are directed at providing a high-quality teacher in every classroom, and giving teachers the tools and support they need to raise the standards of academic performance. . . .

This new plan—known as "A Call to Action"—emphasized improving the early literacy experiences of children. Kindergarten teachers received new training. Full-day kindergarten became available in more schools, and during this day a ninety-minute block of time was now devoted to literacy.[1]

Just as the new superintendent was investing millions of dollars in K–2 education at the local level, the state was making changes that could also influence literacy. No longer were local standards enough. Now each student has to pass state tests in subject areas.

The state has already created tests on a number of subjects, said Susan Spencer, an instructional specialist with the MCPS. "In the first phase, the state created tests in biology, algebra, government, geometry and English. Additional tests will be added in other subjects in phases 2 and 3. Eventually students will need to pass these tests in order to graduate."

So a teacher needs to look at the state content indicators, which could be described as the topics to be covered on the test, to know what the kids need to pass the state tests, she explained. "If I look at content indicators for a test in government, I know what the students will need for success on the high school assessment in government. If my students know those standards, that content, then I can enrich the curriculum."

Spencer said that the time required to cover the topics in the state curriculum does influence the local high schools. "Time is an issue when you have numerous tests and all the obligations to fulfill in the curriculum." She recommends the use of biographies and social histories if time allows.

Wonderful books are available to supplement textbooks, she added. Two books that she would highly recommend are Tom Brokaw's book about World War II, *The Greatest Generation,* and Doris Kearns Goodwin's social history of life in Long Island, *Wait Till Next Year*. "Doris Kearns Goodwin's social history would be a wonderful book for kids to read. She's a delight to read," Spencer said. "Biographies are also highly engaging and a way to turn kids on to history."

But are these books available? Spencer said she was not close enough to the high schools to know which schools were assigning reading beyond the textbook. Fortunately, homework assignments are now in online databases available to the public.

As the sample in table 7.1 indicates, textbooks seem to be the major source of reading in high school social studies classes in the system, and the reading assignments seem to be very short—when reading had been assigned, which was not every night or even every weekend.

Imagine if the students doing these reading assignments were African American or Latino? Is this undemanding schedule of reading assignments going to help close the reading gap between the races in Montgomery County?

Ty Healey, the resource teacher (department chair) for social studies, said that this snapshot approach may not accurately capture the amount of reading done in biographies, trade books, and other materials since assignments in the online database only cover two weeks, so a biography assigned in March will not show up in the database in May. His information about the database is only correct at first glance; while the default view of the database only covers two weeks, a user can set the database to retrieve up to six months of homework assignments. An analysis of over forty homework assignments in social studies in county high schools in May 2002 did not show a single reference to a biography, autobiography, or trade book. In addition to short textbook reading assignments, teachers were asking students to complete time lines, to critique online PowerPoint slide shows, to analyze short excerpts from primary sources that they had posted online, and to complete a variety of other assignments.

Fortunately, another indicator may show the level of investment in reading in high school social studies. Healey was willing to provide information about the books he had been able to order for his staff of fourteen other social studies teachers and himself. The business manager of his high school explains there are obstacles even for a department chair such as Healey in providing teenagers in Montgomery County with more reading experiences.

Table 7.1. A Sample of Reading Assignments in History Classes, Montgomery County, Maryland, Public Schools, Spring 2002

Subject	School	Assignment	Due Date	Total Pages of Reading Assigned
U.S. history	WJ	Timeline activity on civil rights movement	5/30/02	None
U.S. history	BCC	Read pp. 704–710 (1 + 3).	5/7/02	7
U.S. history	WJ	Read pp. 696–703 in textbook.	5/2/02 assigned on Thursday due on Monday	8 over a weekend
U.S. history	WJ	Read pp. 636–642 and do questions 11, 12, 13 on p. 664	4/30/02	7
Modern world history	WJ	Read pp. 807–810 (rise of totalitarian states) and answer questions 1–3 on p. 810.	4/25/02	4
Modern world history	WJ	Read pp. 801–805; bring text.	4/23/02	5
Modern world history	WJ	No homework	4/20/02	No homework for all classes MHW. Please bring your book Monday.
National, state, and local government	AE	Answer the comprehension questions on the political cartoon worksheet with complete sentences.	5/2/02	1
National, state, and local government	AE	Find a newspaper article about foreign relations. Write a summary of the article in your own words. Turn in the article and the summary together.	5/2/02 One week to complete this assignment	1–2
National, state, and local government government	AE	On the foreign relations worksheet write the foreign policy options available, possible consequences, and your reason for choosing the best option.	5/2/02 one week to complete	2–3

Source: Online database at http://coldfusion.mcps.k12.md.us/cfms/webteam/homeworkboard/.

A teacher in a local high school cannot simply fill out a form, hand it to the business manager, and then have a class set of 150 biographies of *Walking with the Wind*, John Lewis's memoir of the civil rights movement, available for his or her American history course in the fall. Instead, this teacher must compete against the textbook needs of the entire school. This teacher has no direct ability to order supplementary reading materials that might provide more practice in reading and thus develop more fluent readers.

Will these supplementary materials arrive? Will the budget process provide secondary school teachers with a large number of books for students to read during the school year?

Tom Stup, the business manager at Walter Johnson, Healey's high school in Montgomery County, explains the process. "All the resource teachers [chairs of the larger departments] and department chairs who run the smaller departments are informed that an allocation of x dollars has been received from the county for textbooks. They then prepare a justification document for textbooks indicating their textbook requirements for the following year. And in the document they indicate all their reasons such as replacing old dated textbooks or a curriculum change that requires new textbooks.

"Then the document goes to the Budget Committee, an internal committee consisting of the principal, the business manager, two resource teachers, one department chair, and one or two students. The Budget Committee reviews requests and determines the school's budget for the year. All of the allocations are released to the school so that everyone can see what everyone is getting."

At this high school in an affluent section of the county, the budget process provided little but textbooks for students to read in the three required social studies classes. Healey provided the numbers for purchases of textbooks and supplementary reading for the current year (see table 7.2).

As table 7.2 indicates, the records of book purchases by Healey's department show few orders for anything but textbooks. Collectively his staff of fifteen was only able to order two books in addition to textbooks among all of them in one year. Healey explained his department began the year with just the new textbooks. He said the new textbooks were available at the beginning of the year, while the money for the two supplementary books, *Thirteen Days* and *Savage Inequalities*, did not appear un-

Table 7.2. Social Studies Department Book Purchases School Year 2001-2002, Walter Johnson High School, Montgomery County Maryland Public Schools

Class	Quantity	Title
American History	70	**Textbook:** *The Americans-Reconstruction though the 20th Century* (McDougal Littell)
American History or Government	84	**Tradebook:** *Thirteen Days* (W.W. Norton & Company)
American History or Government	60	**Tradebook:** *Savage Inequalities* (Harper Perennial)
World History	72	**Textbook:** *World History: Patterns of Interaction* (McDougal Littell)
National, State, and Local Government (NSL)	40	**Textbook:** *West's American Government* (Glencoe McGraw-Hill)
AP Sociology	35	**Textbook:** *Sociology and You* (Glencoe McGraw-Hill)
AP U.S. History	25	**Textbook:** *The Unfinished Nation* (Glencoe McGraw-Hill)
AP World History	72	**Textbook:** *The Human Record* (Houghton-Mifflin)
AP World History	152	**Textbook:** *The Earth and Its People* (Houghton-Mifflin)
AP Psychology	160	**Textbook:** *Psychology: Myers in Modules* (Von Holtzbrinck Publishing Service)
Honors American Government (APEX Program)	65	**Textbook:** *American Government* (Houghton-Mifflin)

Source: Ty Healey, social studies Department, Walter Johnson High School.

til midyear when the business manager announced that there was money available for additional books. Healey also explained that his department had some additional titles to supplement textbooks. "Examples I can think of right now include *Why We Can't Wait, Nectar in a Sieve, Animal Farm, Black Like Me*," he said.

Not surprisingly, the homework assignments available at this high school depend heavily on textbooks. "In this department, most people use the textbook to provide a lot of background and supplement it with newspaper articles," Healey said. A sample of homework assignments supports Healey's conclusion: very short reading assignments in textbooks with occasional assignments of newspaper articles.

This strategy on relying on short textbook assignments, teacher-constructed worksheets, and so on, may not be challenged in Healey's school. After all, students there graduate with SAT scores at the top of the county—far above the Maryland and national averages. But can this standard curriculum, with its modest reading assignments year after year from sixth through twelfth grade, help close the reading gap between the races in the county's high schools, where achievement is much lower? The gap in SAT verbal scores is over 100 points, and it is not closing.[2] In fact, in high schools in the eastern part of the county, which are heavily African American and Latino, SAT scores are declining.

VIEWS AND RECOMMENDATIONS

What should Superintendent Jerry D. Weast be doing to close this achievement gap?

One voice argues that Weast may not be running one but three separate school systems. This situation may complicate his planning. According to Brigid Schulte of the *Washington Post,* "In recent years, the 'world-class' Montgomery County school system has evolved into three distinct systems, school officials say: the elite, high-performing school district that rivals any private school, an above-average suburban district, and an 'urban fringe' system with many of the same problems of high poverty and low performance that plague urban schools."[3]

Schulte goes on to describe the plan for a new network of smaller high schools in the "urban fringe" area. "The consortium plan for Montgomery Blair, Albert Einstein, John F. Kennedy and Wheaton high schools, and for Northwood High when it reopens in 2004, centers on four principles: make these massive schools, which range from 1,300 to 3,000 students, smaller and more personal; get great teachers and principals; offer an engaging curriculum; and raise expectations."

"Research shows it works everyplace else," Superintendent Jerry D. Weast said. "It should work here."

The plan for improvement in the five low-performing high schools are detailed. According to Walter Gibson, the director of the Downcounty Consortium, "To reverse course, the first thing these large schools are doing is attempting to become smaller and more personal, so fewer students fall through the cracks. They have a $1.95 million grant from the federal government and $1.4 million from the county to help them get started.

"Each school has created a ninth-grade academy. When classes start next week, freshmen will be divided into teams of one hundred students and taught by a core of teachers whose job it will be to get to know each of them intimately. Already, administrators at each school have combed through data on each student, including test scores going back to fourth grade, to determine what each one needs. High performers are to be pushed. Calls have been made through the summer to students who were not recommended for honors but show promise, to get them into these high-level classes.

"Students who lack basic skills—25 percent of the freshmen entering Wheaton and Einstein read at the sixth-grade level or below—are being assigned double-period algebra and intensive literacy classes," Gibson continued. "Most freshmen will take a new class called 'Connections,' which is designed to teach them study skills and time management, and help them see how school ultimately helps them to the career they want.

"For the upper grades, each school is also creating 'smaller learning communities,' or schools within the schools, to appeal to a variety of student interests.

"The idea of the special programs is to draw out students' passions and set them on fire. Or at least to keep them in school. We want to give kids a reason to stay in school and persist," said Gibson.

But much is missing in this Downcounty Consortium plan.

1. *Waiting until high school to intervene is not a best practice.* If one believes the research that reading is developmental and that only practice, practice, and practice builds reading skills, then why wait until high school for double periods of literacy, as the Downcounty Consortium Plan intends to do? If the goal is to build the habit of reading in all youngsters, why don't the superintendent and his leadership team begin demanding monthly reports from elementary and middle school teachers about the reading and writing assignments in their classrooms? There are simply no debates in the research about the need to practice reading in order to build fluency. No one is arguing in the *Reading Teacher, Reading Research Quarterly* or the psychology journals that there are other paths to fluency. If practice is the only path, why wait until ninth grade for an emphasis on literacy? Won't all the children of the county schools be better served by an emphasis on building the habit of reading much earlier?

2. *Montgomery County's underspending on books is not a best practice.* Of course, for more books to appear in classrooms, the county

cannot continue with the situation at Walter Johnson High School, described earlier in this chapter, where an entire social studies faculty was able to acquire copies of only two trade books for supplementary reading for an entire academic year. Unfortunately, this situation—the same lack of funds that shaped buying books at Walter Johnson—is common practice throughout the system. Both middle schools and high schools are spending less than $50 per year per teenager on books—an amount not even sufficient to replace textbooks on a six-year cycle much less buy large numbers of biographies and trade books to build the habit of reading. Montgomery County must spend much more on books in the middle school years and make teachers more visible guides to reading, and more accountable for the amount of reading accomplished, in order to prepare teenagers for success in high school. The changes at the middle school level that are being implemented may be too little, too later. (See tables 7.3 and 7.4 for spending on books in Montgomery County's secondary schools.)

3. *Keeping teachers away from decisions about books is not a best practice.* Teachers have many roles in school systems from checking attendance to planning the daily lecture or class discussion, but their role in developing literacy is often not officially prescribed. Maybe it should be. Maybe the importance of teachers as guides to literacy should receive official recognition, since in the bureaucratic school systems where they work, if a function is not embedded in the school regulations, it isn't important.

Some researchers feel that unless the poor can find guides and sponsors to literacy, little will change. The well-to-do will continue to become literate without too much difficulty, and the poor will find the path to literacy filled with so many obstacles that success is uncertain.

Deborah Brandt is one of these researchers. She argues that to track literacy, one must move "beyond SES shorthand" and look at how individuals have encouraged each other to read throughout the past.[4] She suggests that developing literacy may be more complex than just handing out survey textbooks once at the beginning of a semester. A teacher's enthusiasm for a new book may matter. A teacher's willingness to recommend what comes next for a student may matter; what are the next books to read, who are the next teachers in the school who can help with writing skills. Brandt writes that

Table 7.3.   Spending on High School Texbooks at Montgomery County Public Schools (Maryland), 2000–2002

No	School Name	FY 2000	FY 2001	FY 2002	Number of Students	Per Pupil
406	Bethesda CC	$ 49,807	$ 56,088	$ 62,126	1338	$46.43
757	Blair	123,181	126,789	142,119	3087	$46.04
321	Blake	151,290	62,860	73,239	1567	$46.74
602	Churchill	74,889	76,581	85,981	1875	$45.86
701	Damascus HS	70,122	73,329	85,454	1937	$44.12
789	Einstein	66,959	69,899	74,532	1708	$43.64
551	Gaithersburg HS	81,393	85,536	90,962	2001	$45.46
424	Johnson, W	67,805	70,211	79,754	1885	$42.31
815	Kennedy	60,187	58,672	64,378	1476	$43.62
510	Magruder	75,646	79,344	91,824	2102	$43.68
201	Montgomery, R.	68,340	69,587	77,838	1711	$45.49
246	Northwest	137,946	59,697	72,281	1743	$41.47
315	Paint Branch	65,088	65,177	73,287	1700	$43.11
152	Poolesville HS	28,690	29,225	33,195	726	$45.72
125	Quince Orchard	73,819	73,641	82,053	1854	$44.26
230	Rockville	48,560	48,515	48,235	1145	$42.13
104	Seneca Valley	62,281	63,395	69,934	1614	$43.33
503	Sherwood HS	76,492	77,027	84,160	1945	$43.27
798	Springbrook	86,650	79,834	93,166	2081	$44.77
545	Watkins Mill HS	81,838	82,106	83,298	1973	$42.22
782	Wheaton	55,598	55,465	59,013	1402	$42.09
427	Whitman	74,844	77,161	83,633	1847	$45.28
234	Wootton	78,586	80,101	92,016	2045	$45.00
	Total Allocations	$1,760,010	$1,620,239	$1,802,478	40762	$44.22
	Total Expenditures	$1,758,501	$1,767,985	$1,713,110	40762	$42.03

Source: for financial data: Mr. Brian J. Porter, Director of Communications, MCPS for school enrollment data: http://www.mcps.k12.md.us/departments/dea/saag/.

Table 7.4. Spending on Middle School Texbooks at Montgomery County Public Schools (Maryland), 2000–2002

No	School Name	FY 2000	FY 2001	FY 2002	Enrollment	Per Pupil	Met Local 6th Grade Reading Standard
823	Argyle	$ 25,054	$ 25,766	$ 30,656	687	$45	No
705	Baker	29,904	31,862	32,668	581	$56	No
333	Banneker	40,362	42,587	48,619	927	$52	No
335	Briggs Chaney	36,001	34,043	36,021	914	$39	No
606	Cabin John	39,027	38,626	44,691	960	$47	Yes
157	Clemente	31,017	33,286	36,069	826	$44	No
775	Eastern	38,003	37,647	38,895	977	$40	No
507	Farquhar	31,284	28,614	31,614	896	$35	No
248	Forest Oak	37,959	39,116	43,876	977	$45	No
237	Frost	43,432	45,924	50,822	828	$61	Yes
554	Gaithersburg MS	34,888	31,862	32,141	1,013	$32	No
228	Hoover	43,432	45,746	48,619	981	$50	Yes
311	Key	38,938	40,584	44,687	954	$47	No
107	King MS	35,511	38,226	43,385	909	$48	No
708	Kingsview	41,430	51,220	56,762	986	$58	No
818	Lee	26,700	23,986	27,782	735	$38	No
557	Mont Village	29,504	30,394	30,608	729	$42	No
115	Neelsville	33,776	33,998	38,363	918	$42	No

413	North Bethesda	131,837	92,523	30,551	676	$45	Yes
812	Parkland	47,882	50,819	55,986	1,049	$53	No
155	Parks	42,186	37,469	45,710	950	$48	No
247	Poole MS	17,667	16,821	19,783	500	$40	No
428	Pyle	54,468	54,023	58,869	1,139	$52	Yes
562	Redland	30,616	32,085	40,332	792	$51	No
105	Ridgeview	38,626	38,226	44,595	1,014	$44	No
707	Rocky Hill	31,061	31,150	33,759	751	$45	No
521	Shady Grove	157,365	110,610	34,775	800	$43	No
647	Silver Spring Int	182,007	128,659	43,757	923	$47	No
778	Sligo Middle	50,997	54,869	55,940	1,216	$46	No
755	Takoma Park MS	42,587	42,008	44,739	751	$60	Yes
232	Tilden	36,535	28,035	31,231	723	$43	Yes
211	West	38,315	38,938	47,517	1,096	$43	No
412	Westland	40,317	44,678	46,361	1,029	$45	No
811	White Oak	33,687	35,155	43,158	984	$44	No
820	Wood	36,357	38,404	45,361	1,000	$45	No
	TOTAL ALLOCATIONS	$1,648,723	$1,527,951	$1,438,702			
	TOTAL EXPENDITURES	$1,541,421	$1,338,384	$1,409,179			

Source: Mr. Brian J. Porter, director of communications, MCPS.

intuitively, *sponsors* seemed a fitting term for the figures who turned up most typically in people's memories of literacy learning: older relatives, teachers, priests, supervisors, military officers, editors, influential authors. Sponsors, as we ordinarily think of them, are powerful figures who bankroll events or smooth the way for initiates. Usually richer, more knowledgeable, and more entrenched than the sponsored, sponsors nevertheless enter a reciprocal relationship with those they underwrite. They lend their resources or credibility to the sponsored but also stand to gain benefits from their success, whether by direct repayment or, indirectly, by credit of association. *Sponsors* also proved an appealing term in my analysis because of all the commercial references that appeared in these twentieth-century accounts— the magazines, peddled encyclopedias, essay contests, radio and television programs, toys, fan clubs, writing tools, and so on, from which so much experience with literacy was derived. As the twentieth century turned the abilities to read and write into widely exploitable resources, commercial sponsorship abounded.

Brandt also states that "unequal conditions of literacy sponsorship . . . lie behind differential outcomes in academic performance."[5] She argues that what is seen as a failure of values in low-caste racial groups—a failure to care about literacy—may in fact be a failure of access to literacy. (Do school systems such as Montgomery realize that parents of the poor may not be able to hand their teenagers cash for a trip to the local Barnes and Noble or Borders? If they did realize that some households can do far more than others to encourage literacy, would they not be much more conscious of how teachers are handling the responsibilities of developing literacy?) She writes:

A focus on sponsorship can force a more explicit and substantive link between literacy learning and systems of opportunity and access. A statistical correlation between high literacy achievement and high socioeconomic, majority-race status routinely shows up in results of national tests of reading and writing performance. These findings capture yet, in their shorthand way, obscure the unequal conditions of literacy sponsorship that lie behind differential outcomes in academic performance. Throughout their lives, affluent people from high-caste racial groups have multiple and redundant contacts with powerful literacy sponsors as a routine part of their economic and political privileges. Poor people and those from low-caste racial groups have less consistent, less politically secured access to literacy sponsors—especially to the ones that can grease their way to academic and economic success. Differences in performances are often attributed to family background (namely education and income of parents) or to particular norms and values operating within different ethnic groups or social classes. But in either case, much more is usually at work.

If you believe even part of Brandt's analysis that contact with a teacher or another figure with access to materials or information about literacy matters to teenagers, then a school system needs to move far beyond data such as SAT scores to measure the intellectual lives of teenagers. It needs to look closely at the volume and quality of reading and writing assignments—not just in English classes but also in social studies classes.

4. *Limiting book-length reading assignments to English classes is not a best practice.* Research tells us that reading is a developmental process depending on practice at every age. When I examined the assignments in English classes in the county's homework database (mentioned earlier in this chapter), much more reading was being assigned in English classes than in social studies. Informal interviews with current county high school students confirmed this. Social studies seems to be the area where little reading and writing are being accomplished. Since the content of social studies classes is closely tied to state curriculum objectives that cover content rather than the development of literacy, school leaders face choices.

Parents seeking evidence of the state's neglect of literacy in social studies classes should turn to the state education department's own documents. In almost forty pages of curriculum goals for government, U.S. history, and world history, not a single book or writing assignment is mentioned.[6] Montgomery County warned its teachers in 2000 that the new state objectives were now to shape local curricula. "In the following pages you will find the first attempt at directly creating Montgomery County Public Schools high school social studies curriculum out of the standards assessed by the state."

As we'll see in the next chapter, one alternative is to connect each era of history with a long list of reading. Should the leadership in the county school system give parents the choice: a long list of readings that will take time and may lead to some complaints from teenagers (e.g., "It's too much work," "It's too hard") or business as usual, very modest assignments from one textbook for the entire year?

6. *Keeping information about books from parents is not a best practice.* Parents may need to ask more questions of the Montgomery County Public Schools if they want to see teachers become effective sponsors of literacy in secondary schools. The county school system needs to prepare parents for encounter with teachers at "Back to School" nights and on informal occasions. Parents need to ask questions that will elicit the necessary information about the development of literacy from the teachers they meet:

- How many books do you plan to assign for my son or daughter to read this year in history and English classes?
- What are the titles? Do they include writers published in the last twenty years? Will the system keep assigning Thorton Wilder and *Our Town* for another fifty years, or will Toni Morrison and *The Bluest Eye* eventually become an acceptable assignment?
- Are these readings to be solitary, individual activities for book reports, or will the whole class read and discuss and then write about *Dead Man Walking* by Sister Helen Prejean and other books on topics that help define a nation?
- When will teachers in county schools have the authority to order books, to build syllabi around biographies and trade books, and to make these syllabi visible to parents before a semester starts rather than using the one book fits all method recommended by the state education department?
- When will parents and their teenagers be able to choose among English and social studies courses based on their publicized reading lists (as is done in the private school described in chapter 12)?

So far, the leadership team at the Board of Education headquarters in Montgomery County has stayed cautious. They have not touched the curriculum in the county's secondary schools in social studies or English — a curriculum now controlled by state curriculum objectives. They have not considered giving more authority to the teachers in classrooms to select materials. And, not surprisingly, little has changed. Until teachers have the authority to order several books, it is difficult to see how teenagers are going to have a large number of books to read. For the first four years of his administration, the new superintendent has not seen improvements in the achievement gap in county schools. Can he really believe that improvements in early childhood education and the new plans for a Downcounty Consortium of at-risk schools will be enough to close the achievement gap?

So far, the leadership in Montgomery County—despite the area's wealth and political clout in the state capital—has operated in exactly the same manner as Schools Chancellor Crew in New York City in the late 1990s: many initiatives in the early childhood education, and neglect of reading after grade 5 when secondary school starts. This approach will not work.

Fortunately, alternatives exist, as we will see in the next chapter.

NOTES

1. Montgomery County, Maryland, Public Schools, *A Call to Action: The Citizens Budget, FY 2002* (Bethesda: Author, 2002).

2. SAT data available from the Montgomery County Public Schools (MCPS) do distinguish between students who have spent their entire careers in county schools, called "stayers," and those who arrived in middle school or even later in high school. While the gap in SAT scores between African American stayers and white stayers is considerably lower than the aggregate gap, it is still over 200 points. And the percentage of African American teenagers taking the SAT is only 57 percent in 2001, as compared to 82 percent of white stayers, so the actual size of the gap cannot be accurately determined. See p. 11, table 6, in a memorandum from Jerry D. Weast, superintendent of schools, to members of the Board of Education, "Subject: 2001 Results of the Scholastic Assessment Test (SAT)," dated August 28, 2001; available at www.mcps.k12.md.us/info/pdf/satreport2001.pdf.

3. Brigid Schulte, "Downcounty, a Year of Change—and Hope: Officials Eye Reforms, Programs at Consortium with Anticipation," *Washington Post*, August 22, 2002, p. GZ14.

4. Deborah Brandt, *Sponsors of Literacy* (Albany, N.Y.: National Research Center on English Learning and Achievement, 1997); available at http://cela.albany.edu/sponsor/index.html.

5. Brandt, *Sponsors of Literacy*, 3.

6. Maryland State Department of Education, *Social Studies Core Learning Goals* (Baltimore: Author, August 1999).

Chapter Eight

Alternatives

Communicating with Parents

Imagine an on-the-fence, undecided, uncertain school administrator in the suburbs in Maryland or in any other area with a diverse school population. This administrator has promised to close the achievement gap, but, as we saw in the last chapter, results have been hard to come by. So far this educator has only intervened in early childhood education in an attempt to close the achievement gap; the secondary schools are running as they have always operated. And even this educator—at the top of the hierarchy in a school district with a budget of over a billion dollars—may lack the complete freedom needed to make changes. His or her state is imposing mandate after mandate. In addition to the state curriculum, now state exit exams are being phased in. By the end of the decade, students may have to pass state tests in a variety of areas to graduate. In this educator's professional judgment, some of these mandates may not be all that is needed to build the fluency in reading and writing necessary for success in college and other postsecondary pursuits, but challenging state mandates is not a common political practice. What could this educator tell parents about what is really needed for all teenagers to become more fluent in their native language?

What would alternatives to the state curriculum in the humanities look like? How could this superintendent explain the need for alternatives to busy parents—who are perhaps more worried about paying for college than about what is being read in high school?

This superintendent could start by telling parents that only reading a great deal of books builds fluency in reading. Newsletters and handouts with references to the cognitive psychologists and the research in applied linguistics could be produced to show parents that fluency will only result when teenagers read, read, and read. Our superintendent needs to make it clear that the state curriculum in the humanities—especially in history—is so broad that only a survey textbook can be used. But fluency will not improve handing each teenager a single textbook each semester, as is the current practice in grades 6 through 12 in Montgomery County's public schools.

The next step would be to bring in experts from across the political spectrum who can speak to parents about the quality of books used in our schools. Superintendent Weast in Montgomery County might begin by reprinting excerpts from *American Memory: A Report on the Humanities in America's Schools* by Lynne V. Cheney and sending these excerpts to parents. Cheney argues that the modern textbook is now so filled with name after name and cause after cause, that it has become "a fleamarket of disconnected facts."[1] She makes it clear that textbooks are not enough to pass on our nation's cultural heritage:

It is hard to imagine that youngsters are spurred on to learning by these textbooks. What we give them to read seems particularly vacuous when compared to what grade-schoolers once studied. In the early decades of this century, they read myths, fables, stories from the distant past, and tales of heroes. They learned about Daedalus and King Arthur, George Washington and Joan of Arc, exercising their imaginations and beginning to develop a sense of life in other times.

Textbooks used to teach American history are also disappointing. The advisory group on history and literature looked at samples used in high schools. They were large (weighing about three pounds each), heavy with facts, but seldom were those facts made part of a compelling narrative, part of a drama with individuals at center stage. The human ambitions and aspirations that are both the motivating force of history and its fascination were largely absent. One textbook's account of the Constitutional Convention, for example, mentioned only James Madison's age and the fact that he took notes. A second recognized him as a "profound student of government," credited him with being "the Father of the Constitution," but provided no further explanation. A third set forth his contributions to the Convention in some detail, but beyond describing him as "the most astute political thinker of his day" gave little sense of the character of this shy and driven man.[2]

Cheney continues:

> Missing also was a sense of the significance of the historical record. A reader was left with little notion of the ideas that inform our institutions, the arguments and debates that helped shape the kind of nation we are, the reasons behind the choices we have made or why those choices are important. As NEH Deputy Chairman John Agresto observed, "At the end of each chapter, I could imagine any student saying, 'So what?'"

History textbooks have become so weak, Cheney argues, because they have fallen into the "mentioning problem," in which people and events are mentioned by the hundreds but never in enough depth to stick and resonate and connect and engage teenagers. She blames the needs of publishers to satisfy state curriculum checklists for the mentioning problem.

Cheney clearly shows how state curriculum guidelines shape the reading experiences of American teenagers:

> Publishers are frequently blamed for textbooks. It should be noted, however, that when they decide to put out new books or new series, they first consider what various states and localities say they want. As textbook consultant Harriet Tyson-Bernstein explained to the advisory group, publishers look to state and district curriculum guides and adoption checklists for guidance. Curriculum guides, thick manuals full of lists and charts produced by education specialists, set forth what students are to know—skills for the most part, though in the case of history there will often be many pages of topics to be covered. Checklists detail what adoption committees look for, including whether or not textbooks fulfill the requirements of the curriculum guides.
>
> Many checklists specify reading levels, thus bringing readability formulas into play. Checklists also provide a way for various interest groups to make their influence felt. Feminists, environmentalists, ethnic minorities, nutritionists—all have concerns, often important ones. But adding them to the checklist of textbook requirements frequently results in what critics call the "mentioning" problem. A native American will be mentioned or a suffragist pictured, but no full account given of his or her contributions. Name will be heaped upon name, cause upon cause, until the textbook becomes an overcrowded flea market of disconnected facts.
>
> Many checklists have an entry about whether the textbook is likely to engage students; but as one item among many, it is of no more consequence than whether the textbook has a recent copyright date (the most common

question on checklists) or whether it will withstand wear and tear. Even if adoption committees were to focus more on content and quality of writing, one has to wonder how textbook editors and writers could meet their expectations. They have dozens of curriculum guides and adoption checklists to try to satisfy as they work. Some are more important than others. More than twenty states adopt textbooks on a statewide basis; and when those states are large and the number of textbooks they approve for each subject is small—as in Texas and California—their demands receive extra attention. But since publishers want to sell books in as many places as possible, editors and writers must also try to keep the requirements of other states and localities in mind. "They are so tied up in knots accommodating this cross-referencing that they forget they are editing real material or writing about real events," Tyson-Bernstein observed.

Cheney then goes on to describe the fear that shapes the content of the books teenagers see: the fear of the controversial.

Fearful that controversy will keep them out of important markets, publishers have tried to avoid controversial subjects like religion. This strategy has come under attack in recent years as critics across the political spectrum have pointed out that history makes no sense unless the driving power of religious belief is taken into account. To describe the Crusades or the pilgrims or the Civil Rights movement without talking about religion is to distort the past, but wary textbook publishers have done it.

Her solution is what many teachers would love to see: Stop centralized adoptions of textbooks. Give teachers and faculties the power to select books they believe will work with students. Cheney continues:

One possibility is to move away from centralized book adoptions. Let teachers and faculties decide what textbooks they will use and hope that when individuals and small groups choose, they will do so by asking a few important questions: Is this a book a child might love? Does it tell him or her about things that really matter? . . .

One step that should be taken is to assign textbooks a less important role. Let teachers enlighten their students with real books—real works by real authors in the same form which they are read by the rest of us. Many teachers do this now, often paying for books out of their own pockets since their own schools' book budget are consumed by textbooks.[3]

Cheney's suggestion of providing "real books" makes great sense and in itself might provide more opportunities for historical literacy in American secondary school, but this cannot happen until superintendents begin to tell parents about the damage done by the survey textbooks. Superintendents need to explain to parents how the curriculum checklists, with topic after topic generated by state education departments, force the adoption of survey textbooks in history classes and thus limit the education of American teenagers. A debate of the quality and quantity of reading assignments in American history classes needs to begin, as Cheney urges. In messages to parents, superintendents could include commentators who charge that our textbooks are actually miseducating our young by omitting information necessary to understand American history. Educator and author Herbert Kohl believes that the stories we tell young people matter, and that in some situations, our textbooks have not been telling the entire story. He says that stories are a way "to convey power to children and to enable them to take control of their own lives." He warns "that stories can also be used as a way to deprive children from seeing their world as it is."

One case he describes is that of Rosa Parks and the Montgomery, Alabama, bus boycott. Kohl examined a number of children's books and looked at how Parks was treated. He found that these books obliterated, removed, and wrote out the civil rights movement of which Parks had been a member for years. In these children's books, Parks was the individual hero. She was not part of a group. The civil rights movement of which Parks had been a member for years did not exist. She refused to give up her seat on that bus because she was tired that day, not because she and the movement had planned and strategized and organized for years before the boycott began. These books fail to mention that Parks had been selected to challenge the laws because the National Association for the Advancement of Colored People (NAACP) leadership believed she had the strength to deal with the racist police force and the publicity.[4]

Kohl believes that youngsters should know that Parks had been a community activist for years. He believes that readers should know that her defiance was planned and that a civil rights organization stood behind her ready to mobilize. He believes they should know that when Parks was arrested, she was the secretary of the Montgomery chapter of the NAACP. He believes also that young readers should know that the struggle was difficult, pointing out that the bus boycott lasted 381 days. He also believes that the children's books about Parks that refuse to use the word *racism* are not providing an accurate picture of the Jim Crow era in the United States.

In a newsletter to parents offering local alternatives to the state's sanitized curriculum of one book a year, little challenge/little growth curriculum, our superintendent could also discuss the ideas of Vincent Harding from *Hope and History: Why We Must Share the History of the Movement.* Like Kohl and Cheney, Harding believes that what we read in school influences our attitudes toward politics and history. He argues that "those of us who teach cannot avoid the disturbing reality that faces us every day: we know more about the nurturing of capitalism, athletics, pop culture and high technology than we do about the care and development of democracy."[5] Offering the civil rights movement as an example of citizen participation and struggle that reshaped American life, Harding believes that studying the history of this movement can still inspire American youth; it can give them the idea that political change is still a possibility.

When we look carefully and with insight, it soon becomes evident that few bodies of knowledge are more filled with such living signs of hope than the story of the Black freedom movement in the United States. (Indeed, human struggles for liberation and resurrection, wherever they occur, are often rich in such lively, translucent testimonies, personified in men and women of amazing possibilities.) Interestingly enough, our students seem to have already intuited something of the power of this biographical treasure. For not long ago they provided an important surprise to some educational experts when, in the course of a national assessment of historical knowledge among school seniors, their response revealed that one of the figures in American history who was best known among the students was Harriet Tubman, the indomitable heroine of the Underground Railroad and the Civil War, who later became a pioneer in the postwar care for the aged.

The scholars who reported the strength of the Tubman/Underground Railroad image in the minds of our students were not sure why it was so real. They suggested that the "inherent drama and conflict" of the subject matter might help account for its presence, as well as the fact that the testing had been done shortly after a national television treatment of the topic. These, of course, are likely enough factors, but at a deeper level it may well be that the students caught the essence of the "drama and conflict," recognizing that in the case of Tubman and others like her they were being confronted by powerful, authentic personalities, rooted in a great human determination to overcome the forces of darkness within the systems of domination and destruction around them.

When we turn to Harriet Tubman's great-grandchildren, to the lives that flowered in the Black-led freedom movement of the post World War II period, we are flooded with opportunities to provide our students with access to authentic signposts whose biographies may challenge, illuminate and inspire young people and adults—across lines of race, class, gender, and nationality. There are literally hundreds of well-documented examples and thousands more still waiting for their compelling stories to receive the documentation that groups of curious of committed students and teachers could provide. The potential subjects of such explorations are living and dead, Black and white, urban and rural, poor and not-so-poor, people of varied religious and nonreligious persuasions, a marvel of hope. Each provides us with a vivid opportunity to use biographical study as a teaching tool, to allow the life stories of significant women and men to draw students into their light, and to make it possible for all of us to reassess our own understandings of what makes for a "significant" life.[6]

While Cheney, Kohl, and Harding are persuasive, they offer few facts—little real data—to support their assertions that history textbooks are failing American youngsters and that teenagers are not learning American history successfully under the current arrangements. Superintendents need facts if they are going to be able to persuade parents to give local teachers a chance to write curricula in history, as Cheney advocates. Fortunately, these facts exist.

According to a federal report, young Americans are not learning their own history, and this situation is not improving. A majority of American twelfth graders—some 57 percent—scored "below basic" on the most recent survey of historical literacy from the federal government released in May 2002. According to this report from the National Assessment of Educational Progress, this very weak performance was unchanged from 1994.[7]

This most recent evidence shows that state standards are not linked to higher achievement in history.[8]

With the rise of the movement for standards-based reform in K–12 education, an increasing number of states have adopted standards for history or social studies. . . . About two-thirds of the students had teachers who reported that standards were used to a large extent in planning instruction (63 percent at grade 4, and 69 percent at grade 8). There were, however, no statistically significant differences in students' performance at either grade 4 or grade 8, based on whether or not there were standards or on the extent to which teachers reported using standards for planning social studies instruction. Because state and local standards are diverse and are used in various ways, readers should interpret this data with caution.[9]

As with much data from research, the warning in the last sentence is certainly appropriate. Without in-depth interviews from teachers, it is difficult to determine the extent to which state curricula shape local schools.

VIEWS AND RECOMMENDATIONS

By now in the letter to parents, our hypothetical superintendent has explained that changes are needed in the status quo. Business as usual is not providing either historical literacy or many opportunities to gain fluency in reading and writing. What else can a new curriculum based on in-depth reading in fewer topics provide?

One obvious model is the "Doing the Decades" approach sponsored by the Assembly on Literature for Adolescents of the National Council of Teachers of English (ALAN). At the heart of this curriculum is book after book after book. Here's a brief description:

> At a high school or middle-school not far from you, they're "Doing the Decades." Students, guided by social studies and English language arts teachers, work in learning teams to explore the ins and out of the 1920s, 1950s, or other periods. They examine major historical events, inventions, life styles, the cost of groceries and automobiles, sports, and other aspects of the social landscape. They may interview family members about what teen life was like in the decade *du jour,* view old movies, and learn the "latest" songs and dances. They may examine photo albums, their parents' high school annuals, or collections of historic photographs. They may listen to classic radio programs.[10]

Of course, many schools are using the oral histories of older neighbors and relatives to supplement textbooks. The curriculum from the National

Council of Teachers does much more; it emphasizes reading a large amount of historical fiction:

> Young adult literature of two sorts may help teachers Do the Decades well in their classrooms. First, there is a wealth of historical fiction set in each period of American history. In these works — in, for example, novels such as Carolyn Meyers' *White Lilacs* — writers painstakingly recreate times and places consistent with historical records. The San Francisco earthquake, the Depression, the Civil Rights Movement, the Viet Nam War — these and other pivotal events of history may bore young people when they come straight out of the history book or a teacher's lecture. When linked to young characters *experiencing* those events in a work of fiction, however, the same history may capture the interest of many teens.[11]

The reading list offers ten to twenty books from each era. The entire list can be seen online at http://scholar.lib.vt.edu/ejournals/ALAN/spring99/brewbaker.html.

Each era has a long list of reading associated with it. These are not two- or three-page excerpts from primary sources or teacher-constructed worksheets with names and dates to memorize for Friday's test. They are "real books — real works by real authors in the same form which they are read by the rest of us," as Cheney advocates.

This is an example of one decade:

1970–1979: Vietnam and After, Watergate, and Social Unrest
In the early 1970s, Americans were deeply divided as the country pulled out of Vietnam with more than 56,000 young men killed in combat. They experienced the resignation of President Richard Nixon as the climax of the Watergate scandal, and they uneasily witnessed a rise in urban violence, homelessness, and drug addiction. More often than not, they viewed these events on the evening news rather than learn about them from newspapers.

Walter Dean Myers' *Fallen Angels* is perhaps the best Vietnam era novel for teenage readers. Its realistic language has sparked censorship in some communities, but its honest portrayal of a squad of young soldiers, each with his own story, is memorable. Gary Soto's *Jesse* is set on the other side of the world, in California, yet the specter of the military draft — always a greater threat to the poor than it was to the affluent — is always just on the horizon. Jesse and his brother, Mexican Americans, join the protest movement led by Cesar Chavez, who represented migrant farm workers. Mathis'

A Teacup Full of Roses, set about 1970, follows three brothers attempting to rise above the worst of urban life, particularly drugs. The youngest is a talented basketball player. Despite its earlier publication date, the easy-to-read novel appeals to many contemporary teens. Cormier's *After the First Death* introduces the subject of terrorism in a nail-biting narrative. In it Kate, a heroic school bus driver, tries to save the children she is transporting. Writers may be too close to the 1970s and 1980s to set historical fiction in these relatively recent times. Having said that, one may observe that other superior novels set in Nixon and Carter years, Judith Guest's *Ordinary People* among them, not only tell a good story but mirror the times in which they were written.

Literature for Young Readers Set in 1970–1979
Cormier, R. *After the First Death.* Pantheon Books, 1979.
Guest, J. *Ordinary People.* Penguin, 1993.
Mathis, S. B. *A Teacup Full of Roses.* Viking Press, 1972.
Myers, W. D. *Fallen Angels.* Scholastic Paperbacks, 1991.
Soto, G. *Jesse.* Harcourt Brace, 1994.
Pulitzer Prize Winners from the Decade
Welty, E. *The Optimist's Daughter.* Random House, 1972.
Shaara, M. *The Killer Angels.* Ballantine Books, 1974.

Of course, local teachers could supplement these choices or replace them entirely. Providing the names of books being used in classrooms might help reassure parents that local decisions did not mean a "dumbing down" of education. In a system where homework assignments routinely appear on the web—listed teacher by teacher systemwide—this communication would seem easy to accomplish. The Montgomery County Public School system, the subject of the last two chapters, does an excellent job providing parents with information about homework assignments through an online database at http://coldfusion.mcps.k12.md.us/cfms/ webteam/homeworkboard/. But this same county, which uses technology so well in places, is not communicating to parents about books and the need to build fluency in reading and writing through practice, practice, practice. The leadership is staying with what the state wants in spite of the lack of any link between state standards in the humanities in improvements in literacy of teenagers.

The choices of what books will best engage and inform teenagers should be left to the adults actually working with these teenagers, not to education "managers" in remote state capitals. In the previous two chapters, we saw that political power was not devolving to teachers in the classroom. Is power devolving elsewhere as states grapple with the challenge of preparing teenagers not for factory work but for success in higher education? In the next chapter, we will examine the record of California in providing more resources and more authority to classroom teachers and more opportunities for literacy to teenagers.

NOTES

1. Lynne V. Cheney, *American Memory: A Report on the Humanities in the Nation's Public Schools* (Washington, D.C.: National Endowment for the Humanities, 1987), 17.

2. Cheney, *American Memory.*

3. Cheney, *American Memory,* 19.

4. Herbert Kohl, *Should We Burn Babar? Essays on Children's Literature and the Power of Stories* (New York: New Press, 1995), 2.

5. Vincent Harding, *Hope and History: Why We Must Share the History of the Movement* (Maryknoll, N.Y.: Orbis, 1991), 31.

6. Harding, *Hope and History,* 17.

7. M. S. Lapp, W. S. Grigg, and B. S.-H. Tay-Lim, *The Nation's Report Card: U.S. History 2001,* NCES 2002– 483 (Washington, D.C.: National Center for Education Statistics, 2002).

8. Lapp et al., *The Nation's Report Card.*

9. Lapp et al., *The Nation's Report Card,* 91.

10. James Brewbaker, "Doing the Decades," *ALAN Review* 26, no. 3 (1999): 49–54. ALAN is the Assembly on Literature for Adolescents of the National Council of Teachers of Literature. This work is available at http://scholar.lib.vt.edu/ejournals/ALAN/spring99/.

11. Brewbaker, "Doing the Decades."

Chapter Nine

The California Experience

Can Standards Lift the State's Public Schools off the Bottom?

California, with its almost six million students in classrooms and with a teaching corps of over two hundred thousand, is a major enterprise, and it is an enterprise whose quality of services is uncertain. In the 1990s, researchers told parents what some of them had already known: California was not only scraping the bottom with its reading scores but also is falling faster than the national average.[1] According to reports, the indicators showed that achievement in California was closer to that of the traditional bottom dwellers in the ranks of American states: Alabama, Mississippi, and Louisiana.

This is how one research institute describes California:

California student scores on the National Assessment of Educational Progress math and reading exams showed students performing far below proficiency. California's fourth-grade reading scores ranked next to last among the states. . . . In 1994 California's public-school graders tied Louisiana's fourth-graders for dead-last, with an average score of 199. In 1998 California's average public-school fourth grade reading score inched back to 200, but the state still ranked next to last, edging out only Hawaii.[2]

In addition to a next-to-last ranking on the respected tests from the National Assessment of Educational Progress, the institute also reported very low high graduation rates for California teenagers: "In 1998, the graduation rate in California was 67.2 percent. In other words, nearly 33 percent of ninth-graders who were enrolled four years previously did not graduate."

Those who did manage to graduate from high school were often not very well prepared for college. "Systemwide in 1998, 54 percent of California

State University (CSU) incoming freshmen had to enroll in remedial math, while 47 percent had to enroll in remedial English. At CSU Dominguez Hills, 87 percent of entering freshmen needed remedial math, while 80 percent needed remedial English."[3] See table 9.1 to review the percentages of teenagers forced to take remedial courses in public colleges.

Statewide, over 60 percent of African American and Mexican American and other Latino students who enrolled in the CSU system needed remediation in English.

Not surprisingly the political system responded in dramatic fashion to the crisis in the newspapers and on television. California's attempt to reduce class size became national news as school district after school district struggled to find teachers to work with all the new smaller classes. But class size reduction is only one aspect of what the educational planners in the state capital had in mind for California. They had plans for California's youngsters for the rest of their years in the school system:

- A new system of annual tests to measure achievement on a school-by-school basis.
- A new system of intervention to force changes in schools with weak results on these new state tests.
- A new system of content standards defining what should be covered in each subject in each grade.
- An on again, off again attempt to spend more money on classroom resources such as books. A new program to supplement state spending on books lasted for three years from 1998–1999 to 2001–2002, but in the fall of 2001, Governor Gray Davis vetoed an attempt by the legislature to continue this program, citing "the rapid decline of our economy and a budget shortfall of $1.1billion through the first three months of this fiscal year alone."[4] Passage of a new bill to extend this funding was caught up in the state's budget crisis in the summer of 2002, and it finally passed in September 2002.

While this program of reform appears logical, details are missing about the opportunities to gain fluency in reading and writing in California public schools.

Parents may wonder, for example, whether any of these models of change bring extra books with them for their children to read. They may

Table 9.1. California State University Placement Data, Fall 2000 (Regularly Admitted First-Time Freshman Remediation Systemwide)

Ethnicity	Number of Freshmen	Number Needing Remediation in Mathematics	Percentage Needing Remediation in Mathematics	Number Needing Remediation in English	Percentage Needing Remediation in English
American Indian	216	107	49.54	85	39.35
African American	2,028	1,511	74.51	1,306	64.40
Mexican American	5,657	3,665	64.79	3,656	64.63
Other Latino	2,120	1,368	64.53	1,231	58.07
Asian American	5,026	1,786	35.54	3,191	63.49
Pacific Islander	210	99	47.14	108	51.43
White Non-Latino	14,420	5,298	36.74	4,004	27.77
Filipino	2,220	1,031	46.44	1,194	53.78
Unknown	4,043	1,811	44.79	1,603	39.65
Nonresident	715	248	34.69	547	76.50
Total	36,655	16,924	46.17	16,925	46.17

Gender	Number of Freshmen	Number Needing Remediation in Mathematics	Percentage Needing Remediation in Mathematics	Number Needing Remediation in English	Percentage Needing Remediation in English
Female	21,081	11,346	53.82	9,959	47.24
Male	15,574	5,578	35.82	6,966	44.73
Total	36,655	16,924	46.17	16,925	46.17

	Overall Mean High School GPA	Number of High School GPAs for Students Needing Remediation in Mathematics	Mean High School GPA of Students Needing Remediation in Mathematics	Number of High School GPAs for Students Needing Remediation in English	Mean High School GPA of Students Needing Remediation in English
Overall Number of High School GPAs	3.27	16,887	3.16	16,842	3.18
36,542					

Source: California State University Placement Test Data, at www.asd.calstate.edu/remediation01/remediation/2001-ftrnr023.htm.

wonder whether shortages of textbooks will return to Los Angeles and other cities that struggled with inadequate supplies of books throughout the 1990s as the state's budget crisis continues.

Parents who love reading and believe that a central purpose of high school is to immerse teenagers in books that engage imaginations and stretch intellects may have other questions for the state planners. Will educational reform make books more visible? Will a list of reading and writing assignments from each teacher be available for students and parents to review? Are reading and writing assignments going to be connected so that teenagers will have to actually read the entire assignment to pass the writing assignments? And will there be someone with the time to read all these new writing assignments needed to prepare for success in college? Parents may also wonder whether their teenagers will work with teachers who have time to actually grade their papers and write comments on them rather than just noting that the assignment was turned in.

Parents who are interested in preparing their youngsters for the more rigorous writing assignments of college may ask if school reform models from Sacramento are bringing teachers realistic numbers of students. As English teachers know, when the student load is 150, 160, or 170, the number of writing assignments shrinks. Few teachers are willing to go home with 160 essays to grade each weekend.

So we have a list of concerns for our conversations with state planners and with the local administrators and teachers who march to the music of school reform being played in Sacramento. Is school reform—as instituted through the reform models—going to fundamentally improve the opportunities for literacy for teenagers in California? Will supplies of even the most basic instructional material, textbooks, be reliable after being unreliable in large cities in the 1990s? Will the new emphasis on standards and the new emphasis on state intervention lead to more literate teenagers?

This chapter looks at what California expects of its youngsters through its standards movement. California's standards for its teenagers are by now well known. They are detailed and explicit. There is no uncertainty about what California expects its teenagers to learn in the state's secondary schools, but will lists of hundreds of topics to cover create teenagers who are fluent readers and writers?

For example, seventh grade includes a survey course of world history in the last two thousand years. Eleven separate topics are included; sixty-one subtopics follow the major topics (one example is presented here). Not a single suggested reading is included after these eleven topics. Writing assignments are not mentioned. Reading in these survey courses is usually limited to a single textbook for the year.[5]

7.1 Students analyze the causes and effects of the vast expansion and ultimate disintegration of the Roman Empire.

1. Study the early strengths and lasting contributions of Rome (e.g., significance of Roman citizenship; rights under Roman law; Roman art, architecture, engineering, and philosophy; preservation and transmission of Christianity) and its ultimate internal weaknesses (e.g., rise of autonomous military powers within the empire, undermining of citizenship by the growth of corruption and slavery, lack of education, and distribution of news).
2. Discuss the geographic borders of the empire at its height and the factors that threatened its territorial cohesion.
3. Describe the establishment by Constantine of the new capital in Constantinople and the development of the Byzantine Empire, with an emphasis on the consequences of the development of two distinct European civilizations, Eastern Orthodox and Roman Catholic, and their two distinct views on church–state relations.

In another example, in tenth grade, teenagers turn to the topic of World History, Culture, and Geography: The Modern World. Now they are expected to know how political philosophy influenced political events of the modern world.

Students in grade ten study major turning points that shaped the modern world, from the late eighteenth century through the present, including the cause and course of the two world wars. They trace the rise of democratic ideas and develop an understanding of the historical roots of current world issues, especially as they pertain to international relations. They extrapolate from the American experience that democratic ideals are often achieved at a high price, remain vulnerable, and are not practiced everywhere in the world. Students develop an understanding of current world issues and relate them to their historical, geographic, political, economic, and cultural contexts. Students consider multiple accounts of events in order to understand international relations from a variety of perspectives.

A sample topic and its subtopics:

10.2 Students compare and contrast the Glorious Revolution of England, the American Revolution, and the French Revolution and their enduring effects worldwide on the political expectations for self-government and individual liberty.

1. Compare the major ideas of philosophers and their effects on the democratic revolutions in England, the United States, France, and Latin America (e.g., John Locke, Charles-Louis Montesquieu, Jean-Jacques Rousseau, Simón Bolívar, Thomas Jefferson, James Madison).
2. List the principles of the Magna Carta, the English Bill of Rights (1689), the American Declaration of Independence (1776), the French Declaration of the Rights of Man and the Citizen (1789), and the U.S. Bill of Rights (1791).
3. Understand the unique character of the American Revolution, its spread to other parts of the world, and its continuing significance to other nations.
4. Explain how the ideology of the French Revolution led France to develop from constitutional monarchy to democratic despotism to the Napoleonic Empire.
5. Discuss how nationalism spread across Europe with Napoleon but was repressed for a generation under the Congress of Vienna and Concert of Europe until the Revolutions of 1848.

Should tenth grade be a time to read paragraphs in a textbook about the Congress of Vienna and the Concert of Europe or to read a four-hundred-page biography about Thurgood Marshall by Michael D. Davis and Hunter R. Clark each night, or perhaps the more recent biography of Justice Marshall by Juan Williams? Which approach to language is going to develop fluent readers, a couple of pages in a textbook each evening or chapter after chapter in biography after biography?

By now a reader can see the pattern: Youngsters face a variety, literally dozens, of topics and subtopics to master each year without any emphasis on reading or writing assignments. Curriculum planners in Sacramento have decided that exposure to dozens of different topics in one survey history textbook is more important than the fluency that might result from actually reading biographies, autobiographies, and historical fiction as private school students often are able to do.

By now, in tenth grade, students are in their fourth year of secondary school studies, and book lists are nonexistent. If a tenth grader wants to read four or five books during a semester on crime and punishment in California or on American social movements or American business leaders, the state says no. Tenth grade is time to plow through a survey textbook with its snippets of information comparing the Glorious Revolutions and the French Revolution. The opportunity to actually do a great deal of reading on a single subject is not available since the state says tenth grade is time for yet another survey course. The opportunity to write for an audience—for example, to produce a newsletter on topics—is not part of their school day in social studies. The state curriculum must be followed.

OPPORTUNITIES IN THE CENTRAL VALLEY

Debra Schneider is a teacher from a town in the Central Valley just over the mountains from the Bay area. Once primarily an agricultural area, it is now becoming a bedroom community for San Francisco. Her story is of opportunities lost in high school.

"The funding for books isn't enough even to buy the textbook in social studies," said Schneider when I talked to her in early 2002. In her school, she explained that the only reading in her world history and American history classes came from the textbook and short excerpts from primary texts. Biographies, autobiographies, and historical fiction were not available to the students in her history classes, she said. A much wider range of materials were available in English classes, where novels were available to supplement the textbooks.

Schneider said that the teachers in her high school would like to bring in an American studies program that would combine English and history and offer more opportunities for reading, but the district would not provide the release time for planning.

Schneider explained that in the middle school where she had previously taught, there was much more time to build fluency in reading in the students. That school had a three-hour core: reading, writing, and social studies—hence more time to give up forty-five minutes for free voluntary reading, with the goal of building fluency and taste in reading. "Often they liked books from the same series, such as the Babysitters Club, that didn't stretch their vocabulary too much. My approach was to read new books to them out loud so they would hear the content from these new sources. If they wanted to read the Babysitters Club, that was OK, but I would try to entice them to move away from the series and move into 'better' literature." And it worked, she said. "Kids would approach me and ask the name of the book they had listened to that day."

One favorite was *Lupita Mañana* by Patricia Beatty. Migrant kids were enthralled by the book, Schneider said. "I knew I had touched them with the book. I recommended the book to a very bright, disaffected Latino boy. Later he whispered to me, 'Did I have any more books like that one?' With *Lupita Manana*, kids got to know that books spoke to them and they didn't know that." She also recommended *Yellow Raft in Blue Water,* a book that her high school students had loved.

She said that if she were free to make decisions about the curriculum in her high school, there would be an American studies program built around themes. "We would have four themes with a choice of four or five books in each theme. And there would be literature circles where [students] would read and then meet with each other. One job would be to come up with questions about the text. Another job would be to make a map and so on. There would be five or more roles in a literature circle," she explained.

Time is an obstacle to fluency in reading in her high school, Schneider added. "As kids get older, they get much busier, and they don't have the same amount of time to read on their own. In the middle school, we provided that time with the free voluntary reading period of forty-five minutes. In high school, I can't set aside forty-five minutes from a fifty-eight-minute history period for reading."

Schneider said that she has seen two especially successful approaches to literature in her district. One English teacher requires students to go around and ask teachers about the best book they have read in the last year. The process of talking to someone who is positive about a book gets kids interested in books.

Another teacher has a class called Senior Odyssey. Book choices are made by community people, and a book list with descriptions of these books is posted for the class to see. Kids sign up for a book and then read it and meet with the community person who recommended it. "When they came to my house to talk about the book, they stayed until 9:30 in the evening. I couldn't get them out of my house," Schneider said.

"It's not enough just to assign the book," she said. "It's about a relationship between the person who loves the book and the person who wants to read the book."

Schneider said she was not certain that the new standards begun in 1999 would lead to improvements in youngsters' reading and writing skills. "People feel pressured and judged unjustly. Some badmouth the test; others harangue the departments. At times, the standards teach X and the tests test Y." The connection between the test and the standard state curriculum varies from subject to subject, she said. For example, in world history, there is a wide gap between the state standards and the questions about world history in the Stanford 9 test. "In American history, the test and the standards are much closer together, and our students do much better as a result."

Do the obstacles that Schneider mentions—a lack of time to read during social studies and a very limited range of materials to read, only the textbook in most classes—also apply to English? Or are English teachers free to select books that will engage their students and to create writing assignments closely tied to the readings as the private schools described in chapter 11 do?

Carla Hanson, a teacher in the same high school, said teenagers in her school are able to read outside the textbook in her English classes. They read novels like "*Of Mice and Men, The House on Mango Street*, and *The Joy Luck Club*—books that are pretty much part of the canon. Some of them were selected before they entered the canon," she said, "such as *Yellow Raft and Blue Water.*"

One obstacle Hanson did mention is that all of the books used in her classes must be preapproved by her school district. She does not have the authority to simply order books from a best-seller list or books that she has enjoyed on her own and thinks will engage her students.

"Before the new high school in town opened," Hanson said, "the English teachers selected titles with a clear rubric in mind as to what we were after. We chose books that would be appealing but also had literary merit and we tried to get some breath. Junior year is American lit, but we didn't necessarily follow that mandate. Then we convened a committee of teachers and parents to evaluate the books on suitability. After this committee met, there was time for the community to look at the titles. The reading list with the new proposed titles was published in the newspaper, and the public could go and look at the books. After that, the titles had to go to a curriculum council, a group of teachers and administrators. Finally, the Board of Trustees [of the school district] approved the titles.

"I think the district established this process because there is a strong group of Mormons and other religious groups here that are concerned with the literature we teach. The adoption process does give us protection from the parents," Hanson explained. "Each year that I taught *Beloved* [by Toni Morrison], I had parental concerns. The associate superintendent called me and said that some parents had complained. Since the book had been adopted and approved, I was able to continue teaching it. Some parents last year objected to *To Kill a Mockingbird*. This year we have parents who think that kids shouldn't read *The Catcher in the Rye* because of the strong language."

Hanson said that although the lengthy process does provide protection, it also keeps some excellent literature out of the classroom. "I love teaching *Beloved;* I would like to teach *The Bluest Eye*, but I won't even try to have *The Bluest Eye* adopted. I think the incest would drive everyone mad. It's short and it's so powerful, and it's the kind of literature kids become involved with. And it would make them examine their own lives even though it's set some years back. I had a student who is biracial—raised on the white side of the family—say she wanted to be blond and blue-eyed, so it's still pertinent. But *The Bluest Eye* will be available soon," Hanson said. "I got through an anthology called *Seven Contemporary Novels,* and it's in there. I can teach it and, when the furor starts, blink my eyes and innocently say, 'It's been approved.'

"If a parent is adamant about a book, I'll ask their child to read something else," Hanson added. "The student can go to the library and read *The Scarlet Letter* rather than *Beloved.*

"Another book that I would like to teach is *Reservation Blues* by Sherman Alexie. I'd also teach anything by Barbara Kingsolver. She's a very good essayist, and her novels are fabulous."

Another obstacle that keeps teenagers in Hanson's high school from reading more is a lack of time. "They work. They have video games and just the fact that they are so social. The biggest thing is that we don't provide them enough time. The kids who are not readers think that reading is what the teachers tell them to read."

Her solution is to provide some time to read silently during the school day and to allow the students to choose the book that they will read during this period. "I operate by the principle that if it's valuable, I have to provide class time. We have fifteen minutes of silent reading three days a week. Now I have a group of girls running around reading the Nicholas Spark story. It's a lame love story, but they're running around excited about the fact that they got to choose what their group is going to read."

Nancy Atwood writes about kids who take ownership of reading, and this ownership has to be combined with time, Hanson said. "I also have kids reading the Wally Lamb book—it's nine hundred pages. Sometimes if a teacher can create a community of readers even the nonreaders start reading."

Hanson was less optimistic about the opportunities for teenagers to become fluent writers in her high school. Since each English teacher has up to 36 students in a class and five classes, or at a total of 180 students, this schedule becomes an obstacle to literacy.

"The schedule is a crime against society. I'm not exaggerating. I don't think the level of instruction can be maintained. For many teachers, it becomes a situation of controlling a mob. With 180 kids a day, the paper load for an English teacher is impossible.

"Personally, I have the kids write a lot of essays. Not all teachers are able to manage that for a variety of reasons, but I am committed to doing it because it's the most important thing so they write literature response essays. Most of my prompts are from things that they can't find on the Net. I try not to give the standard prompts. In an attempt to avoid plagiarism, we do a lot of in-class timed writings.

"We follow the writing process introduced by Jane Schaffer in San Diego," Hanson explained. "The process is very prescriptive. The people who object to it don't understand what the kids get who learn the process. Until I found Schaffer's approach, I wasn't a very good writing teacher. She provides a model, a recipe, a training wheel with an emphasis on things like concrete details."

Another obstacle Hanson mentioned is the increasing number of new teachers without credentials who do not have student teaching experience. "Because of the shortage of teachers, we are getting people right out of college who are not credentialed and have no experience and no practicum, and the kids eat them alive. Teaching process writing is laborious, especially with teenagers who are not motivated. I advise people I mentor that to make it through the year, you are going to have to jettison some of the writing."

She explained that the district required few writing assignments from its English teachers. "Two essays a year are all that's required. I could assign those, and that would be it," she said. "I don't think that happens, but it could. We had teachers who after they left, we found out that they really weren't doing anything.

"I'm not saying our kids exit writing well; some of them do. But what I do is that if they want to learn how to do it, they can learn it from me. There are a lot of people who don't see the merit in that, and I don't blame them at all. Our burden is ridiculous."

Are Hanson's complaints justified? Is it as difficult as she says for teenagers to become fluent writers in schools where each teacher has 160 to 180 students to respond to on each writing assignment—a number that discourages assigning a lot of writing?

Fortunately, data are available to assess her complaints. The writing placement tests California teenagers face when they enter the California State University system will give some indication of the writing skills they bring to college. And the writing difficulties are not limited to teenagers whose parents may speak another language at home. California high schools are not providing adequate writing instruction for African Americans, either, as table 9.1 shows.

But the numbers in table 9.1 actually underreport the language crisis in California for a number of reasons. As any Californian knows, only teenagers in the top third of their graduating class are admitted to the California State University system to stand for these placement tests. An elite 1 or 2 percent are admitted to the University of California campuses at Berkeley, Davis, UCLA, and so on, while the majority of California teenagers interested in higher education attend public community colleges.

Sadly, since only half of Latino teenagers who enter high school in California ever graduate to take placement tests at any level of higher education, presumably their writing skills are also worse than the placement results in table 9.1.

So what is a fair estimate of the writing deficiencies in the entire cohort of eighteen year olds in California? Sixty percent? Seventy percent?

Does it matter that these deficiencies exist? Can't these teenagers just take a remedial course or two in college and be on their way?

According to a researcher at UC–Berkeley, students "who think that they can easily make up during college the learning they have failed to do in high school" should be forewarned. The data W. Norton Grubb cites shows how difficult it is for students with severe deficiencies to graduate even from a community college—the lowest level of higher education. "Students with three deficiencies had a much harder time than students with one deficiency: only 42 percent of the former group corrected all three deficiencies and only 9 percent of these students graduated within three years, while 63 percent of students with one deficiency corrected it and 28 percent of these graduated."[6]

Therefore, the teachers in this sample are correct to complain about the literacy practices in their high schools. The deficiencies that students leave high school with have consequences for their careers in higher education.

The teachers in this sample have identified a number of literacy practices that may influence the development of reading and writing skills in California:

- *The custom of providing one survey textbook as the only reading for an entire year of social studies.* Biographies, autobiographies, and historical fiction used in private schools are not available and would provide a much larger volume of reading experiences for California teenagers. Research says that the volume of reading accomplished is the variable most closely associated with the development of reading skills. The custom of making decisions about books is far above the heads of teachers. An instructor enthusiastic about the novels of Barbara Kingsolver can't use this writer unless the texts have already been approved by the local school district.
- *The lack of time for students to read silently during the school day.* Many students—especially those in low-income neighborhoods—are busy with jobs after school.
- *Heavy workloads for teachers.* With up to 180 students a day to respond to, the workload of English teachers may influence the frequency of writing assignments and thus the development of teenagers as writers.

Are planners now working to reduce these obstacles to literacy in states such as California? In the next chapter, I will look at some indicators that may show what teachers can expect in the future in their classrooms in California and elsewhere.

VIEWS AND RECOMMENDATIONS

By now a large number of reports on the new statewide policies in Califor-nia in the 1990s have been published. One of the most comprehensive is *Crucial Issues in California Education 2000* from the Policy Analysis for California Education Center at Berkeley (available at www-gse.berkeley.edu/research/PACE/pace_publications.html). In the section of this report on governance, Michael Kirst and his coauthors describe the increasing centralization of power at the state level in the hands of the governor, the state Board of Education (which the governor appoints), and an elected state superintendent of public instruction. But at the same time, Kirst and his colleagues maintain that there is still room for local control of curricula and that the state standards are a "framework rather than a prescription."

In my small sample, I do not see any evidence of such a benign arrangement. Kirst et al. may need to look at the ecology of California's secondary schools much more clearly. For example, if a high school chooses to keep English and social studies as separate subjects in secondary school, as the state suggests, for the last seven years of public education from grades 6 to 12, each child will be one of 150 to 180 students each teacher sees every day. This fundamental decision is strongly influenced, if not controlled, by the state, yet many researchers do not even acknowledge the existence of this decision. Instead, they see curriculum just as subjects, not as ecology. They continue to believe that the official curriculum reflects the experiences of students in schools. I would argue that the "unofficial curriculum" includes how a subject is delivered. Is the English teacher delivering the subject to 80 students or 180? If your job is to respond to teenagers' written work, this number of students matters. It is not a detail; it is a fundamental part of the curriculum. Does the schedule of English teachers matter in California with so many students whose native language may not be English? In fact, the curriculum may be much more the ecology of the school than the official list of subjects. Being one of 180 students a teacher faces may shape a student's day far more than the details of the subject at hand.

Merely by offering the standard state subjects, school districts are forced into the ecology described in this chapter: English teachers with 180 students are overwhelmed, while social studies teachers have no official responsibility for language development. Just by keeping these subjects separate, as the state does, the local school is forced into a factory model with little attention for the individual student. If researchers included the voices of teachers and students from time to time, the influences of ecology (i.e., teacher workload, school size, etc.) might receive more attention in their reports.

I think the curriculum is what the students experience in a secondary school. It is how they are treated in addition to the official list of subjects. If a teenager is rarely given writing assignments because a teacher with 180 students has little time to read them, this experience is part of the curriculum. If a homework assignment is checked in a log book but not graded, that also is part of the experience. If Kirst and his coauthors expanded their definition of curriculum, they might see schools through different eyes, and the influence of state regulations might be more visible to them.

NOTES

1. Presentation by Marshall S. Smith at a November 19, 1992, seminar sponsored by the California Education Policy Seminar and the California State University Institute for Educational Reform. See the January 1998 report on the seminar, "Putting Schools to the Test: California's NAEP Scores and The National Testing Plan," available online at www.calstate.edu/ier/materials.shtml.

2. Pacific Research Institute, *Index of Leading Education Indicators 2000*, 11; available at www.pacificresearch.org/pub/sab/educat/00_ed_index/.

3. Pacific Research Institute, *Index of Leading Education Indicators 2000*.

4. To read Governor Davis's veto message of October 10, 2001, see www.leginfo.ca.gov/pub/bill/asm/ab_0001-0050/ab_50_vt_20011010.html.

5. California State Board of Education, *History–Social Science Content Standards for California Public Schools, Kindergarten through Grade Twelve* (Sacramento: Author, 2000); available at www.cde.ca.gov/cdepress/downloads.html.

6. W. Norton Grubb, *From Black Box to Pandora's Box: Evaluating Remedial/ Developmental Education* (New York: Community College Research Center, Teachers College, Columbia University, 2001), 22–23; available at www.tc.columbia.edu/ccrc/PAPERS/grubb2.pdf.

Chapter Ten

Improving the Capacity of Teachers

The Experiences of Three States

Like many parents, Richard F. Elmore, a professor at the Harvard University Graduate School of Education, does not believe that the current management of high schools is adequate. Elmore writes that U.S. high schools "are probably either a close third or tied for second as the most pathological social institutions in our society after public health hospitals and prisons."[1]

Elmore also does not expect the "tough standards" movement now in place around the nation to improve low-performing schools. He argues that new state tests will not add to the capacity or the ability of weak schools to improve.

The working theory behind test-based accountability is seemingly — perhaps fatally — simple. Students take tests that measure their academic performance in various subject areas. The results trigger certain consequences for students and schools — rewards, in the case of high performance, and sanctions for poor performance. Having stakes attached to test scores is supposed to create incentives for students and teachers to work harder and for school and district administrators to do a better job of monitoring their performance. If students, teachers, or schools are chronically low performing, presumably something more must be done — students must be denied diplomas or held back a grade; teachers or principals must be sanctioned or dismissed; and failing schools must be fixed or simply closed. The threat of such measures is supposed to be enough to motivate students and schools to ever-higher levels of performance.

This may have the ring of truth, but it is in fact a naïve, highly schematic, and oversimplified view of what it takes to improve student learning. The work that my colleagues and I have done on accountability suggests that in-

118

ternal accountability precedes external accountability. That is, school personnel must share a coherent, explicit set of norms and expectations about what a good school looks like before they can use signals from the outside to improve student learning. Giving test results to an incoherent, atomized, badly run school doesn't automatically make it a better school. The ability of a school to make improvements has to do with the beliefs, norms, expectations, and practices that people in the organization share, not with the kind of information they receive about their performance. Low-performing schools aren't coherent enough to respond to external demands for accountability.[2]

In Elmore's view, federal efforts to reform schools through the recent No Child Left Behind legislation depend on states who themselves lack the ability to transform local schools. Elmore urges new investments by states in capacity of schools: "internal accountability and instructional improvements."

The work of turning a school around entails improving the knowledge and skills of teachers—changing their knowledge of content and how to teach it—and helping them to understand where their students are in their academic development. Low-performing schools, and the people who work in them, don't know what to do. If they did, they would be doing it already. You can't improve a school's performance, or the performance of any teacher or student in it, without increasing the investment in teachers' knowledge, pedagogical skills, and understanding of students. This work can be influenced by an external accountability system, but it cannot be done by that system. Test scores don't tell us much of anything about these important domains; they provide a composite, undifferentiated signal about students' responses to a problem.

Test-based accountability without substantial investments in capacity— internal accountability and instructional improvement in schools—is unlikely to elicit better performance from low-performing students and schools. Furthermore, the increased pressure of test-based accountability, without substantial investments in capacity, is likely to aggravate the existing inequalities between low-performing and high-performing schools and students. Most high-performing schools simply reflect the social capital of their students; they are primarily schools with students of high socioeconomic status. Most low-performing schools also reflect the composition of their student populations. Performance-based accountability systems reward schools that work against the association between performance and socioeconomic status. However, most high-performing schools elicit higher performance by relying on the social capital of their students and families rather than on the internal capacity of the schools themselves. Most low-performing schools cannot rely on the social capital of students and families and instead must rely on their organizational capacity. Hence, with little or no investment in capacity, low-performing schools get worse relative to high-performing schools.[3]

Elmore believes that in the diverse American educational system, where states have operated for generations with different standards and different resources, these states have not developed "the institutional capacity to monitor the improvement of teaching and learning in schools." He also asks whether states have begun to support teachers—"to support the development of new knowledge and skill in teachers and administrators."

For Elmore, school reform is blocked by a weak knowledge base in teachers, weak internal accountability, and states that do not have the ability to intervene. Too many teachers simply are not effective instructors and they are not accountable for this lack of skill.

Other commentators have a somewhat different approach to the obstacles to school reform. Samuel Bacharach, a professor of organizational behavior at Cornell University, and his research team have focused on how the working conditions of teachers influence their effectiveness—their capacity to teach. Bacharach warns that the efforts to reward teachers through merit pay and career ladders—while politically attractive—would "fail to address the most critical obstacle to improving the educational system: the characteristics of the learning workplace. Only when we begin to examine the conditions that exist and the resources that are available in this workplace in America's schools will we be able to establish focused and strategic reforms that produce real and lasting improvement."[4]

After sending out a survey questionnaire to teachers, Bacharach and a team of researchers found a workplace where teachers faced obstacles in a variety of areas. This is what the data from their survey, which they call CART (conditions and resources of teaching), show:

- Teachers do not feel that they receive the resources they need to carry out their jobs effectively.
- Teachers do not have the opportunity to bring their professional expertise to bear in decision-making.

- Communication between teachers and building-level administrators is less frequent then desired.
- Teachers feel that building-level administrators do not exhibit the characteristics of supportive leaders.[5]

Citing the empirical results of this survey, Bacharach argues that school reform has been going in the wrong direction. He believes that the reform efforts of state legislatures to motivate teachers through merit pay and career ladders fail to make the changes that teachers need in the workplace. He says that "education reformers have ignored the basic lesson of decades of research on organizational effectiveness: before a job can be performed effectively, it must be properly designed."[6] Bacharach wants the role of a teacher in a school to be the central focus of school reform. He writes, "to a large extent, the job design of the role of teacher determines just how effective an individual *can* be as a teacher."[7]

Bacharach believes that "the resources necessary to perform the job of teacher may be grouped into five categories:

1. *Authority.* Every job requires that decisions be made to complete the tasks assigned to the position. The right to make those decisions is authority. The authority structure of the organization, i.e. who has the right to make what decision, is a critical component of an examination of resources.
2. *Time and space.* Each teaching responsibility requires a certain amount of time to fulfill. It is quite possible to assign a mix of responsibilities that cannot be fulfilled in the time allotted.
3. *Human support.* Few jobs exist in isolation. Teachers must coordinate their activities with others in order to ensure task completion. For teachers, human support may be thought of as both advice and feedback and assistance.
4. *Equipment, supplies, and materials.* [M]ost teaching responsibilities also depend on adequate supplies and material. These resources are covered in the CART survey by questions on:
   - classroom supplies
   - A.V. materials
   - A.V. equipment
   - textbooks
   - workbooks

- other published materials
- money to purchase supplies.

5. *Knowledge, skills, and information*."[8]

Using a combination of indicators contributed by Bacharach and El-more, it is possible to examine the ability of our three states to support the effectiveness of teachers in secondary schools. We need to create measures of the conditions and resources of teaching, as Bacharach suggests, and measures of internal accountability, as Elmore suggests.

Let's begin by measuring the adequacy of resources. In states such as New York that have created a separate allocation of state funds for textbooks, the amount of this allocation would seem to be a valid measure of resources. If researchers had considered the issue of school resources more carefully in the past, this question of support for teachers may have gained national attention some time ago. In his landmark study in the 1960s, the late James S. Coleman used the number of books in a school library as a measure of school resources, a choice that ignores the need of teachers to assign a single book as a source of common reading and writing assignments for an entire class.

In urban districts such as New York City, traditionally this state allocation has been it; New York City has not spent local funds to supplement the state allocation on textbooks.

The New York State Textbook Law—usually called NYSTL, or "nistil," by teachers—currently provides $57 per pupil per year. After adjustment for inflation, this amount is lower than when the program began in the 1960s. Is this amount adequate after it is divided up for use by six or seven subject area teachers? If our history teacher receives one-sixth of this amount, he or she will have approximately $13 to provide all the reading materials for an entire year. This will provide perhaps one trade book; it will not provide the trade book a month that may be needed to close the reading gap between the races in the United States or prepare students for the rigors of college.

What this low level of funding does is perpetuate a system of textbook-centered education for all teenagers across a state. For the children of upper-middle-class college graduates, the need to read widely outside textbooks may not be urgent in high school. They hear the vocabulary of the college educated at the dinner table; they have access to home libraries and newspaper and magazine subscriptions. They have relatives providing books at holidays and credit cards to buy books at Barnes and Noble and Borders. College graduates seem to reproduce themselves without difficulty under current arrangements. But for the children of the poor, who may have entered high school reading below grade level, the opportunity to prepare for the rigors of college and the workplace through reading a large number of books in high school courses may be crucial to their success in college. The carnage that results when the underprepared enroll in open admissions community colleges is well documented, as in the study by Norton Grubb described in the last chapter.

A teacher in a history or a humanities course would need a budget of at least $100 per pupil per year to provide a large reading list, and the same amount for an English teacher—not a share of the $57 that Governor George E. Pataki and the New York state legislature are currently providing. Of course, there is no guarantee that even in the presence of more resources, teachers will step up and assert themselves and write syllabi and craft assignments that can only be completed by doing the assigned reading. Richard Elmore's point about the need for internal accountability is well taken and will be addressed later in this chapter.

What is Maryland—the second case study—doing in this area of providing resources? According to one national report, Maryland is doing well in the adequacy of resources category. It received a grade of B from the most recent rankings (2002) by *Education Week*.[9] But after further analysis, this ranking is suspect because the reviewers made no effort to see how much of total resources went to the classroom where it might influence achievement. For these reviewers, the total amount of spending was enough to evaluate a state's commitment to education. As the teachers indicated in chapter 7, this large amount of aggregate spending in Montgomery County did not reach their classrooms or improve their ability to provide a large volume of reading for the teenagers they face.

But the state of Maryland does not inquire into what happens in actual classrooms. The state does not have a separate state textbook fund, nor does it require that local school districts spend a fixed amount of money each year on books. It only "requires that local boards of education provide an instructional textbook for a core curriculum course for each student in a public school." The result of this hands-off approach to textbooks and other reading materials is very low spending on books even in counties with high total spending on education. In 1998, the average spending by county was only $38, with some counties spending as little as $25 per child per year on books. (See table 10.1 for recent textbook spending levels throughout Maryland.)

What is California doing in this area? Is the state providing adequate funding for books? Has this state, which has been notorious for textbook shortages as late as 1998, changed its ways? In California, the archives of the *Los Angeles Times* are full of stories about textbook shortages throughout the 1990s. A search of Lexis-Nexis at a university library will provide dates and bylines on the search term "textbook shortages and California." There was a slight improvement in this situation at the end of the 1990s, when a special state allocation provided four years of supplemental funds for books from 1998 to 2001. (The actual aid in this supplemental bill, called the Schiff-Bustamante Standards-Based Instructional Materials Program, was not generous. At the secondary level it added $41.86 to the basic state aid of $20.77, providing a total of $62.63 for all reading materials and textbooks for a high school student for a year.[10] As recently as 1997–1998, total state book aid at the secondary level was only $18 per year. See table 10.2.)

In addition to four years of supplemental funding, the California state education department, in the spirit of public schools around the nation, has created a new bureaucratic safeguard to ensure that local school districts spend an adequate amount of money on textbooks. California now trusts local school districts so little in this area of providing adequate reading materials that it actually requires a hearing by each school board in the state on the topic of adequacy of textbooks as the warning below shows.[11] Here is an illustrative message from the superintendent of the San Bernardino school system:

REMINDER! SUFFICIENCY OF TEXTBOOKS AND INSTRUC-
TIONAL MATERIALS
    Remember to hold your board meeting on sufficiency of textbooks and instructional materials in order to pass a resolution for FY 2001/02. Send District Advisory Services a copy of the resolution and Notification of

Table 10.1. Maryland Spending on Textbooks by County, Fiscal Year 1998

County	FTE Enrollment 9/30/97	Instructional Costs	Textbook Costs	Per-Pupil Textbooks Costs	Percentage of Instructional Costs
Allegany	10,476.75	$ 31,587,591	$ 444,388	$42.42	1.4
Anne Arundel	69,843.50	204,858,808	1,749,034	25.04	0.9
Baltimore City	98,972.25	282,892,761	4,648,263	46.97	1.6
Baltimore	97,921.25	314,229,794	4,257,488	43.48	1.4
Calvert	13,982.50	41,142,262	677,001	48.42	1.6
Caroline	5,261.50	15,382,069	254,127	48.30	1.7
Carroll	25,633.00	70,764,134	697,976	27.23	1.0
Cecil	14,320.50	39,779,606	548,622	38.31	1.4
Charles	20,367.75	57,629,791	731,995	35.94	1.3
Dorchester	4,777.75	15,738,978	70,926	14.85	0.5
Frederick	32,752.50	96,632,973	923,573	28.20	1.0
Garrett	4,987.75	15,250,781	150,310	30.14	1.0
Harford	36,274.25	105,151,003	1,708,754	47.11	1.6
Howard	38,501.50	123,100,004	1,440,019	37.40	1.2
Kent	2,653.00	10,673,176	122,815	46.29	1.2
Montgomery	118,016.25	459,065,028	3,608,510	30.58	0.8
Prince George's	120,505.50	353,030,764	4,228,540	35.09	1.2
Queen Anne's	6,125.75	18,848,418	247,406	40.39	1.3
St. Mary's	13,611.75	39,391,999	609,288	44.76	1.5
Somerset	2,877.75	10,521,638	288,407	100.22	2.7
Talbot	4,263.00	13,035,043	196,636	46.13	1.5
Washington	18,901.25	56,880,421	1,183,676	62.62	2.1
Wicomico	13,137.25	39,598,145	889,846	67.73	2.2
Worcester	6,401.50	22,505,237	352,745	55.10	1.6
Statewide	780,565.75	$2,437,690,424	$30,030,345	$38.47	1.2

Source: Department of Legislative Services, "Selected Financial Data, Maryland State Department of Education," March 2000.

Table 10.2. California Instructional Materials Program: Annual Spending per Student on Textbooks from State Aid

	97/98	98/99	99/00	00/01	01/02
K-8					
6110-186-0001 allocated (ADA)	$110,251,710	$121,655,674	$123,664,891	$128,869,688	$137,013,000 $134,936,032
rate	$27.06	$29.79	$30.87	$31.85	$33.08
Grades 9-12 (enrollment) CBEDS					
6110-185-0001 allocated	$28,209,138	$30,899,794	$32,116,000	$33,591,500	$35,827,000 $35,425,501
rate	$18.077	$19.167	$19.39	$20.00	$20.774
Schiff-Bustamante 4yr program 98/99-01/02 (K-12) (enrollment) CBEDS					
allocated		$250,000,000	$250,000,000	$250,000,000	$250,000,000
rate		$43.65	$42.82	$42.42	$41.866
Total per pupil textbook allocation					
K-8	$27.06	$48.96	$73.69	$74.27	$74.95
Grades 9-12	$18.077	$62.82	$62.21	$62.42	$62.64

Source: Carol Presnell, Schools Fiscal Services Division, California Department of Education.

Compliance (Attention: Adrienne Williams). This is pursuant to Bulletin 02-010. The notification form was attached to the bulletin. Districts have until 6/30/02 to comply or are in penalty of losing ALL textbook and instructional materials funding including Restricted Lottery, K–8 Instructional Materials, K–12 Schiff-Bustamante Instructional Materials, etc.

ADDITIONALLY . . . Districts must post a notice of this board hearing 10 days prior to the hearing in three public places. Districts are still receiving audit findings in 2000–01 for not complying with these posting requirements. If districts do receive audit findings for 2000–01 for failure to hold a public hearing or missing the 10-day posting requirement, they can submit a specific waiver request form and certification to try and alleviate any fiscal penalties. Contact Teri Kelly for further information.

This strategy is a little puzzling. If local school districts—called local education agencies, or LEAs, in California—have underspent on books for decades, why are they now able to evaluate how much spending is enough? Requiring hearings does not seem a serious approach to the problem of adequate resources in California; raising state aid for instructional materials from its current level of $63 per pupil to $250 might be a more realistic approach, especially if federal aid for classroom materials became law. And trusting each teacher with the authority to order books—subject to building level review process—might also be useful.

AUTHORITY

As cited earlier in the chapter, Samuel Bacharach asks whether teachers have the authority needed to "complete the tasks assigned to the position." If developing the reading and writing skills of the students in front of them is a desirable task for a high school teacher, then Bacharach's conclusion that teachers lack authority would also hold for the three states in this study. In these three states, almost twenty years of school reform has not improved the authority of teachers in such areas as providing books. Teachers are not becoming high-impact, high-influence professionals able to design rich cognitive environments for their students. And it is surprising, at least initially, that teachers' unions are not aggressively bargaining for increased authority. While a detailed look at the political goals of teachers' unions is not within the domain of this book, it is disappointing to read document after documents on union websites without seeing calls for increased authority. There are union position papers on topic after topic, but authority does not seem to be a subject of much urgency to the union movement.

Professionals have highly developed skills and the authority to use these skills and make decisions. But redefining teaching to make it a more substantial, more powerful profession is not yet a priority of the union movement. Instead, unions fight for smaller class size but ignore other aspects of working conditions that make them more effective in secondary schools and gain the appreciation of their customers: parents and students, and taxpayers.

An aspect of education closely related to authority—the ability to make decisions—is having the time and space necessary to fulfill a responsibility, as Bacharach reminds us.

FORTY-TWO HOURS TO RESPOND TO EACH WRITING ASSIGNMENT

"Each teaching responsibility requires a certain amount of time to fulfill. It is quite possible to assign a mix of responsibilities that cannot be fulfilled in the time allotted." As the English teacher explained in the last chapter, the workload facing an English teacher with 150 to 170 students is impossible. The results of this workload include infrequent or short writing assignments or even the use of multiple-choice tests that can be graded by machines. The National Council of Teachers of English (NCTE) makes clear the cost in time for a teacher who responds to 125 different essays:

> Policymakers must realize that when a teacher spends 20 minutes reading, analyzing, and responding to each paper for a class of 25 students, the teacher must have 500 minutes for those processes alone. A teacher with 125 students who spends only 20 minutes per paper must have at least 2500 minutes, or a total of nearly 42 hours, to respond to each assignment. Therefore, responding to one paper per week for each of their 125 students requires English teachers to work over 80 hours a week.[12]

One solution proposed many years ago by Theodore Sizer, and discussed in more detail in chapter 13, is to combine English and social studies classes so that each teacher will have only eighty students, but this commonsense solution is still not common practice in the high schools in the states in this study.

The NCTE goes on to caution that changes in workload such as reducing class size or the total number of students a teacher works with each day will not influence achievement unless instructional methods change. For example, how does a principal encourage a veteran social studies teacher with tenure that teaching is more than leading class discussions each day, assigning a couple of pages in the textbook to read a couple of times a week, and then creating a multiple-choice and short test every two weeks?

In this hypothetical new literacy-centered school that this principal and her leadership team are creating, teachers in the humanities will have new responsibilities:

- Locating and assigning books that engage teenagers.
- Planning a syllabus that leads teenagers to complete a large number of books during the school year.
- Responding to students' resistance to reading. Would an in-class silent reading program work to convince teenagers that this new school is serious about reading?
- Tying all writing assignments to reading assignments as a way to encourage and monitor the amount of reading being accomplished.
- Responding to the writing itself. Is each error to be corrected and to become the subject of grammar lessons, or are instructors just to read for content? Over the semester, can grading move from correcting each error to just flagging errors so that students can revise their own work? Are peer groups enough audience for drafts of essays, or do students need to write for publication in school or class newspapers to see the importance of revising their drafts?
- Sequencing writing assignments. How can teachers help students develop confidence in their voices? Is James Moffett correct? Do young writers need to begin with monologues and personal narratives, before writing essays that involve arguments and the audience of the outside world? Can writing assignments that allow teenagers to comment on the personal as well as the historical events help them stay interested in writing? One example might be to compare your education with what

Thurgood Marshall experienced in his years in the Baltimore public schools, at Lincoln University, and at Howard Law School.
- Possibly locating placement tests for writing from universities so that high school students can evaluate their skills in relation to the outside world.

INTERNAL ACCOUNTABILITY

Perhaps the teachers in this school are progressive and welcome more opportunity to become professional, with more authority, more resources, and more time to develop the literacy skills of each student. In this case, our principal and her team could probably continue and develop some new measures of teacher productivity. They could move this new school closer to the performance review system common in private industry. Goals could be established around common benchmarks of student achievement: the number of books assigned, the quantity and quality of the students' responses to these readings, the growth of the students as readers and writers during the year. In some cases in some jurisdictions, the political barriers might deter any change in the reward structure of teachers. It is difficult to generalize about the possibility for changes in states where there are so many different jurisdictions each with a different contract with its teachers. New York alone has 905 separate school districts; California almost one thousand. Each has a separate set of arrangements with its teachers.

But there are other models of reading beyond the survey textbook or the guide book to prepare for state exit tests. In schools where the heavy hands of the state curriculum and the union contracts—with all the emphasis on seniority rather than productivity—do not shape education, what are the literacy practices? What are private schools doing with the freedom they enjoy? Researchers, by now, have a clear idea of what should be provided to develop the language skills of teenagers. And some public and private schools are providing these environments. The chapters in part 2 look at the research and best literacy practices in public and private schools. The voices of both practitioners and researchers speak about what is needed and what is working with teenagers and reading and writing.

NOTES

1. Richard F. Elmore, "The Limits of 'Change,'" *Harvard Education Letter Research Online* (January/February 2002); available at www.edletter.org/current/limitsofchange.shtml.

2. Richard F. Elmore, "Unwarranted Intrusion," *Education Next* (Spring 2002); available at www.educationnext.org/20021/30.html.

3. Elmore, "Unwarranted Intrusion," 8.

4. Samuel B. Bacharach, C. Bauer, and Joseph B. Shedd, *The Learning Workplace: The Conditions and Resources of Teaching* (Ithaca, N.Y.: OAP, 1986), 1 (ED 279-614).

5. Bacharach et al., *The Learning Workplace*, 3.

6. Bacharach et al., *The Learning Workplace*, 5.

7. Bacharach et al., *The Learning Workplace*, 5.

8. Bacharach et al., *The Learning Workplace*, 8–11.

9. See *Education Week* online at www.teachermagazine.org/sreports/qc02/templates/state_data.cfm?slug=17qcmd.h21.

10. Telephone interview with Carol Presnell, Schools Fiscal Services Division, California Department of Education, August 2002.

11. The actual law mandating these hearings is California Education Code, section 60119, which "requires the governing board of any local agency receiving instructional materials funds from any state source to hold a public hearing or hearings on the sufficiency of textbooks or instructional materials." See www.cde.ca.gov/ and search for "instructional materials fund."

12. National Council of Teachers of English, "Statement on Class Size and Teacher Workload: Secondary, 1990," available at www.ncte.org/positions/class-size-second.shtml.

Chapter Eleven

What Does the Research Say about Reading?

Print exposure is a variable over time "that accumulates into enormous individual differences."

—Anne E. Cunningham and Keith E. Stanovich (1998)

What does science say about how teenagers become strong, fluent readers? While some students do come to high school with third and fourth grade reading skills and may require special help on the fundamentals of reading, many others arrive in ninth grade only reading two or three years below grade level. What do these teenagers need? Most of them are past the need to learning decoding. They can translate letters into sounds effectively, but they still read years below teenagers in wealthier suburbs. As this chapter will show, the research suggests that they need immersion in print, but questions remain about what immersion is and how it can be offered in the context of public schools with a variety of existing rules and regulations.

Jeanne Chall of Harvard University, the author of *Learning to Read: The Great Debate* and *Stages of Reading Development,* is one of the best-known researchers on reading in the postwar period. She has written both on general questions of reading development and on the gap in reading skills between the races in the United States.

According to Chall, the accessibility of books is the single most powerful influence on reading development:

Probably the most important factor in reading development is the wide reading that depends on the easy accessibility of books. From the earliest studies of adults and children (Marston, 1982) accessibility was found to be the most important factor, with readability and interest following. This means that books (and magazines and newspapers) are read when they are at hand, are readable and are interesting. A classroom library collection, a school library collection, or books at home bought or borrowed from the public library are, therefore, very important. Textbooks are important, but they are not enough.[1]

A LARGE VOLUME OF READING IS NECESSARY

Subsequent research in cognitive development has made clear that the volume of reading students accomplish matters. "Furthermore, many researchers are convinced that volume of reading, rather than oral language, is the prime contributor to individual differences in children's vocabularies," write Anne E. Cunningham and Keith E. Stanovich, both developmental psychologists, in "What Reading Does for the Mind" (*American Educator,* Spring/Summer 1998). They argue that "early success at reading acquisition is one of the keys that unlock a lifetime of reading habits. The subsequent *exercise* of this habit serves to further develop reading comprehension ability in an interlocking positive feedback logic."[2] Note their emphasis on "the subsequent exercise of this habit."

In another study, Stanovich and Cunningham investigated whether exposure to print still correlates with general knowledge in an age of television and other electronic stimuli. They sought to see which of a set of variables, including exposure to print, correlated most strongly with a test of practical knowledge.

Their test was not elitist. The knowledge they asked about was practical. They asked about "how a carburetor worked, who their U.S. senators were, what a capital-intensive industry was," and so forth. They write, "In this study we examined whether individual differences in print exposure—and differences in exposure to other media—can account for individual differences in acquired declarative knowledge. . . . Not only was print exposure a significant unique predictor, but it was a more potent predictor than the ability measures."[3] The ability measure included high school GPA, Raven Advanced Progressive Matrices, a mathematics test, and Nelson-Denny Reading Test—Comprehension Subtest. They state that print exposure is a variable over time "that accumulates into enormous individual differences."[4]

Exposure to television, they conclude, is negatively correlated with knowledge measures: "In cases in which television did display associations with knowledge measures, the relationships tended to be negative."

Recent research funded by the federal government comes to the same conclusion that the exercise and practice of reading is crucial to the development of reading skills. "Fluent readers can read text with speed, accuracy and proper expression. Fluency depends upon well-developed word recognition skills, but such skills do not inevitably lead to fluency. . . . There is common agreement that fluency develops from reading practice."[5]

Phrases such as exercise *of reading, practice of reading, volume of reading,* and *exposure to print* dominate the literature. After youngsters acquire decoding skills, there is fundamental agreement about what is next. This is not a field divided into camps of whole language versus phonics. There is agreement that "environmental differences (cultural opportunities, parental modeling, quality of school) all influence language development."[6] There is agreement that practice and exercise of reading matters—whether is it inspired by parental modeling, a school assignment, or a book recommended by an aunt or uncle.

If the volume of reading matters so much according to the research, why aren't the goals of reading a great deal at the heart of the secondary school curriculum? What forces continue to shape curricula in American schools? What do researchers say about how curriculum decisions are being made today in the American school system?

OBSTACLES TO A CURRICULUM DESIGNED
FOR IMMERSION IN LANGUAGE

"We do have a national curriculum," states Michael W. Apple, a professor of education at the University of Wisconsin–Madison. "But it's not determined by a democratically-elected body and it's not determined by a central ministry of education. The curriculum is determined by the textbooks, and the textbooks—by and large—look the same all over the United States."

We ought to think about textbooks as the tip of the iceberg. Here are problems with texts, but texts are only there because of the ways schools are organized, because we have a lack of time for teachers to find other materials, because there's not a lot of alternative material being produced any-more, and because we have a system where everything is centralized and highly bureaucratized. In order to alter texts, we have to think ecologically. How does this text fit into administrative regimens, lack of resources, lack of time?[7]

Lack of authority could also be added to Apple's analysis of the ecology of the American high school.

Frances Fitzgerald focuses attention on how textbooks are written and then selected by state adoption committees in her well-known book *America Revisited: History Schoolbooks in the Twentieth Century*. She also believes that textbooks drive the national curriculum.

> The big basic history textbook thus seems here to stay, at least for a while, at least for a bit, and to stay just about what it has always been in this century—a kind of lowest common denominator of American tastes. . . . Since the public schools across the country now spend less than one per cent of their budgets on buying books (textbook publishing is only a seven-hundred-million-dollar-a-year business), publishers cannot afford to have more than one or two basic histories on the market at the same time. Consequently, all of them try to compete for the center of the market, designing their books not to please anyone in particular but to be acceptable to as many people as possible. The word "controversial" is as deeply feared by textbook publishers as it is coveted by trade-book publishers. What a textbook reflects is thus a compromise, an America sculpted and sanded down by the pressures of diverse constituents and interest groups.[8]

Fitzgerald's distinction between the textbook—designed to be dull and unoffensive and thus to appeal to a variety of markets—and a trade book—designed for its narrative and flow and ideas and to sell to real readers, not captives in a school system—seems fundamental, but it does not seem to have received much subsequent attention. Of course, being able to provide trade books would also allow more books to be available for teenage readers.

Clearly, providing each youngster with one textbook for social studies and one for English is not enough. This tradition of one textbook so common in our secondary schools does not serve to provide the volume of reading and the redundancy in reading that research says are best practices. Even if teenagers read every word of a six-hundred-page textbook, they have read only one book for the year. Why is this tradition of depending on textbooks as the primary source of literacy so dominant in American schools?

The political benefits of textbooks in the humanities are obvious. Textbooks provide safety; citywide administrators at headquarters know that each ninth grade social studies teacher at each school in Brooklyn, or Bethesda, or Silver Spring is listening to lectures about ancient Rome, or ancient Africa, or ancient Asia at the same time in the fall semester. The administrators at the building level are also safe. They are complying with state curriculum laws that mandate global history in ninth grade, American history in tenth grade, and so forth. While these mandates vary somewhat from state to state, the directions seem to be the same. Americans hope that providing years of surveys of foreign and domestic history will prepare our children for citizenship. We hope that memorizing the names of dozens of treaties, compromises, and presidents for a test on Friday (and forgotten by Monday) will build historical literacy in our young.

HISTORICAL LITERACY, SURVEY TEXTBOOKS, AND THE VOLUME OF READING

One of the best-known proponents of historical literacy is Paul Gagnon, a professor of history at the University of Massachusetts; his critique of existing practices in the teaching of history in high schools is rich and detailed. For someone who has not taught history for many years, Gagnon is an eye-opener. He reminds readers of periods when the majority sat by idly for generation after generation as labor unsuccessfully tried to organize since labor never represented the majority of the American public. He also reminds readers of the constant challenge presented by capitalism: how to maintain the energy of the economic engine without tolerating the oppression of labor. He asks that we bring "the gigantic forces of the modern age under democratic guidance without slowing the parade of benefits."[9] He writes with so much enthusiasm about the nation's Founders, Abraham Lincoln, John Atgeld, Theodore Roosevelt, and Jane Addams that one is inspired to read more about these historical figures. As he writes his critique of the standard American history textbooks, he takes his readers on a lively journey through the events and themes of American history.

He begins by noting Fitzgerald's complaint that while the problems of the poor are mentioned, "the causes of their problems are still not probed."[10] Thus, a poor teenager might sit in history class year after year and think that the condition of his or her family is a personal "disease" rather than a political condition that might have been different with different government policies.

Gagnon is also critical of the dull march through chronology that many textbooks present to young readers. He would have more drama, more zest. He quotes Gilbert T. Sewall's study of "the literacy quality of the texts and their clarity of organization."

"One consequence," Sewall says, "is that students find history and social studies dull and worse, unrelated to their lives. To the extent that textbooks are responsible for student indifference, they contribute to 'a wholesale loss of national heritage,' preparing the day when we may resemble 'a ship of fools, without anchor or compass.'"[11]

My main objection to Gagnon is that he does not take his own conclusions far enough. In the end, he stays with the survey textbook in spite of page after page of criticisms of these very survey textbooks. While he urges changes in the textbooks and the use of more themes and fewer dates and names, he stays with the use of the standard textbook as the central reading assignment in American high school social studies. This is a significant decision, as social studies represents one half the opportunity to gain language skills in secondary schools. Gagnon and many other experts who are happy to prescribe the content of what teenagers are to learn during adolescence assume that one curriculum can serve all entering freshmen regardless of the reading skills and cultural backgrounds of these teenagers. This assumption needs examination since "the one best curriculum" still controls our schools and so far has been unable to bridge the gap in reading skills between the races in the United States.

There are advantages to allowing teachers to move beyond the standard curriculum with its one textbook to read for the year. Providing more reading assignments than the one standard textbook might reduce the reading gap. It might also allow teachers to craft reading lists far closer to the interests of students. And to craft writing assignments tied to the reading as is done in private schools. It might also allow teachers to use books they are committed to, rather than what is left over in the book room after the senior teachers have made their choices.

There are alternatives to the four or five standard American history texts Gagnon criticizes. Imagine a thirteen-year-old starting high school in Boston, or Brooklyn, or Baltimore where the urban poor graduate from high school with grammar school reading skills. Imagine if this student was taken as seriously as eighteen- or nineteen-year-old college freshmen and sophomores. Rather than trudging through one paragraph summaries of ancient Aztec emperors and Indian sultanates in a world history or global studies textbook, this teenager could choose from courses on crime and punishment with readings from Mike McAlary's work on police corruption in *Buddy Boys,* to his account of the search for a cop killer in *Cop Shot,* to Sister Helen Prejean's argument against the death penalty in *Dead Man Walking,* to the earlier account of how *Gideon v. Wainwright* expanded the legal rights of the poor by Anthony Lewis. These books offer the drama and zest and rich characterizations that Gagnon is seeking. They can teach the basics of constitutional law through dissonance. "What's this paragraph about the Fourteenth Amendment mean?" was a typical response to a chapter in Prejean when I taught this text. Similar readings are available about the public health crisis of AIDS, about the civil rights movement of the past, and about the civil rights crisis of today—about unequal opportunity in the United States. These topics might engage the imaginations and intellects of high school freshmen far more effectively than the better survey textbooks Gagnon wants.

Alternatively, the student could choose a reading list with texts from the urban topics of the criminal justice system, the AIDS crisis, and police corruption, but still the student would have the privilege of making a choice rather than receiving the one book for the year choice of the state. And with these choices, the school could communicate that the books will be read and responded to in written assignments, or the course will be failed. The current practice of "getting over" of passing tests by listening to class discussions rather than actually completing the reading assignments would be much more difficult.

Unlike a semester with half of a survey textbook, these lists of four or five books in a semester would offer a volume of reading. These books would do far more than a textbook to prepare youngsters for the much larger reading lists in higher education. And there may be ancillary advantages we are not aware of. Choice may matter in education. It may matter to a student entering high school reading below grade level that at least he or she will finally have some voice in what the readings will be. For once, these students will work in an environment where their voices become part of the institution in a positive way.

But some readers would certainly point out that something is lost in this approach that emphasizes developing language skills through a variety of texts that will vary from school to school just as they do in private schools, rather than the standard journey through American history. One of the most vigorous proponents of the standard journey is the historian Arthur Schlesinger. In his well-known work *The Disuniting of America: Reflections on a Multicultural Society,* Schlesinger argues that more attention to ethnic identities in the curriculum will end the cohesion we need to stay together as a nation.

> The militants of ethnicity now contend that a main objective of public education should be the protection, strengthening, celebration, and perpetuation of ethnic origins and identities. Separatism, however, nourishes prejudices, magnifies differences and stirs antagonisms. The consequent increase in ethnic and racial conflict lies behind the hullabaloo over "multiculturalism" and "political correctness," over the iniquities of the "Eurocentric" curriculum, and over the notion that history and literature should be taught not as intellectual disciplines but as therapies whose function is to raise minority self-esteem. . . . [I]f separatist tendencies go unchecked, the result can only be a fragmentation, resegregation, and tribalization of American life.[12]

Schlesinger makes many assumptions that should be examined given the widespread failure of American teenagers to learn history within the current curriculum of survey textbooks year after year. The data from the recent most national assessment of the history skills of American children mentioned in chapter 8 and earlier NAEP assessments show that current classroom practices are not developing historical literacy. But Schlesinger does not look closely at classroom practices. He still advocates control from above. His fervor also opens a window into how decisions are made about secondary curricula.

To begin with, Schlesinger wants to continue presenting European history as the heart of the social studies curriculum, and he wants decisions about curricula to still be made from above. He asks readers, "Is the Western tradition a bar to progress and a curse on humanity? Would it really do

America and the world good to get rid of the European legacy?"[13] In Schlesinger's world, the authority should continue to reside far above the classroom, in the historians and professors of literature whose role it is to argue and finally make decision for classroom teachers. His essay is a response to what he sees as the excesses of ethnic studies in higher education and also to the new multicultural curricula in K–12 in New York and California. He blasts educators in these states for a new emphasis on global history and less emphases on American history. He fears that youngsters will now learn less about the "American Creed."[14]

But isn't an allegiance to the American Creed boosted by literacy itself, by teenagers who grew into the habit of reading, by year after year of exciting reading experiences in school? Schlesinger, like many historians prescribing from above, does not look below to see what weak books are doing to youngsters' reading habits. These scholars who are willing to advise state education departments and prescribe in detail what should be taught in secondary schools', have not bothered to learn the basic features of the lives of the secondary schools' teachers. Unless these historians and other "experts" from academia begin to look into the lives of classroom teachers and the books available to them, we will continue with scenes such as the following one.

Theodore Sizer, one of the most important critics of our current high schools, shows how standard issue textbooks—the heart of the curricula in many school systems—damage the lives of teenagers. Here is his portrait of a teenager and a textbook:

> Dennis' bright eyes deadened as the class proceeded. His paper was as neat as his haircut and tennis shirt, but it was clear that he could barely write. It was as though he were copying nonsense ideographs. He persisted for a while and then slowly sank, head downward, asleep, propped up by his over-eight-hundred-page world history textbook, virtually none of which he could either read or understand. Roman fires and sewers, Chinese horses, Indian cities, dates B.C. and A.D., were light years from this youngster. Morpheus put him out of his misery.[15]

There are alternatives to the boredom of the survey textbook and the survey course that Sizer describes. It might do the teenagers of the United States a great deal of good—especially those reading below grade level— to have the freedom to choose which topics they are going to spend three or four months with. It might do American teachers some good to select the books they are going to be using rather than what is available in the departmental bookroom.

What would this system actually look like in a real school? The next chapter examines the literacy practices in private schools that have abandoned survey textbooks and force teenagers to select what they will read. Not surprisingly, these private schools also tie all writing assignments to the readings, so that the common public school practice of listening to the class discussions to prepare for tests, rather than doing the reading, doesn't work very well. In these schools, you actually have to do the reading to pass the course.

What would more choice from a wide range of humanities courses with long reading lists look like? Would teenagers develop allegiance to each reading assignment or would they still try to "get over" and pass courses without doing the reading? The experiences of teenagers in private schools operating outside the state curricula may provide some insights into these questions.

NOTES

1. Jeanne S. Chall, *Stages of Reading Development* (New York: McGraw-Hill, 1983), 107.

2. Anne E. Cunningham and Keith E. Stanovich, "What Reading Does for the Mind" *American Educator* (Spring/Summer 1998).

3. Keith E. Stanovich and Anne E. Cunningham, "Where Does Knowledge Come From? Specific Associations between Print Exposure and Information Acquisition," *Journal of Educational Psychology* 85, no. 2 (June 1993): 224.

4. Stanovich and Cunningham, "Where Does Knowledge Come From?" 225.

5. *Report of the National Reading Panel: Teaching Children to Read* (Washington, D.C: 2000); available at www.nichd.nih.gov/publications/nrp/report.pdf. Chapter 4 on fluency is especially interesting.

6. *Report of the National Reading Panel.*

7. Michael W. Apple, "Whose Knowledge Do We Teach?" in *Focus in Change: The National Center for Effective Schools Research and Development* (Spring 1992): 2.

8. Frances Fitzgerald, *America Revisited* (Boston: Little, Brown, 1979), 46–47.

9. Paul Gagnon, *Democracy's Half Told Story: What American Textbooks Should Add* (Washington, D.C.: American Federation of Teachers, 1989), 87.

10. Gagnon, *Democracy's Half Told Story,* 11.

11. Gagnon, *Democracy's Half Told Story,* 12.

12. Arthur M. Schlesinger, *The Disuniting of America: Reflections on a Multicultural Society* (New York: Norton, 1992), 17–18.

13. Schlesinger, *The Disuniting of America,* 126.

14. Schlesinger, *The Disuniting of America,* 68.

15. Theodore Sizer, *Horace's Compromise: The Dilemma of the American High School* (Boston: Houghton Mifflin, 1984), 97.

Chapter Twelve

Private School Literacy Practices

"We spend a lot of time on the French Revolution and the Industrial Revolution, but not all the dates, battles, and wars in between. But if they give you tests, you have to teach all those things. You can't have any creative teaching," is how one private school official explained his opposition to the state tests.[1]

What is ironic is that just as President Bush and Congress rush toward more testing as a foundation for school reform, our private schools—considered the most rigorous and effective in the nation—continue to reject the idea that testing and a standardized curriculum to prepare for tests are the best methods to educate teenagers.

In New York City, where the weak public education system has made private schools especially important, a number of private schools have rejected the state's curriculum and its efforts to measure their students. These private schools do not bother preparing their students for the state tests. They do not boost the percentage of graduating seniors who have passed the state tests, called the Regents. Instead, they market themselves by advertising SAT scores and acceptances into elite colleges.

What are private schools doing with this freedom from the state education rules? What books are they assigning? How much reading is being assigned? How are reading and writing being connected? Are there literacy practices at work in these private schools that could be used effectively in the nation's public high schools?

SARA HENDERSON—A TENTH GRADER AT BERKELEY CARROLL IN PARK SLOPE IN BROOKLYN

Sara's experiences show how much reading is expected of students in this private school. Her comments also show that even in private schools, not every assigned book is read by each student. Finally, Sara who attended a public school, Erasmus Hall, last year, was able to compare how books and reading are presented in a public and in a private school.

First, her reading assignments differed both in volume and in content from the public school students who have been interviewed. In addition to assigning a great deal more reading than the public high schools in Brooklyn, Berkeley Carroll also assigned much newer fiction and more American fiction. Some of the novels were as little as two decades old. Titles such as *Wuthering Heights* from European fiction, which public school students had objected to, are missing from English classes at Berkeley Carroll.

Choice exists at this private school. Students at Berkeley Carroll are able to choose the books they will read during the next semester from a list of courses and readings. "You choose your English class. You have maybe two or three courses each year. The teachers describe the courses, and then you choose."

Sara's first-semester English course was about Native Americans; for second semester of tenth grade, she chose an English course titled "Literature and Psychology." The other choice for second semester was "Men and Women—How Men and Women Are Portrayed in Literature."

Preparing for the SATs

Sara also explained that other factors in her private school motivated students to read. To begin with, her private school made the connection between reading and success on the SATs clear. Scoring well on the SATs was a concern at her private school. She had taken the SATs this year as a tenth grader and would take them two more times in junior year, before finally taking the ones in her senior year that would be submitted to college. She said that the average scores at her school were "around 600" and that she hoped to improve her own scores.

Sara said that she felt less encouragement to read in the public school she had attended the year before.

Getting Over in Public Schools

"Even if they'd assigned more books in public school, I wouldn't have read them," Sara said. "You can get away without reading them. You can just listen to the discussion and then write a general essay with a little bit of information from the discussion.

"I just felt that I didn't want to read the book for myself when I was in public schools because of what I said about SAT scores. They don't emphasize the importance of the SATs [in public schools]. They don't emphasize the importance of reading."

Her classmates in her public school were also different. "Maybe because of the people I was around, I was more narrow-minded and not concerned with reading information and forming my own opinions," she said.

Finally, her private school also encouraged reading by assigning essays that require having read the books. "Also in Berkeley Carroll, we're called upon to write more deep essays, and I feel like without really reading the book, I'm selling myself out in the essay."

But even with all this encouragement to read, the nature of the book itself may still be a major factor as to whether it's read—even in a private school—as we will see.

Getting Over in Private Schools

Even in private schools, students don't complete reading assignments. Of the paperback books assigned in her history class, Sara said, "*Night*, I thought was really good. *All Quiet*—I read like two chapters—it was OK. The rest I didn't open."

Why?

"It wasn't really necessary. We didn't have to write an essay on it. I could get all of the information I needed from the discussions and from asking people."

Not surprisingly, how much she liked the book influenced how much she read of the book. And this was true both for history and English.

"The worst book assigned so far this year in English class was *Lonesome Dove*. Only one person read it. His name was Dave. They called him Lonesome Dave for the rest of the year. The teacher only had us read up to the middle of the book.

"I hated *Lonesome Dove*. I just thought it was really boring. Also, I didn't get into it. I didn't give it much of a chance.

"The same with *Ox-Box Incident, Huck Finn,* and *Little Big Man*. They were OK."

She enjoyed the English books of second semester much more. "In the second semester, I read each book." She said that she would recommend *The Great Gatsby* and *Slaughterhouse Five* to a friend.

The worst book assigned in history was *Hard Times*, she said. "I should have read *Hard Times* since he gave a test on it, and I didn't do good. It was a surprise test. He didn't give us tests on the previous three books."

Of the five books assigned for history, Sara said she read one and a half.

Thus, while the private school assigned a great deal more reading and seemed to use a number of tactics such as surprise tests to motivate this reading, the quality of the book still mattered for this student. It would be interesting to see whether this private school has developed a mechanism to obtain feedback about books and other reading assignments.

JON WEISS—A NINTH GRADER AT
BERKELEY CARROLL IN BROOKLYN

Jon provided details of both his reading and writing experiences as a freshmen at Berkeley Carroll. And he showed how the reading and writing were closely connected:

"We've read the Bible, but not religiously, but literary. We read the *Odyssey*. We read *The Immigrant Experience*, a book on immigration. *The Miracle Worker. Bridge over San Luis Rey. I Heard the Owl Call My Name*."

The writing assignments came from these books. "We write essays on themes that run through the books, Jon said. He explained that essay assignments might be on transformation or unification. He said that *transformation* is "a person starting their life and then changing their views." *Unification* is how people under hard times can unite and solve their problems. Another essay topic from the reading was fate versus free will. "It's a big one," he said. Death is also a big topic, especially in *The Bridge of San Luis Rey*, he said.

The writing assignments were due every couple of weeks and varied from short three- to six-page handwritten essays done in class to ten- to fifteen-page essays done at home and usually typed.

Computers were available for keyboarding the essays. "Everybody has access to computers. There's a computer room, and you're free to use it. The whole computer room is Macintosh. As of next year, the library will also be Macintosh.

"English is a fun class," Jon said, but he didn't like every book that he had been assigned to read as a freshman.

"I think they're all important to read. Some are dry. *Bridge over San Luis Rey* I didn't particularly like. It's slow reading. The details are implicit. Other books like the Bible are most interesting I think. We didn't read the Bible cover to cover. We skipped around. We read most of it, more than half."

Jon said that he would recommend the *Odyssey* to a friend to read.

Like the ninth graders in public school, Jon's social studies class was Global History. "We studied China starting with the Chinese Cultural Revolution. We covered all the revolutions until the present. We did all of Asia, the legacies left from each empire. We did the European influence on Asia. Right now we are on India, talking about Gandhi."

In addition to a textbook, Jon said, "We read little passages from *The Communist Manifesto*, and bits and pieces of Mao's book. We don't do much reading in the class. We watch a lot of videos—reenactments. We're watching *Gandhi* now."

Beyond the textbook and passages from *The Communist Manifesto* and *Mao's Little Red Book*, Jon said that his social studies and geography class had read a book called *Through African Eyes* and also *Burmese Days* by George Orwell. He added that "we read little bits and pieces of other stuff by Orwell."

Jon said that his school should assign more reading "because in books, there's more there than in lectures or class discussions." He said that he would like the school "to add more of the type of books that I like. More about philosophy."

Jon's personal reading habits outside school were interesting. He said that he bought five to ten books a year with his own money and that he was expecting a book that day as a gift from his parents: "I'm hoping to get a book today called *Life after God* about the lack of religious teachings for this generation and what happens when they grow up and have no religion to fall back on.

"I read more when I was younger because I had a much broader spectrum of books I liked.

"I like reading philosophy. I like reading books about my generation, which is kind of weird, not teeny books. People from my generation writing about it, saying what's wrong with it and stuff, and what we can do about it. There aren't very many people who write on that topic. Usually when they do, they've had a critique written which would make my parents not want to buy it for me."

Jon said that the next book that he was planning to read after *Life after God* had been recommended by a senior who said it was "poetic."

The *New York Times* is delivered to his house each day, and Jon said that he read the "Style section and sections of the Science Times and anything that looks of interest." He said that he usually had time to read this newspaper only on the weekends.

He said that he had a subscription to *Rolling Stone* and his parents subscribed to the *New Yorker* and *Time,* and his dad gets computer magazines, which he said he didn't read.

He also spent his own money to occasionally buy *Entertainment Weekly* "if there's something in it I like. I also buy guitar magazines that have music transcribed."

His feelings about his teachers were very positive: "They're always there if you need them. They're always offering extra help. They understand if you have a problem with an essay you're writing. You can get an extension if you explain it.

"That's about it. They're nice people. They work hard."

SUSAN MILLER—A TWELFTH GRADER
AT FRIENDS SEMINARY IN MANHATTAN

Susan's courses this year looked more like college than secondary school in New York City. In her last semester at Friends Seminary, she was taking AP calculus, physics, Greek, a course on Indian literature and film for English, and sculpture. One course during first semester, Italian Cultural Studies, included a trip to Italy for twelve days.

Unlike the public high school students in this survey, Susan had significant involvement in extracurricular activities at her school. She was head of the life-drawing club and art editor of the yearbook. In her neighbor-hood, she was copresident of her temple's youth group.

Her English class included the readings, quizzes, and films. She said there was "a test or essay on each book." The readings for the current se-mester were as follows:

Kanthapura by Raja Rao
A book of Indian fables
Bachelor of Arts by R. K. Narayan
The Guide by R. K. Narayan

In first semester of twelfth grade, in a world literature course, she read these works:

Great Short Stories by Tolstoy
King Lear
Great Ponds by Elechi Amadi
"And a lot of short stories that were photocopied"

One advantage of this private school, at least for a researcher, is that by requiring its students to buy all books, each student could look at his or her bookshelf after four years and see what had been assigned. Thus, it was easy for Susan to compile a record of her reading for English over four years (see table 12.1). Susan added that in English class she also saw and discussed a movie a week.

Unlike public school students, who had textbooks and only textbooks in social studies classes, Susan also had novels and trade nonfiction in her history classes.

She said that tenth grade social studies included "a mystery novel, *Daughter of Time*, by Josephine Tey, and a nasty world civilization textbook." She also read *Candide* by Voltaire, about which she said, "I've read better books."

In the history course this year, which was only first semester, she read *Plunkett of Tammany Hall* and a book on public education in New York.

Susan provided a fairly complete description of her social studies course, Politics of New York City: "We had to do stuff like write our con-gresspeople, city council members, state senators, et cetera. We wrote po-sition papers and had to present them to a group like the city council."

Table 12.1.   Private School Reading Experiences: Susan Miller's English Curriculum at Friends' Seminary in Manhattan for 1990–1994

Ninth Grade
>   The Bible
>   *The Crucible*
>   *Taming of the Shrew*
>   *East of Eden*
>   *Look Who's Talking*—a short storybook
>   *Black Boy*
>   *Immortal Poems of the English Language*

Tenth Grade
>   *Wuthering Heights*
>   *Canterbury Tales*
>   *The Philology of the Comedy*

Eleventh Grade
>   A book of poetry and *American Short Stories*
>   *The Scarlet Letter*
>   *The Awakening*
>   *The Adventures of Huckleberry Finn*
>   *The Great Gatsby*
>   *Go Tell It on the Mountain*
>   *Walden and Civil Disobedience*
>   Viewed and discussed the film *Citizen Kane*

Twelfth Grade
>   *Great Short Stories* by Tolstoy
>   *King Lear*
>   *Great Ponds* by Elechi Amadi
>   "And a lot of short stories that were photocopied"
>   *Kanthapura* by Raja Roa
>   A book of Indian fables
>   *Bachelor of Arts* by R. K. Narayan
>   *The Guide* by R. K. Narayan

Like the first private school student in this survey, Susan did a great deal of reading on her own. She said she bought ten to fifteen books a year with her own money. She said so far this year she'd read on her own *Vampire Chronicles, Carolyn and the Raiders, A Tree Grows in Brooklyn,* and "sometimes supermarket trash. Reading is lots of fun," she said. "It's very interesting. It's company. I'm an only child. I like to write, too—poetry and short stories." She said the amount of reading done fluctuated with the amount of time she had. "During college applications, there was little time to read. Now, I'm reading more."

Two newspapers are delivered to her house, *Newsday* and the *New York Times.*

ALLISON MCCALL—A SENIOR AT ST. ANN'S IN BROOKLYN

"I'm extremely atypical," said Allison. "Most St. Ann's students don't read Harlequin romances," she explained as she pulled the four romance novels and one science fiction story she was currently reading out of her book bag. Her books in her bag that day were *A Thousand Roses* by Bethany Campbell (Harlequin), *Sweet Hannah* by Lori Copeland (Dell), *Heart of Fire* by Linda Howard (Pocket), *Stargate* by Dean Devlin and Roland Emmerlich (Signet), and *Bandit's Brazen Kiss* by Kay McMahon (Zebra). "I average [reading] about four a day," she said. "I'll read a book more than once; a good book is like a friend you keep coming back to.

"I started reading so much because my entire family reads," Allison said. "My romance novels are probably not representative of the private school mentality," she explained. In addition to romance novels and science fiction, Allison said she read action-espionage writers such a Clyde Cussler, who has written "tons of books about Dirk Pitt." She said reading "gives her mind something to do. For a little while, you're not here. You're in the world of the book. If it's a real good book, you're no longer here, you're there. It's not just pages and ink. You totally forget yourself."

Her reading list for her classes so far this year was also long (see table 12.2).

Allison said that some of this reading had been tough going. "Socrates is pretty arrogant, in my opinion. He sits in the agora and talks to the

Table 12.2.   Alison's Reading, Senior Year (September–January 1995), St. Ann's in Brooklyn

Class	Title	Author
English	*Civil Disobedience*	Henry David Thoreau
	Walden	
English	*Billy Budd*	Herman Melville
	Bartleby the Scribner	
English	*Washington Square*	Henry James
English	*Young Goodman Brown and Other Stories*	Nathaniel Hawthorne
English	*Winesburg, Ohio*	Sherwood Anderson
English	*Five Short Stories*	Willa Cather
History	*On Liberty*	John Stuart Mill
History	*The Last Days of Socrates*	Plato
History	*Gorgias*	Plato
History	*Democracy in America*	Alexis de Tocqueville
History	*U.S. Senate*	George Reedy

youths all day. He may be the only honest man in Athens, but we don't need to hear it every two minutes. Socrates' ideas on law and the statesman are sheer genius, but he's hard reading."

She said she especially liked Tocqueville but found *On Liberty* by John Stuart Mill "good, but kind of dry and hard to get into." Like all of her classmates interviewed at St. Ann's, she said that she prefers the current practice at the school of assigning the same book for all students to read rather than allowing individual choice for book reports. "I come at a book from my own prejudices. It's cool to see how other kids come at it."

PRIVATE SCHOOL STRATEGIES

Interviews with teenagers from three private schools in Brooklyn do not provide a sample of what is happening in private schools nationally. Nevertheless, the strategies in these schools are quite different than what students report in Brooklyn's public high schools.

These private schools take the quality of books seriously. They have moved beyond *The Story of America*, a 1,222-page textbook used throughout the public secondary schools managed by the New York City Board of Education. Novels, biographies, autobiographies, and even historical fiction are the primary reading materials.

Unlike the public schools, some private schools actually respect the tastes of teenagers. At the Berkeley Carroll School in Brooklyn, for example, the opinions of teenagers matter. The teenagers choose their teachers and the readings. Electives are allowed in the first year of high school. They are allowed to choose the humanities courses they take based on the reputation of the teacher and the reputation of the readings. Berkeley Carroll makes its commitment to electives and choice and connections between reading and writing, and between English and history, clear:

> All Upper School English courses are comprehensive in nature, applying skills learned in the Middle School. They involve reading, writing, vocabulary, grammar and usage, speaking and listening, and research. Both analytical and expressive writing assignments are required.
>
> The English Department has agreed on a list of essential readings that all students will have encountered before they graduate, regardless of the elec-

tives they choose. At the same time, the elective system allows for the consideration of works of literature from a number of different cultures in the same course, giving the program an international and comparative aspect. Finally, where appropriate, readings are coordinated with the work that students are pursuing in their history courses.

The program integrates knowledge and skills so that students can make connections and build on what they already know in order to achieve a more mature understanding of themselves, of communicating with others, and of the world around them.

The characteristics of this private school curriculum, the electives early in high school, the interesting books, the high volume of reading assignments, the connections between reading and writing assignments, and the freedom of teachers to build reading lists and to advertise their classes based on these reading lists are all important literacy practices. As we will see in the next chapters, these "best literacy practices" are also present in some public schools. The practitioners in these chapters had a vision for literacy based on research; they were patient and persistent even in the face of resistance from their own colleagues.

NOTE

1. Neil S. Rosenfeld, "Private Schools Spurn NY Course Plan," *Newsday*, November 9, 1985, p. 11.

Chapter Thirteen

Successful Practitioners and the Quality of Reading Assignments

In an era of electronics, part-time jobs for teenagers after school, and state-mandated textbooks that do not encourage reading, what is to be done? Can secondary schools change the reading habits of teenagers?

Unfortunately, American children read less as they get older, according to government reports.

Each study of reading habits shows that as American children continue in school, they read less. "Not all American students seem to be 'hooked on books'. . . students seem to be less book-oriented as they progress through school. In fact, by the time they near high-school graduation, students seem to have little to do with reading activities beyond those required in school," according to a federal report.[1]

Are there solutions to this decline in literacy as youngsters progress through schools? Would assigning better books and providing more time for reading in school influence reading skills and reading habits? This chapter looks at two practitioners who found that better books led to more reading. The next chapter looks at a three-year struggle to increase the time devoted to silent reading in a secondary school.

One teacher in Brooklyn received unusual recognition for her leadership in literacy. She has won a citywide award for excellence in teaching from the New York Alliance for the Public Schools and has been named Teacher of the Year in her own district in Brooklyn. And now the reading program she began is being replicated in District 15.

Who is this teacher, and why are her ideas attracting such attention?

A NOVEL AS A FOCUS ON THE ENTIRE CURRICULUM

Carmen Fariña of Public School 29 in Cobble Hill, Brooklyn, says children should be able to read for pleasure just as adults do. "Too often reading is taught as a skill rather than a pleasure," she said.

To show her students that books are to be enjoyed, she assigns novels rather than the basal readers common in elementary schools throughout the city.

"Novels have ideas," Fariña said; "basal readers just have words. Novels have developed characters. The reading selections in basal readers are rarely long enough to develop characters."

She said that for a novel to succeed with her class, it must present a real issue and often a controversial issue. In this way, the novel becomes the central focus of the classroom, she said. "We read it, and we discuss the issues it raises."

Recent examples of novels in her third grade classroom are *The Cay* by Theodore Taylor and *Sadako and the Thousand Cranes* by Eleanor Coerr.

Perhaps one reason Fariña's philosophy has attracted so much attention is her ability to use a novel as a focus of the entire curriculum. She ties together social studies, science, and writing as well as reading through the assigned novel.

The Cay, for example, is a story of an elderly black man who cares for a white child shipwrecked on a Caribbean island during World War II. "As we read *The Cay*, students discuss race relations," she said. "Their writing assignment is to interview an adult who lived through World War II. We also use the setting of the Caribbean for geography lessons and for science lessons on trade winds and hurricanes."

According to Fariña, a major advantage of using novels is that the novels draw the students into history. The characters in the novels engage the children's imaginations and motivate the children to learn more about the events the characters experienced.

"As students read about a boy in Vietnam, they ask questions about the Vietnam War," Fariña said. "This is when I introduce the history of the war."

Fariña said that once the children's imaginations are engaged, they often ask for more historical material on their own. "I don't have to assign this new material," she said. "They ask for it themselves." One result of all this reading is "test scores three to four years above what would be expected," she added.

Fariña emphasized that novels do more than promote the reading skills so easily measured in standardized tests. She feels strongly that the class discussions that originate in the novels also improve the verbal skills of her students.

"A major difference between public schools and private schools is the degree of verbalization in the classroom," Fariña said. By discussing novels in the classroom, public school children become more verbal and better able to defend their points of view, she said. Fariña added that she also encourages the parents of her students to read the novels assigned in her class so that the children can also discuss the stories with their parents.

Not surprisingly, this enthusiasm for books and the test scores has led District 15 to begin to emphasize a literature-based approach to reading above the second grade. Fariña herself is now free on Fridays to present model lessons in classrooms throughout the district when she is invited.

Hindy List, curriculum director in District 15, has definite opinions about using novels in the classroom. "Carmen Fariña's program is excellent," she said. "She's very energetic and she's doing a terrific job. It's a very stimulating program for the kids." Fariña integrates the novels with the social studies program, List said. "In this way she brings the novels to life, and she brings social studies to life."

List said that the district has used both after-hours training sessions and classroom visits by Fariña to disseminate information about the use of novels. Last spring Fariña worked with thirty volunteers who wanted to learn more about using novels in their classrooms.

"Carmen Fariña's novel-based program is all positive," said Steven Tribus, the director of communication arts at the Board of Education. "She demonstrates that you can teach basic skills through good literature without losing the basic skills," he said. "Her program is consistent with the research we see. Research shows that students need experience with quality literature of all kinds."

Tribus said that through state funding there are now programs in six districts in the city that use literature as the central focus of the classroom.

SUCCESS IN A LABORATORY SCHOOL: CLASS DISCUSSIONS, READING, AND WRITING

The Urban Academy is a laboratory school funded by the New York City Board of Education under the Inquiry Demonstration Project. It was founded to provide a setting for experimental education that could also be used in traditional Board of Education sites. The Urban Academy now enrolls seventy students.

"Education is more than good reading skills," said Ann Cook, the director of the Urban Academy, during our interview in May 1990. "I'll admit that having kids do more reading will improve their vocabularies, but we need to do more than this." For example, more reading is not enough to make kids better writers, she added.

"Kids need to learn to analyze; they need to learn to argue analytically. They need to be able to support their positions with evidence and research. They can't do this on their own in writing unless they have practiced it hundreds of times in classroom discussions," she said.

"For students to be truly literate—for them to be able to read, and write and argue a position—we have to pay attention to discussion," Cook said. "And we have to be careful about the quality of these discussions. In the typical Board of Education developmental lesson plan, the discussion is contrived. The teacher leads the class from point A to point B and then finishes at point C. These discussions do little more than follow the outline of the textbook the class is using.

"Our discussions are open-ended; the conclusions are not contrived," Cook said.

"We also bring in guest speakers and have panel discussions and debates between adults so that the kids can see adults arguing," she continued. "They need to see adults disagreeing who are using a normal adult vocabulary, rather than in the more restricted vocabulary teachers might use with kids. This is one way for kids to learn the language in addition to reading. Kids can learn language by listening to adults speaking and discussing and arguing.

"We waste the talents of our teachers in the United States," Cook said. "We use teachers only as funnels to pour information into the heads of kids. We also need to use teachers as models of inquiry and language. Kids need to see teachers debating with other teachers. They need to hear the more elaborate vocabulary that teachers use in discussions with each other."

LITERACY AND PRINT

You have to be careful to pay attention to literacy in more than just a print sense, Cook said. "There is a high correlation between kids coming to school language-deficient and the kids who have trouble reading," Cook said. "We need to look more at the relationship between oral language and reading and writing.

"For example, District 2 is now going to look at kids in kindergarten and identify the ones who will have trouble reading even while the kids are prereaders. If the kids can't verbalize, they are going to have trouble reading. If the kid can't think abstractly, reading will be difficult. Reading is an abstract activity—translating words into images.

"The kids who can't verbalize often come from language-deficient homes where there is not much language spoken," Cook said. "If the kid doesn't have the resource—the idea—to attach the new word to, it's difficult."

MIXED MESSAGES

"In reading, we do a lot of undermining of what reading skills are for," Cook said. "We say that we want kids to read for pleasure and enjoyment, but we do very little to support it. We give the kids mixed messages. We have lofty goals for reading, but we translate these goals into practice in bizarre ways.

"We fill up the curriculum with workbooks and basal readers and engineered books. We aren't setting good standards for reading.

"Here in the Urban Academy, kids have good reading experiences in short stories in English classes. We also have a Novels course and a course like the one on censorship that I taught last year," Cook said.

"We brought in fifty or sixty banned books. We talked about why books get banned. This is an ungraded, untracked school, so the kids selected books at their reading level. The range of reading materials was vast. Kids could plug into any book. And they kept records of the books they had read. The one book that we all read together was Nat Hentoff's book on Huckleberry Finn."

"The kids bring from these books the issues being considered. They discuss why a book was banned, and they discuss the rights of individuals in our society.

"In our novels course, kids select a book to read, and then we look at what is good reading and good writing. The novels range from Stephen King to more traditional authors. As they read books, the kids are asked to bring in samples of what was good writing and to demonstrate and define what good writing is.

"I hope sometime to offer a course on children's literature here," Cook said. "A lot of poor readers missed the experience of reading good children's books. There are marvelous children's books that can be read from the perspective of critiquing them.

"Although the Urban Academy doesn't have a separate period devoted to recreational reading during the school day, the students do attend a homework lab where they can read silently."

Cook's point that reading and writing need to be connected cannot be overemphasized. She also reemphasizes the importance of using classroom discussion to warm up topics to be used in students' writing assignments. These connections among classroom discussions, reading assignments, and writing assignments might seem easy to engineer to parents and other outsiders. But remember, shortages of books in city secondary schools are commonplace; the authority to order books is almost never given to individual teachers in public schools—at least in the highly bureaucratic systems of large cities. And as Andy Hargreaves points out in chapter 14, some teachers are so balkanized into departments that literacy is not their job; they are state-certified social studies teachers, and their job is to push teenagers through the material the teenagers will see on state exit exams. Reading and writing are the jobs of the English department.

The administrator in the next chapter had another idea. She lengthened the school day to allow more time for the practice of reading.

NOTE

1. National Assessment of Educational Progress, *Learning to Read in Our Nation's Schools: Instruction and Achievement in 1988 at Grades, 4, 8, and 12*, Report No. 19-R-02 (Princeton, N.J.: Educational Testing Service, 1990), 36.

Chapter Fourteen

The Fork in the Road and Volume of Reading

For many city children, junior high is the fork in the road. Here the well-to-do turn in one direction and begin to prepare for high school and college. And here the sons and daughters of the poor too often veer off the road and begin to disengage from American institutional life. But this separation of classes may not be inevitable. In some inner-city schools, the junior high years are a time to keep pace with the much more affluent, not to fall behind.

Many cities have several such schools. They are places where teenagers achieve even as neighboring schools continue to fail. In the nation's capitol, one of the conspicuous successes over the last twenty years has been Jefferson Junior High. The achievement at Jefferson has attracted presidents. President Reagan visited in 1984; President Clinton visited in 1992.

To begin, it is clear that the attention that Jefferson has received is deserved. "The school serves a depressed area," said Dr. James T. Guines, associate superintendent for Instruction, in a 1981 interview. "The test scores at Jefferson were not expected. It serves a population of young people from the housing projects. . . . We first noticed the scores three years ago and they seem to be holding their own." Guines went on to attribute much of the success of Jefferson to the leadership of the principal, which is undoubtedly true. The literature on improving schools is filled with anecdotes of the energetic principal, capable of organizing a new school out of an institution that had been failing. Guines mentioned "her insistence on academic instruction and her ability to separate 'administrivia' from the priorities of what a school leader should be. She focuses on instruction, not on taking children's hats off."

This description seems accurate. In my visits to Jefferson, principal Vera White was often in the halls between classes asking students about their homework—she didn't spend time reminding them about their hats. But White talks about more than homework and instruction and time on task. She also tells visitors to her schools about the silent reading program that begins the school day at Jefferson. At Jefferson, each day begins with "Project Read," a thirty-minute silent reading period. In this period, students are not handed textbooks that will be difficult for those with reading problems and of little interest to more powerful readers. Instead, students select the paperbacks, newspapers, and magazines of their own choice from a library in each classroom.

White believes that the opportunity to read each day is the basis of the improved reading scores at Jefferson. According to White, "dramatic improvement in students' test scores did not occur until silent reading became a daily activity."

But she cautions that Project Read was not an instant success. "Project Read began in 1975," she said, "but reading test scores did not show dramatic improvement until 1978."

White did not abruptly impose Project Read on the students and faculty of Jefferson. Instead, she remembers a regional meeting in the late 1970s.

She had just transferred from Western Senior High School to work with a new principal, James E. Campbell, at Jefferson. In this regional meeting, they received a coded report without the name of their building but with a number indicating that Jefferson had the second lowest scores in the region. Dr. Dorothy Johnson, the regional superintendent, suggested that an evaluation of the school was appropriate.

Campbell and White, then the assistant principal, organized a school committee for this assessment. A parent and a student from each of the school's homerooms, a teacher from each subject area, three lay persons, and a union representative participated. This group and later smaller groups worked for six months evaluating the school's program.

The "rule of fives" increased the number of parents at evening community meetings. Parents attending initial meetings had to return with five additional parents to be readmitted.

Parents, teachers, and students agreed. They decided reading, mathematics, and discipline were to be the basis of the new curriculum at Jefferson. White emphasized the support of parents for Project Read: "We were changing a program, we were dropping courses. Parents had to support these changes if they were to succeed."

But even with the support of parents, there were still difficulties. "Many of the faculty did not initially buy into the program," said White. "There was resentment about a new program that encroached upon time previously devoted to history, science, and other subjects in a junior high school curriculum." There were also disagreements about scheduling. Would it work best late in the afternoon after students had their traditional subjects? Or should Project Read begin the day?

In 1975 when Project Read began, students read silently only on Friday afternoons. But a faculty evaluation committee was unhappy with the results. Student progress did not meet faculty expectations.

The time devoted to silent reading increased in the 1976–1977 school year. Now students read for twenty minutes, three times a week. Still there was dissatisfaction. Some faculty members were not effective role models. White remembers that some faculty members used the afternoon silent reading periods for their own work. They prepared lesson plans rather than read themselves as role models for their own students.

Then, in 1978 a decision was made to lengthen the school day. Classes began at 8:45, rather than the usual 9:00 A.M. opening in the District of Columbia. White believes that this change enabled Project Read to work. With the schedule change, Project Read became a daily activity. After the early morning announcements about basketball games and bake sales, Project Read would begin promptly at 9:00, and students would read books of their own choice until 9:30.

Susan White, an eighth-grade teacher at Jefferson, said that she looks forward to the silent reading period. "I have never been in a school that encouraged a program like this. I think it is a fine program. The students seem to enjoy it. I note that as a result of the program the students take more of an interest in reading in general. Last year there were three books assigned by the English department. This year there is more of a free-choice approach. . . . A couple of students really digest the newspaper and ask me questions afterward. I have a school librarian in the class who logs books in and out. This keeps the silent reading period from being a totally teacher-directed activity."

Germaine Armstrong, who teaches seventh and eighth grades at Jefferson, said that "the program motivates students who otherwise might not read. I feel that a lot of reluctant readers use the time they normally would not find during the day to do some type of reading. We provide magazines of interest, high-interest title books, and they can bring in the books they want to read. And the good thing about it is that teachers can read at the same time. I think that seeing the teachers read motivates some of them."

In addition to the silent reading period, some students at Jefferson also spend one period a day working on phonics. "Seventh graders reading more than four years below grade level are placed in a phonics program," says White. "These students often have difficulty recognizing sounds or identifying configurations of letters."

Each student at Jefferson also works in a reading skill lab each day on activities such as word analysis, vocabulary building, and literal and critical comprehension.

Principal White acknowledges that there are problems in the schedule of some seventh graders who take a period of phonics, a period of reading skills, and two periods of mathematics in addition to the silent reading period. "Sometimes parents object when their children cannot take science until ninth grade."

LOCAL ADMINISTRATORS AND JEFFERSON

"Sustained silent reading in school gives students practice in reading for enjoyment," said John J. Campbell, a professor of education at Howard University. "And by having sustained silent reading, the school is saying we value reading for enjoyment without anything attached—no homework, no testing.

"Sustained silent reading should take place in addition to textbook reading assignments," Campbell noted. "When a teacher assigns chapter 3 in a history book, the students have to generate purposes for reading. Students may decide that they are reading because the teacher wants them to, rather than because they want to. Sustained silent reading gives students the opportunity to read for themselves."

Dr. Helen Turner, the supervising director of reading instruction in the public schools of the District of Columbia, was also certain of the value of silent reading. "As soon as the capacity to read exists," she said, "students should have the opportunity to read silently each day. . . . When students are reading silently, they are more comfortable. The threat of mistakes that occur in oral reading is removed. Sustained silent reading should be practiced because people know it affords students a chance to select material on their reading level."

Vera White understood that the goal of an effective school is to build the habit of reading. Assigning textbook chapters to read is not enough to do that. But few of her peers understood what she was doing in the early 1980s. What did local administrators think of Jefferson, a school with ideas and a leader far from the mainstream?

"I am not aware of other schools that have adopted sustained silent reading [SSR] in the region," said Dr. Reuben G. Pierce, the assistant superintendent for Region A. (A survey of the principals in the seven junior high schools in Region A confirmed this information.)

Pierce does believe that the silent reading period is an important part of the success at Jefferson. "Jefferson test scores would indicate that their program for the improvement of reading skills is paying off." But he was reluctant to select either the silent reading period or the reading skills period as the more important factor in the success of students at Jefferson.

"It's hard to isolate a particular factor," said Pierce. "It's the program taken as a whole. If I had to isolate a particular factor, I would say it is the limitless energy of the principal. She is directly involved in virtually every activity that the school engages in. She is personally involved."

A second administrator did not think that silent reading was essential at Jefferson or elsewhere. According to Guines, silent reading is one way to devote a defined amount of time to reading each day, but oral reading would serve equally well.

A third administrator, J. Weldon Greene, the director of the Office of Program Development, worked on both the competency-based curriculum and an intensive junior high school curriculum first used in the 1981–1982 school year.

According to Greene, "neither curriculum specifically recommends the establishment of sustained silent reading programs such as the program at Jefferson Junior High."

However, Greene adds that the competency-based curriculum does recommend the silent reading that might occur during a homework assignment. A typical silent reading assignment could be "Tonight, read chapter 3 in your history book and answer questions one through eight," Greene said.

Administrators Guines, Greene, and Pierce missed the research on silent reading that White had studied. The research talks about modeling and the importance of teachers sitting in front of the class reading themselves as models.

The success of Vera White is that she tore up the page and that she was technical enough to know what to do after tearing up the page. She succeeded because she was energetic and determined, as her colleagues say, but also because she had read the research. Her vision came from the research journals. She can talk about details of silent reading programs and how some of her teachers did not originally buy into it.

If the goal is to increase the volume of reading in the lives of teenagers, it is clear that the silent reading programs begun by principal, now assistant superintendent, Vera White are extremely valuable. Another valuable strategy may be to increase the amount of reading youngsters accomplish during the summer. Several researchers believe that unless low-income children improve their reading skills during the summer, the gains they make during the school year will not be enough to close the gap with the middle class, as we will see in the next chapter.

Chapter Fifteen

Summer Reading

What Should Be Done?

> My son plays basketball during the summer. Basketball is enough. He doesn't need to read during the summer.
>
> —A parent in an education class at the
> Bedford-Stuyvesant campus of
> the College of New Rochelle

We are told that private schools are better for a number of reasons. The late James S. Coleman and his colleague Thomas Hoffer emphasized the shared goals in private schools, in the sense of community in these schools, and how sense of school and home working together influences achievement. In a study done many years later, John E. Chubb and Terry M. Moe explained how higher expectations in private schools led to higher achievement.

But we have less information about what is happening in the long periods when American children are not in their private schools or public schools. What are the millions of mothers and fathers and aunts and uncles doing to encourage reading at home? Are they providing books? Are they talking about their favorite books? What is happening during summer vacation? Are all youngsters making the same improvements in reading skills during summer vacations and the other long breaks during the school year?

When I began a morning of interviews at St. Ann's, a private school in Brooklyn Heights, perhaps Brooklyn's most affluent neighborhood, I was using the long list of questions I had used elsewhere. The list included one or two questions about summer reading. The questions were about school policy on summer reading: Does your school require summer reading? How much of this reading do you do?

The information provided by the student introduced here went far beyond the scope of my questions. He showed how important his family is in providing both books and a time to read.

ROBERT MARSHALL—A NINTH GRADER AT ST. ANN'S

Robert provided a great many details about how teenagers learn to read widely and well. At first glance, St. Ann's policy of providing students with a summer reading list, but not requiring reading of any specific titles, might seem counterproductive or even permissive. In Robert's case, this light hand worked. "The reading list was very long, and it wasn't required," he said. "The reading wasn't required, which made it easier on me to do the reading because I didn't feel pressure to do it. I would enjoy it. The school wanted you to read two or three books. It also said read as much as you can," he said. "I read *All the Pretty Horses*."

Robert also talked in detail about what he read on his own in the summer before ninth grade. "Tom Clancy is bad at characterization, but I love the plots, the ideas he has . . . the plot of *Debt of Honor* is so rich; it has so many levels; it makes you think so much. *Without Remorse* was not that great. *Clear and Present Danger* is my favorite," he added.

Robert said that he had read five Tom Clancy novels the summer before ninth grade. "It's easier to read [during the summer] because you have more time. You don't have homework."

Robert also had the benefit of not working during his previous summer vacation, an advantage not shared by all St. Ann's students. "Most of my reading is done during the summer. I go to camp, but there's no homework at camp."

Robert's family also encouraged him to read in a variety of ways. To begin with, they provided books. "Most of my books are secondhand—handed down from my aunt and uncle, but I bought the new Tom Clancy *Debt of Honor* in hardback," he said. "My mom handed me the *Hunt for Red October*, and that encouraged me to read more because I loved it. She does that a lot. She'll tell me a book that I'll like. She's usually pretty good at it. She introduced me to Robert B. Parker and the *Client*. What's his name, Grisham, John Grisham and Wolfe, a detective mystery. She keeps on telling me she wants me to read it." I told Robert that Ian Fleming was to my generation of high school students what Clancy was to his. He thought that Fleming was even bigger than Clancy. "I've seen all the Bond movies. I read one Bond book, but it was one that they hadn't done a movie about," he said.

Robert said that as he entered high school, in general he was reading more. "I do more of it, but sometimes I have less time to read [during the school year]. Over the summer I do more now than I did two years ago."

KAREN HARRIS—A NINTH GRADER AT ST. ANN'S

Surprisingly, not all the students at this expensive private school enjoyed time off during the summer. The second student at St. Ann's showed that even private schools can present obstacles to reading.

Of the four high school students at St. Ann's, Karen was the only scholarship student and the only African American in my private school interviews. Unlike Robert, she had to work during the summer, a factor in the amount of reading she was now doing.

The amount of reading has decreased as she has gotten older. "There are a lot of things which I do now which I didn't do when I was younger. I work during the summer. When I have my free time during the summer, I relax," she said.

THE RESEARCH ON SUMMER READING

Many factors affect the amount of reading youngsters accomplish during the summer. They need encouragement, the time, the access to books.

Does summer reading matter to American youngsters? What does the research say about summer reading?

Three studies show that unless the poor can make more progress during the summer, they will not be able to catch up during the school year. The first study shows that while effective Title I programs can bring the poor up to the same level of achievement as the middle class during the school year, these federal programs have not been able to improve the reading skills of the "disadvantaged" during the summer. In fact, they find that the disadvantaged student "either makes no gain during the summer or loses a month":

> An extensive search of all the available empirical evidence, however, leads us to conclude that the disadvantaged student does not gain 0.7 month during the summer and therefore does not follow the pattern of the 50th-percentile student. Instead, the disadvantaged student either makes no gain during the summer or loses a month.[1]

They urge attention to summer reading but realize that summer reading is not receiving attention from the federal government:

> Unless the disadvantaged student increases his summer achievement rate, he must achieve at the rate of 1.1 or 1.2 months per month during the school year just to keep up.
>
> Title I projects might be developed that would have positive effects on disadvantaged students in the summer and hence would place less of a burden on school-year effects. To date, however, few Title I projects have specifically attempted to provide positive effects during the summer, and there is no evidence that such effects have occurred spontaneously.[2]

In a more recent study, Doris R. Entwisle and Karl L. Alexander also found that summer matters: "Strong summer gains in reading made by the relatively more advantaged children of both races, however, testify to the critical importance of home resources when school is not open."[3]

When summer reading is missing, it does matters. Research supports the importance of summer reading and makes clear what happens to youngsters who don't read over the summer.

But who is listening to this research? Who is going to provide the encouragement, the time, the access to books during the summer? The authors of the 1976 Title I study asked for attention to summer reading twenty-five years ago, but the federal government has not yet responded.

What would a summer reading program—tied to the current summer jobs program for older youth—look like? Summer job programs for low-income youth have been in place since the 1960s. The responsibilities varied. In Brooklyn each year, teenagers spent their summers painting the miles of fence around Prospect Park and undoubtedly completed other tasks assigned by city agencies, but we may need a new look at what we are asking low-income youth to do as part of a federal summer jobs program if we are to close the reading gap between the races.

VIEWS AND RECOMMENDATIONS

Make reading part of every federal summer jobs program. And have real books involved. Be careful with the money. Mandate the purchase of real books so that all the federal monies won't be spent on hiring friends and relatives. Make all federally funded summer education programs subject to the federal Hatch Act so that the monies will not be diverted to hire cronies out of local political clubs. Make the first hour or hour and a half of every day time for silent reading and writing. Hire teachers who have actually read the literature on silent reading rather than all the aunts and uncles and cousins of the district leader. Employ teachers who are actually readers themselves. These teachers are not impossible to locate. Having them write a letter describing their recent reading experiences would be a start. Or ask them to submit a recommended reading list with descriptions of how youngsters have responded to their choices of books. A recent college graduate may have more enthusiasm for books than a veteran teacher who has struggled with shortages for twenty years and grown weary of the struggle.

For youngsters reading years below grade level, intervene during the summer. These children may need more than silent reading periods. They may not have cracked the code yet. They may not be able to translate letters into sounds confidently. Maybe they need a six-hour school day with trained remedial reading teachers. This is now being done in many cities, but funding these programs from the local tax base is often difficult. When summer reading programs were tried in New York City in the 1980s, it worked in the short run. Reading scores improved. But the city did not have the funding to continue it each summer with at-risk youngsters. After a year or two without summer intervention, their scores dropped back down. By seventh grade, the youngsters who had participated three years earlier were not further ahead than those who did not receive services. (See chapter 16 for more on the history of interventions.)

But with federal help, below-grade readers could receive help every summer; intervention could then be effective. Money will have to be found for new summer programs, and the funding may have to be federal.

Cities such as New York, Cleveland, and Washington, D.C., have to stretch financially many years just to provide basic educational services. Without federal funding targeted at opening summer reading programs, these programs are not likely to become a regular part of the educational landscape for low-income youngsters.

Titles

Lists of books for summer reading are readily available. Colleges now provide titles and explanations of why individual books were selected. And many of the books on college lists are accessible and would be enjoyed by teenagers with reading skills far below the college level. The books on these lists have been selected carefully.

"At Lincoln University in Pennsylvania, this past summer the entering freshman class was assigned two books: *Gifted Hands: The Ben Carson Story* by Ben Carson and Cecil Murphy and Vincent Harding's *Hope and History*. Our use of the Carson book focused on our desire for entering students to recognize that African Americans can achieve in the face of adversity," reported Charles A. Edington, the vice president of enrollment planning and student life at Lincoln. "Both of these works instilled a sense of pride and direction in our new students." Carson's book is easy reading and could be enjoyed by teenagers at a variety of reading levels.

Rewards and Summer Reading

Encouraging reading can be labor-intensive. School libraries have to be opened during the summer. In some schools, libraries will need to be created in the first place. Stars need to be affixed beside a student's name as he or she reads book after book. With older students, discussions need to be held about what the last book was like and what kind of book they would enjoy next.

Why aren't these summer services in place? Why do so many schools in high poverty areas suffer from shortages of materials during the school year? Why can't parents use the political process to overcome these obstacles to literacy and demand that our educators and politicians bring better literacy practices to our schools? Part 3 looks at such obstacles.

NOTES

1. Thomas C. Thomas and Sol H. Pelavin, "Patterns in ESEA Title I Reading Achievement," Stanford Research Institute Project 4537 (Palo Alto, Calif.: Educational Policy Research Center, 1976), 31.

2. Thomas and Pelavin, "Patterns in ESEA Title I Reading Achievement," 34.

3. Doris R. Entwisle and Karl L. Alexander, "Winter Setback: The Racial Composition of Schools and Learning to Read," *American Sociological Review* 59, no. 3 (June 1994). Also see Doris R. Entwisle, Karl L. Alexander, and Linda Steffel Olson, "Summer Learning and Home Environment," in *A Nation at Risk: Preserving Public Education as an Engine for Social Mobility,* ed. Richard D. Kahlenberg (New York: Century Foundation Press, 2000), 9–30.

Chapter Sixteen

Can We Have a Crumb from the Table?

Parents as Supplicants in the Political Process

Many actors influence the politics of education and thus the literacy practices in a classroom or a school system. Parents, teachers, budget levels, budget practices in local school districts, internal accountability, as Richard Elmore mentioned, and the curriculum created in state education departments all shape the classrooms teenagers occupy. On paper, parents would seem to be a potent force for improving the literacy practices in our schools. No special interest group in the country is larger than parents, and poll after poll tells us that all Americans place education at the top of their political wish list. And the ability to read and write well is certainly high on everyone's definition of an effective education. So it would seem that the political conditions for the success of parent-led initiatives in education are in place.

Can parents turn schools around and persuade local school boards to adopt effective literacy practices and then persuade politicians to fund these new practices? Obviously, better books and teachers who are enthusiastic about these books would improve the literacy of both teenagers and youngsters still in elementary school. Obviously, the reforms advocated by Theodore Sizer and Deborah Meier and others, such as a reasonable schedule of students for each high school teacher, would improve the literacy of teenagers. Few teachers—when questioned very hard—will honestly testify to grading a weekly essay or another piece of writing for a typical high school teaching load of 160 students. What is the power of parents in education in cities as large as New York and much smaller cities such as Washington, D.C., to force the adoption of more effective literacy practices in our schools? What is the role of a PTA in the local political process? Even an elementary school PTA or Parent–School Association

(PSA) can have hundreds of members and could represent a potent political force in elections for the state legislature and for municipal offices such as the city council. Are parents—through PTAs and PSAs—able to project political power and influence policy in education? In short, do parents have the tools necessary to influence the politics of education?

On paper, this would seem a time when parents could influence politics. Envelopes filled with cash to pay election day workers for getting out the vote efforts are now less common in American cities. Local politics has been cleaned up in American cities, and the voices of parents should be easy to hear. In New York City, for example, candidates for city council must file detailed reports with both the City Campaign Finance Board and the State Board of Elections. Each dollar raised and each dollar spent are to be accounted for. The name and address of each donor become part of the public record available for opponents and the press to review.

In reality, much of what is needed for victory is missing from these reports. The first omission is the phone banks, a crucial tool in city and state elections.

Without access to dozens of phones, you need not apply for public office in New York City and in many smaller cities and suburbs. On the phones, your volunteers make the calls to find out who is supporting you in the weeks before the primary. On the phones, your volunteers build their list of voters to visit or call on Election Day. On the phones, your volunteers then call your voters two, three, or even four times on Election Day. You are waiting for each voter on your list to say, "Don't call me again. I've already voted for her." Then your phone bank has done its job.

But phones are expensive. And phone lists that connect the names of voters with their phone numbers are also expensive. The installation of a single phone costs hundreds of dollars in many cities today, so people with phones are friends to hold or enemies to be feared. In New York City, the people with phones are the unions. The larger ones have moved to computerized phones that don't even need to be dialed. After one call is completed, the computerized phone dials the next name in the database. Groups with large numbers of phones such as the United Federation of Teachers and Local 1199 of the Hospital Workers Union shape politics not only through their contributions but also through their technology—their phones and their printing.

The second omission is the under-the-table mailing. The same printing press in the building that prints union newsletters also prints political literature, at times illegally. When the value of a single mailing is thousands of dollars, mailings from unions quickly surpass the $3,000 limit on campaign donations in city council races or state assembly races. The solution is simply not to include all mailings in campaign filings or to attribute only a fraction of their value. (Is corruption rampant in the municipal unions in cites such as New York? The indictment of dozens of union officials—mostly on charges of theft in 1998—gives some idea of the political morality of local union officials.)

Where do these resources needed for political careers come from?

Pillars of political power can provide the resources needed for political careers in American cities: the phone banks, the mailings, the legal muscle to throw opponents off the ballot (especially in New York City), and the volunteers needed on Election Day:

- The municipal unions with their phone banks, volunteers, and occasionally corrupt leadership. See the 1998–1999 scandals in the municipal workers' unions in New York City with expense accounts thefts of as much as $1 million from union treasuries.
- The local developers who want a tax abatement for the next construction project.
- The political clubs seeking control of judgeships. A judgeship is worth far more than a seat on the city council or in the state legislature. With a judgeship, for example, on Surrogate's Court comes the power to control the estates of the deceased who have passed away without wills and appoint guardians—in other words, opportunities for millions of dollars in legal fees for connected lawyers.[1]

Obviously none of these centers of power, the clubs, the unions and the developers have any intrinsic interest in changing the schools.[2] Rather than conversations about public concerns, about education, they have private conversations. What writer should you to hire to do your literature? Which election lawyer can be used to invalidate an opponent's attempt to run for office? Can you raise money with just a letter, or do you have to invite people to an event? Which unions are generous this year? Who are they giving to? There are no conversations about the fundamentals of education. No one is talking about the ecological disasters in our large, overcrowded high schools. No one at these fund-raisers is talking about the fact that our secondary school teachers still see 160 or 175 youngsters a day. No one is talking about the alienation of both teacher and student that occurs when each teacher must see that many students a day. No one is talking about the chronic shortages of books and paper in the high schools. No one is talking about the obsolete reward system in education that provides raises based on seniority rather than on performance.

Parents and PTAs can't compete with the professionals. Parents don't even try. Parents don't have money. They don't have election lawyers. They don't have phone banks. They don't endorse. They don't know the drill. In Brooklyn, parents even in the borough's affluent well-educated neighborhoods such as Park Slope ask politicians for crumbs. "Can we have $20,000 to buy computers for the school's journalism program?" is a typical request.

While the balance of power between politician and parent probably varies from city to city, in New York City, the in-balance is extreme. Rather than demand adequate resources for all schools from their elected officials, PTAs tend to engage in individual bargaining for what is known as "member item money" (i.e., individual grants of public funds, taxpayer money, from a politician to a local group such as a PTA). The unwritten rule is clear. If anyone in the PTA leadership threatens a politician, the member item money ends. The *New York Times* has long editorialized for an end to distributing public funds through the secret negotiations of the member item process. It condemns the power it gives local politicians over citizen groups and the power it gives the leaders of the city council and the state legislature who dole out the member item money to the members of these legislatures on the basis of loyalty to the leadership.[3]

For the most part, citizen action through PTAs has failed to reform public education in urban areas. Parents don't have the tools of professional politicians. (See table 16.1 for a list of the political tools controlled by PTAs.) They don't buy the lists of voters and voting histories from the board of elections. From these lists politicians know who votes in primary and general elections and then can build mailing lists appropriately. Parents don't form alliances with powerful patrons such as unions who have phone banks and printing facilities to share with politicians who cooperate. They don't participate in the politics of education except as supplicants asking for very small amounts of money for very small projects. While generalizations are dangerous, especially in an educational system as diverse as that of the United States, it does not look like parents are go-

Table 16.1. Political Tools in State and Municipal Elections

	A Political Club	A PTA or Parent School Association
Endorsements	Yes	No
Fund-raising help	Yes	No
Volunteers for petitioning (getting on the ballot)	Yes	No
Provide election law lawyers to defend petitions needed to stay on the ballot	Yes	No
Volunteers for canvassing (identifying supporters), via phone banks or door to door	Yes	No
Volunteers for Election Day polls via phone banks or door-to-door canvassing	Yes	No

ing to be a major voice in school reform and the adoption of better literacy practices in our schools.

But there are other actors on the stage, of course, beyond parents and their children. The next actor that could influence the adoption of better literacy practice is the teachers and the teachers' unions, the subjects of the next chapter.

NOTES

1. Jack Newfield et al., "Kings County Princes, Party Faithful Find Favor in Surrogate's Court," *New York Post*, November 9, 1997. Also see Alan Feur, "Prosecutor Heads Inquiry into Politics of Court Post," *New York Times*, February 1, 2000, which describes an inquiry "into whether judges favor lawyers with strong party ties when handing out lucrative court assignments thoroughout the state."

2. See Jack Newfield and Paul Du Brul, *The Permanent Government: Who Really Rules New York?* (New York: Pilgrim, 1981), for an in-depth look at the priorities of the local politicians in New York City.

3. James Dao, Clifford J. Levy, and Raymond Hernandez, "Secret Spending: A Special Report: Tradition and Politics Allow Legislators' Hidden Largess," *New York Times*, July 14, 1996.

Chapter Seventeen

The Political Position of Teachers

Teachers of students in low-poverty schools were about 60 percent more likely to report that they have adequate access to instructional supplies than were the teachers of students in high-poverty schools . . . this basic, and potentially easily solved problem, continues to hamper instruction in high-poverty schools.

—U.S. Department of Education[1]

This "easily solved problem" mentioned here in a federal study of Chapter I schools continues year after year. Teachers working with poor children, whom the Department of Education calls "high-poverty schools," are more likely to work without adequate resources.

Where does this lack of resources originate? Why can't teachers order the resources they need, just as lawyers order dispositions and subpoena witnesses, and just as doctors order diagnostic tests and write prescriptions?

Some writers believe that the political space where teachers live and the authority they have in this space may be the largest barriers to the development of literacy in city school systems. For example, a newcomer to the United States may wonder how it came to be that a teacher with a salary of $50,000 or more with a 30 percent benefit package on top of that does not have the personal authority to order books—the building blocks of literacy. But how did this happen? What factors have contributed to this situation? A number of sociologists and historians have commented on the political authority and the political position of teachers in their organizations.

This lack of the basic resources may be a result of the political position American teachers face—they are at the bottom of very traditional hierarchies. Researchers Ray Marshall and Marc Tucker write that American teachers work in a system of "coolie" labor. They explain that teaching as an occupation was shaped during the industrial period when labor was thought to be stupid and line workers such as teachers were not be trusted with any decisions. They believe that the United States "built a system of 'coolie labor' surrounded by a managerial, technical, and support elite." They admit that "coolie is, of course, a loaded word."

> We have used it deliberately to help the reader gain a perspective on the system, a perspective that might be hard to get in another way because we are all so much a part of the system that it is hard to imagine how things might work differently. We do not mean to imply by the use of the word that management or anyone else now bears responsibility for the way things turned out. Labor, as we noted, did little or nothing to change these features of the system, nor did government.[2]

The sociologist Daniel C. Lortie argues the nature of teaching has led to its highly bureaucratic nature today. Since teaching had to expand in the early twentieth century to reach a mass audience, it became a mass occupation. In manufacturing and agriculture, technology made it possible for fewer people to produce more goods, but in education, this could not happen, Lortie said. The school system was required to maintain "a more or less fixed ratio between teachers and students" so the only way to expand education during the nineteenth and twentieth centuries was to hire more and more teachers. "Mass schooling has inexorably produced a larger and larger occupation."

He also notes that the large number of women in the occupation in its early years influenced working conditions today.

> Continued growth of the public school system required the services of thousands upon thousands of young, single women. The pool of personnel has never produced a high proportion of teachers ready to commit many years to work outside the home; and the problem of turnover was compounded by school board policies which ruled out the employment of married women. (Such restrictions prevailed well into the twentieth century.) In short, teaching was *institutionalized* as high turnover work during the

nineteenth century and the modern occupation bears the marks of earlier circumstance. During many crucial decades of its development, teaching required annual infusions of many new members in order to meet the demand created by expansion and high turnover.[3]

The need for so many new members pushed schools to an "egg carton" or cellular organization with teachers working alone with little contact who could be easily replaced with new teachers, rather than a "team" organization where departures would disrupt a team, Lortie believes.

WEAK SOCIALIZATION EXPERIENCES

Lortie also fears that the early socialization of teachers into the profession, which he believes is quite weak, will not give them enough sense of connection to the field or enough scientific information to overcome their personal attitudes and orientation.

Contrast, for example, pathways to full participation in the Jesuit priesthood, quarterback status in professional football, or diamond cutting on the one hand with beginning work as a waitress, factory worker, or taxi-driver on the other. Among the observable differences are the time it takes to qualify, the arduousness of the preparation, and the complexity of the skills and knowledge needed for full membership.

The comparative impact of initial socialization makes considerable difference in the overall life of an occupation. Where such socialization is potent, the predispositions of newcomers become less important through time; the selves of participants tend to merge with the values and norms built into the occupation. The opposite holds where socialization experiences are weak; in that case, the attitudes, values and orientations people bring with them continue to influence the conduct of their work. The internal structure of an occupation is also influenced by the potency of socialization arrangements. Occupations with highly developed subcultures—that is, with rich, complex bodies of knowledge and technique—differentiate entrants from outsiders, laying the basis for a special sense of community among the initiated. The reverse also holds; where the content of initiatory stages is sparse, the significance of guild is low. Contrast, for example, the internal relationships found in medicine and in retail sales, in airline piloting and in driving delivery trucks, in certified public accountancy and in routine office work.[4]

What Lortie brings to the debate about literacy is the realization that the socialization to a profession matters, that the willingness to identify with the technical side of the profession of teaching matters. It matters if teachers are willing to dig into the *Journal of Reading* or the *Reading Research Quarterly* because they identify themselves as reading teachers and want to add to their knowledge base. Lortie reminds us that attitudes toward the profession may matter a great deal to the willingness of teachers to develop their skills over the years. Weak initial socialization may limit the willingness of a teacher to dig in and acquire the skills needed of an effective teacher rather than a check collector in a bureaucracy. The social studies teacher who is working close to home in order to be able to spend as much time as possible with his or her young children is still responsible for the literacy of the 150 to 165 teenagers as well. Developing the literacy of these teenagers may require strategies that were not acquired during teacher training in a university. Rewards need to be in place to encourage this individual to read the journals, to read the research, to be a member of a profession rather than to be simply a cipher in a bureaucracy.

But other factors also shape the lives of teachers as they spend years in the profession.

Stanley Aronowitz has quite a different look at the topic of weak teachers who are uncommitted to their craft. He argues that as teachers began to become trade unionists in the 1960s, they reduced their commitment to the profession. He states that in much of the push toward smaller work loads in education, the "real intention proves to be a reduction of professional commitment to the institution both emotionally and in time and effort."[5]

Aronowitz writes that "teacher unionism was long overdue when it swept nearly all large Northern cities in the 1960's."[6] But this new unionism did not lead to a new "more intense search for excellence," he notes. Instead, as the newly unionized teachers filled classrooms to gain the new credentials, which meant more pay (e.g., master's degree, master's degree plus thirty hours, master's degree plus forty-five hours of graduate school), "this passion for additional schooling is not the same as the passion for learning."[7]

Aronowitz describes teachers as ticket punchers, acquiring new credentials to increase their income rather than gain new information that might add to their skills as professionals. In his critique, teachers are not managers or owners trying to improve the enterprise but employees doing just what the union contract requires and little else.

But Aronowitz does not present empirical evidence to support his assertion that union membership has led to a ticket punching mentality. He does not bring in the documents from the political landscape to support his arguments.

What evidence now exists that teachers are shaped by their membership in unions rather than their identification with the profession of teaching? The first place to look is the union contract in our large cities. As many readers know, the large cities where public education is especially dysfunctional—New York, Washington, Cleveland, Chicago, Detroit, Los Angeles—are all union towns where teachers are represented by the American Federation of Teachers. (In New York, e.g., the UFT is the city's local of the AFT.) Of course, union leaders and most social scientists would caution that union control of schools and the dysfunctional condition of these schools is not cause and effect. Rather, the poverty of parents shapes the achievement of children, the union would say.

Let's look now at how the central document of union membership—the contract between the union and the Board of Education—may shape teachers' attitudes.

THE SENIORITY INCREASE

"Why should they learn anything new, or improve as teachers? We all get the same raise anyway," is how a teacher in Brooklyn explained the weak teaching in his school. At the heart of a contract between a union and city is the seniority increase. Each teacher gets an automatic increase depending on years of service, not the quality of service. The weak teacher who assigns one or two essays a semester and keeps all reading assignments within the easily available textbook and the zealot who raises money to provide six or seven trade books to his or her class each year and ties biweekly writing assignments to these reading experiences both receive the same annual raise.

If one accepts Aronowitz's argument that union contracts have made a major impact on the commitment of teachers to their craft, then school reform would have to replace local union contracts with a national labor agreement. Seniority increases would end. One can imagine a system of individual performance reviews as used in industry rather than the current system of seniority increases that ignore individual excellence.

In an annual performance review, a chairperson could dole out raises depending on criteria that had been decided at the beginning of the year. The performance review process—if done well, by trained managers— should not be subjective. Completion of clearly defined goals is what should drive performance review. The faculty member who mentors new students and new colleagues receives a raise, the slackers who race to their cars at 2:40 P.M. would not. These raises would not need to be closely tied to test increases—a result always influenced by the quality of students in a particular class in a particular year.

The annual interview with a senior teacher (with quarterly check-ins) would not be difficult to imagine:

Which new colleagues did you mentor?
What do the syllabi of the new colleagues look like?
What were your criteria for evaluating their syllabi?
Are these goals synchronized with the school's plan for building literacy?
What were the reading assignments in their syllabi?
How many books did you assign this semester?
What were students' responses to the reading assignments in your own classes?
Are they just handing in the two typed pages you asked for, or did some of your books inspire five page responses?
What were the types and frequencies of the writing assignments? (Let's look at some sample writing portfolios both in your classes and in the classes of the teachers you are supervising.)
How many at-risk students did you mentor this academic year?
How many of those are still enrolled?
Which articles did you read in the research journals?
Which articles did you contribute to the faculty newsletter?
What did you learn about technology this year?
How did you help your students with technology?

All of these goals could be included in a teacher's performance review. Should Congress develop a performance review form in school districts where children are not being encouraged to read? When will the nation move the reward structure of teaching away from the seniority increase sys- tem at the heart of union contracts with teachers since at least the 1960s to a performance-based approach? Could a Congress interested in education reshape teaching and make it less of a mass occupation with annual rewards based on seniority and more of an individual occupation based on individual skills and expertise as evaluated through annual performance reviews?

This would, of course, require a national debate, but given the condition of teaching and the importance of teaching, this debate is needed. In many areas, national authority has pushed local authority aside in the postwar period. Welfare reform is a recent example of a federal takeover when local initiatives had failed. Clean air and water standards were federal initiatives in the Nixon era that still shape local environments today. And after the tragedy at the World Trade Center in September 2001, Congress has already shaped a new expansion of federal authority in airport security where local standards have failed. But not all commentators on school reform see teacher union and teacher contracts as a barrier to better schools.

The fears of Andy Hargreaves, another prominent educator, about the lives of teachers, are somewhat different. He sees teachers not as victims of the union contracts but as a group being crushed from above by the bureaucracy, and with school reform adding even more bureaucratic pressures on teachers and their time.

Hargreaves argues that the current balkanization into departments in secondary schools severely limits the ability of teachers to learn what they need to be effective. He says balkanization is "characterized by strong and enduring boundaries between different parts of the organization, by personal identification with the domains these boundaries define, and by differences of power between one domain and another."[8] He is not vague. He spells out the damage balkanization causes.

> Secondary schools in particular are in dire need of some of the benefits that a moving mosaic pattern of organization can bring . . . their balkanized, cubby-hole like structure often leads to departmental defensiveness, resistance to changes which threaten departmental identities and lack of opportunities for teachers to work or learn from colleagues in departments other than on their own. Balkanized staffing structures are deeply inimical to effective organizational learning.[9]

In his case studies of two high schools in Canada in chapter 10, Hargreaves describes the conflicts between the new student-centered model of organizing ninth graders into cohorts, and the older, more common high school model when teachers are subject area specialists closely tied to a single department. These departmental teachers do not collaborate with teachers from other subjects and are reluctant to use themes in teaching that must cross departmental lines, Hargreaves writes.

He argues that attempts at public accountability may be counterproductive if these attempts at accountability reinforce the isolation of teachers into departments and subject areas that may be remote from the needs of students. But since his analysis is not directed at understanding the development of literacy, he does not provide details about how these two different organizations of schools might influence the literacy of the teenagers who are enrolled. Are opportunities to develop literacy more available in the new cohort-centered school? Are the themes designed to cut across department delivered just through class discussions and class note taking, or are considerable amounts of new reading in a new range of texts also available? Were the older subject area teachers in his Canadian schools able to order large numbers of trade texts and paperback texts as supplements and even replacements for the standard textbooks?

Nevertheless, Hargreaves provides a framework for understanding the obstacles within a school, the obstacles that are the result of organizing schools into departments rather than making each teacher accountable for carrying out the school's plan to build literacy in each child. Hargreaves makes the cost of this isolation into departments clear. If your only responsibility in a department is to teach social studies from the approved text and you are evaluated by a social studies chairperson who has spent an entire career doing the same thing, why attend the English department workshop down the hall on the writing process or the ESL department's institute on Latino literature?

Hargreaves serves the debate by making the costs of balkanization of secondary schools into departments clear. In expensive seminars, business leaders preach the same message. They urge American corporations to create boundary-less organizations where employees can quickly collaborate on projects and "get up to the plate and take a swing at the bat." They try to construct organizations where initiative is possible and where contact with the external world (i.e., customers) is valued rather than the production of internal charts and reports.[10]

Yet, these same business leaders refuse—probably correctly—to provide any facile solutions to the current educational crisis. Merit pay is one idea mentioned, but as Hargreaves, Lortie, Aronowitz, and others point out, the problem is more complex. Merit pay may not be enough to lower the boundaries of the departments, shine light into the cubbyholes of American classrooms, and radically increase the authority of American teachers. Until teachers as a group can have the same regular access to resources and training as doctors, lawyers, certified public accountants, and other professionals enjoy, it is difficult to see how changes in the development of literacy in the United States will occur. The next chapter looks at the issue of the training of teachers in more detail.

NOTES

1. U.S. Department of Education, *Prospects: The Congressionally Mandated Study of Educational Growth and Opportunity: The Interim Report* (Washington, D.C.: Author, July 1993), 276. For more information on school spending tendencies, also see U.S Department of Education, Office of Policy and Planning, *Reinventing Chapter 1: The Current Chapter 1 Program and New Directions* (Washington, D.C.: Author, February 1993), 15–38; and Wayne Clifton Riddle, *Expenditures in Public School Districts: Why Do They Differ?* (Washington, D.C.: Congressional Research Service, Library of Congress, July 1990).

2. Ray Marshall and Marc Tucker, *Thinking for a Living: Education and the Wealth of Nations* (New York: Basic Books, 1992), 10.

3. Dan C. Lortie, *Schoolteacher: A Sociological Study* (Chicago: University of Chicago Press, 1975), 15.

4. Lortie, *Schoolteacher,* 55.

5. Stanley Aronowitz, *False Promises: The Shaping of American Working Class Consciousness* (New York: McGraw-Hill, 1973), 314.

6. Aronowitz, *False Promises,* 314.

7. Aronowitz, *False Promises,* 313.

8. Andy Hargreaves, *Changing Teachers, Changing Times: Teachers' Work and Culture in the Postmodern Age* (New York: Teachers College Press, 1994), 235.

9. Hargreaves, *Changing Teachers, Changing Times,* 66–67.

10. Jack Welch, "Keynote Address," TechLearn 2001 Conference, October 29, 2001, Orlando, Florida.

Chapter Eighteen

Loosely Latched Doors and Teacher Training

The issue of training of teachers in the schools and the quality of the teachers at the beginning of their careers are huge issues that both political parties duck. John Goodlad, who has studied both the lives of teachers and students in a series of books about American schools, writes that "the gates for admission to teaching in the nation's schools have always been loosely latched."[1]

He accuses the political system of "hard-core neglect in our selection, education, and induction of those who teach our children." He argues that even if a school district can identify and fire low-performing teachers—as Philadelphia is now attempting to do—these teachers will not disappear from education. In a time of shortages of teachers, these individuals will find work elsewhere.

Goodlad shows that the damage from poor teaching can be long-lasting. He is one of the few writers I have read who is able to connect the failure of teachers to the long-term failures of students. He writes of how teachers poorly trained to teach reading often are not able help nonreaders. He shows that poorly prepared teachers cannot help poor readers and that teachers who arrive in classrooms with only having had one course in reading are not prepared to do much to help weak readers.

> Let us look at just one little critically important part of the whole. Most teachers of the primary grades take one course in the teaching of reading. Some take two, so that the average is about 1.3 courses per teacher. . . . It is enough to enable teachers to become quite facile in sorting the children into three—one of good, one of fair, and the other of poor readers whose learning attributes at this

early stage of their school careers were determined largely in the context of home and family.[2]

He also argues that the costs of sending poorly prepared neophyte teachers into classrooms is huge.

> Diagnosis and remediation of the nonreaders lie largely outside the repertoire of teachers whose brief pedagogical preparation provided little more than an overview. Many are fortunate enough to secure the more advanced courses on returning to universities for graduate studies. But many 1st grade children are taught by successive waves of neophytes, large numbers of whom drop out after three or four years of teaching. For many children, their struggle with reading signals a self-fulfilling prophecy of assignment to the low tracks of the secondary school subjects and dropping out. The financial costs of remediation are enormous and the results are far from encouraging.[3]

Where are our major parties on this question of the professionalism of teachers—the only group among lawyers, doctors, certified financial planners, certified public accountants, and others that day after day lacks the training, materials, and schedules needed to be effective? Who is going to provide the training, the materials, the schedules, and the reward system needed to make the adults we place in classrooms effective?

Goodlad calls for a "massive reeducation" of teachers, but our political parties have not responded to his detailed analysis of the preparation and the lack of preparation of American teachers.

Big-city Democrats have not been asleep to the needs of teachers. They have been responding to their constituents—the teachers' unions. Their politics of education have been the politics of spending—much of which goes to the wallets of teachers who need the income to survive in expensive cities. They will pile new programs in schools: work-study, school-to-work transitions, after-school tutoring. All of these programs provide extra income for teachers. Each after school program in New York City pays teachers at the per-session rate set in the teachers' contract; currently this rate is $33.18 in New York City.

The Democrats typically assist teachers—a chronically low-income occupation—by adding new programs to provide extra services to students and extra income to teachers. But this is not a solution. Adding new tutoring in the afternoon programs or new sports programs—as valuable as they may be—do not strengthen the profession. These add-on programs do not provide income to all teachers or training to all teachers and administrators. The junior high school principal who runs an evening GED program at John Jay High School in Park Slope in Brooklyn for extra income should be elsewhere. He could become a better leader by taking a graduate course in cognitive psychology to learn how children develop language skills. He could attend an evening management training seminar to learn how to administer performance reviews. For effective teaching and effective management in schools, educators need their evenings to plan the next day's lessons, to grade the 160 essays from a set of five classes of thirty-two students each.

The Republican response to the failed attempts of local governments to train teachers, to provide teachers with adequate resources so that these teachers will at least have a chance to socialize and educate the poor in the United States, is multifaceted:

- Constantly repeat the mantra that "local authorities know what is best since they are close to the problem." The condition of public education in American cities tends to contradict the assumption that proximity of governance leads to quality governance. Of course, this "localism is best" philosophy avoids any responsibility for rich communities to fund education in cities with large numbers of poor people and the weak tax base that results from the presence of the poor.

- The second aspect—not to be ignored—is skillful advertising of topics that look connected to quality in education. The ability of the Republicans to use public relations to connect themselves to successes in education without doing any heavy lifting in education should not be overlooked. If you can look like a progressive, effective, results-oriented governor to the public without adding expensive training programs, and without adding expensive new resources, you have succeeded. Your message has won over voters in spite of your lack of results. The classic case of message over results is George W. Bush. He touted his success in raising test scores on a state test whose validity has been widely questioned. A number of researchers found the Texas statewide test, called TASST, very basic; they discovered that success on it did not correlate with success on national tests.[4] Even if Texas had improved its scores on national tests at the fourth grade level in addition to the state test, what did this matter? While an improvement in achievement at fourth grade is commendable, few children leave fourth grade for the workplace. Two much more important education indicators of the success of a state education system are the end results: the high school and college graduation rates. The press ignored the fundamental fact that the high school graduation rate in Texas is only 67 percent, still below the national high school graduation rate of 69 percent. (See table 18.1 to see how the number of teenagers enrolled in Texas high schools shrinks sharply from ninth to twelfth grade.) As table 18.2 shows, graduation rates for African Americans, Latinos, and Native Americans are deplorable in Texas as well as in many other states. Texas was not able to increase this high school graduation rate in the 1990s during the years of Bush or his Democratic predecessor, or its college graduation rate.

- Another important aspect of Republican public relations is the use of family members in advertising connected to literacy. This might be called "I am a friend of books" campaign. Former First Lady Barbara Bush appeared in television ads repeatedly touting the success of the Reading Is Fundamental (RIF) program during her husband's presidency. But President Bush failed to restore the cuts to the RIF program made by President Ronald Reagan, and the press never publicized this fact. While individual Bush family members may have genuine enthusiasm for books and reading, funding for books and literacy in secondary schools has not followed to date in the presidencies of either Bush.

When will our Democratic and Republican politicians begin touting successes in high school and college graduation rates in their respective states? When will the press begin publicizing these metrics in their coverage of political campaigns?

In short, the Democrats have responded to the literacy crisis with add-on programs rather than the addition of resources, training, and performance reviews to the lives of teachers. The Republican response has been clever political advertising, without any attempts to restructure teaching through adequate resources for each classroom and adequate training.

Table 18.1. Public School Student Membership, by Grade and State, Fall 1999

	Grade 6	Grade 7	Grade 8	Grade 9	Grade 10	Grade 11	Grade 12	Ungraded
United States	3,564,116	3,541,274	3,496,977	3,934,899	3,415,425	3,033,980	2,781,701	620,779
Alabama	57,703	58,969	56,201	61,150	52,304	46,015	42,576	—
Alaska	10,574	10,683	10,575	11,568	10,217	8,624	8,381	—
Arizona	67,085	66,236	65,338	68,646	60,489	51,771	47,907	3,353
Arkansas	34,397	35,267	35,403	36,657	35,081	31,839	29,316	1,416
California	451,810	439,075	431,730	482,355	444,161	401,348	347,914	82,052
Colorado	54,957	54,856	54,599	58,710	52,548	47,725	41,999	1,261
Connecticut	43,524	42,725	41,205	43,977	39,273	35,160	31,670	—
Delaware	9,014	9,179	8,957	10,150	8,618	7,304	6,490	—
District of Columbia	4,539	4,331	4,408	5,289	4,113	3,550	2,897	4,023
Florida	189,813	186,536	181,574	223,743	177,234	138,667	116,259	—
Georgia	111,603	109,134	106,688	125,388	98,019	82,974	72,351	—
Hawaii	14,441	13,733	13,175	15,629	13,526	12,592	10,818	99
Idaho	18,909	18,827	18,589	20,062	19,833	18,715	17,899	16
Illinois	153,710	148,459	149,397	164,554	145,536	126,866	126,984	3,734
Indiana	76,745	74,743	74,540	81,049	73,532	68,054	64,647	4,769
Iowa	35,819	36,307	37,966	41,394	39,159	37,829	37,124	11,732
Kansas	35,757	36,205	36,759	39,683	36,769	34,333	32,344	11,234
Kentucky	47,662	48,983	48,427	56,678	47,647	43,483	39,111	8,943
Louisana	57,910	58,997	55,710	63,869	52,925	46,144	42,344	11,508
Maine	16,946	17,003	17,493	17,036	15,565	14,237	13,022	2,389

(continued)

Table 18.1. Public School Student Membership, by Grade and State, Fall 1999 (continued)

	Grade 6	Grade 7	Grade 8	Grade 9	Grade 10	Grade 11	Grade 12	Ungraded
Maryland	65,675	64,874	62,776	70,346	60,685	54,737	50,632	6,066
Massachusetts	75,902	74,783	74,545	77,733	68,577	62,424	56,440	4,089
Michigan	123,673	124,554	122,548	135,896	117,408	104,634	96,295	94,153
Minnesota	64,547	64,724	67,705	71,222	69,030	66,375	67,044	—
Mississippi	37,822	38,850	37,344	39,404	34,047	29,391	26,500	15,394
Missouri	68,862	69,534	69,850	75,791	68,523	62,280	56,213	9,356
Montana	12,192	12,607	12,975	13,532	12,877	11,985	11,571	352
Nebraska	21,242	21,786	22,452	24,861	23,064	21,692	21,630	—
Nevada	25,591	24,911	24,268	24,618	22,660	20,549	18,139	710
New Hampshire	17,130	17,249	16,793	17,520	15,297	14,317	12,734	629
New Jersey	96,113	92,672	88,757	89,234	80,654	73,096	69,647	93,703
New Mexico	24,997	25,148	25,322	29,307	25,601	22,054	18,941	—
New York	210,895	206,739	202,221	252,864	212,708	165,159	150,444	152,595
North Carolina	101,621	99,477	96,542	111,493	88,455	75,694	65,558	22
North Dakota	8,523	8,689	9,137	9,677	9,395	9,405	9,306	—
Ohio	140,117	141,628	140,706	156,492	134,736	127,991	120,885	9,863
Oklahoma	46,296	45,737	46,999	50,270	46,441	42,652	40,024	3,137
Oregon	42,023	42,014	42,721	45,619	43,201	40,083	36,827	2,948
Pennsylvania	140,916	141,885	141,714	153,464	137,769	128,787	121,152	28,724
Rhode Island	12,108	12,094	11,592	12,548	11,099	9,966	9,138	3,465

South Carolina	53,544	52,908	51,601	62,883	47,592	36,109	36,471	—
South Dakota	9,934	10,338	10,618	11,247	10,649	9,811	9,693	160
Tennessee	67,708	68,408	66,243	74,699	65,873	58,077	53,160	14,384
Texas	303,447	306,282	300,830	359,368	275,265	243,627	217,670	—
Utah	35,472	34,493	35,170	35,961	36,990	36,905	36,594	10,737
Vermont	8,035	8,040	8,177	8,748	8,356	7,795	7,014	370
Virginia	86,303	85,872	85,092	95,017	80,490	71,917	69,333	22,716
Washington	76,893	76,932	77,543	86,602	80,493	73,383	68,486	—
West Virginia	21,558	22,459	22,409	23,876	22,049	21,142	20,982	634
Wisconsin	64,967	67,103	67,878	78,961	70,934	67,343	64,076	—
Wyoming	7,091	7,389	7,715	8,059	7,958	7,370	7,049	43
Outlying Areas,								
DOD Dependents Schools, and Bureau of Indian Affairs	3,975	3,876	3,691	4,001	3,238	2,422	1,965	—
DOD Dependents Schools,	8,434	7,261	6,423	5,671	4,640	3,871	3,355	206
American Samoa	1,086	1,131	1,047	1,059	926	825	725	43
Guam	2,543	2,445	2,442	3,457	2,234	1,717	1,392	—
Northern Marianas	763	700	694	746	567	441	344	40
Puerto Rico	47,470	49,789	45,842	43,438	43,885	38,037	34,428	19,462
Virgin Islands	1,534	2,033	1,540	2,052	1,569	1,187	1,096	311

Source: http://nces.ed.gov/pubs2001/quarterly/summer/q2-6.asp#Table-1.

Table 18.2.   National Graduation Rates for the Class of 1998

State	Graduation Rate	African American Graduation Rate	Latino Graduation Rate	White Graduation Rate
Texas	67%	59%	56%	76%
National Avg.	71%	56%	54%	78%

Source: The Manhattan Institute online at http://www.manhattan-institute.org/html/cr_baeo_t1.htm

VIEWS AND RECOMMENDATIONS

Nationalize Teacher Training

One solution is to free training and resources from local politics. Nationalize the training component in all teachers' contracts in all school districts where the median reading score is more than six months below national norms. This would put New York City, Los Angeles, Chicago, Detroit, Cleveland, and hundreds of other school districts under federal control of teachers' time. Now training could begin. Now all of July would be training time, and federal funds would pay for this training.

Use two weeks of this month to bring teachers and administrators up to date in how to develop reading skills and a love of reading in teenagers. Have them read the last thirty years of research on reading that says that the volume of reading matters. Use one week to have teachers grapple with technology. Have teachers build computers so that their fear of technology will evaporate. Pedagogy is important—have teachers view videos of successful teachers who do more than write paragraphs on the board for the children to copy. Have teachers visit the homes of the students they will work with in the fall. A month of training would only be a start.

While this could take place at local schools of education, it might be nice to have training at places that did not produce weak teachers in the first place. Bring in outside vendors from private industry. Provide some of the technical training online to reduce travel time and travel costs. Evaluate the training.

Moreover, pay teachers for this training. Respect the reality that today's teachers need the income now made in July working as camp counselors or house painters, or the money they save on child care by being home with their own children.

But training isn't enough.

We need to be comprehensive in changing schools, as William Boyd, a professor of education at Penn State, urges. Training will not be enough if teachers lack materials when they return to schools. Training and materials may not be enough if state curricula still hold teachers accountable for covering centuries of global history each month, rather than bringing in books that teenagers are more likely to read. And writing assignments will accompany these books if our English teachers struggle with schedules of 160 or 170 students a day.

So in low-performing schools, we need to simultaneously do the following:

- Nationalize teacher training both at the end of the school year and during sabbaticals. What is going on now during teacher sabbaticals is ridiculous. Allowing teachers to take exercise walking classes as New York City does as part of "training" during their sabbaticals is theft of our tax dollars and a theft of the skills these teachers need to acquire.[5] This localism is crippling our schools. (See table 23.2 later for a description of classes available for credit during New York City teachers' sabbatical years.)
- Nationalize teachers' access to books, maps, and other classroom materials.
- Nationalize teachers' schedules in the humanities. Forcing English teachers to see 160 teenagers a day in secondary schools dooms the children of the poor to second class or third class language skills. Some junior high schools now assign teenagers to the same teacher for language arts and reading that personalizes education and also gives the teacher a manageable load of 80 rather than 160. This issue of teacher schedule is of national importance and should be dealt with at the national level.
- Nationalize teachers' communication with parents. Make weekly notes to parents mandatory. Type up the weekly reading assignments and other homework assignments and send them home and put them online. Use group e-mail to communicate with parents. (This would be easier if a strong national program of access to technology for the poor existed.)

This reform list is long, but it is well-known and has been proposed by researchers, education activists, and parents many times before. How many of these reforms are now in place as a result of state intervention in weak schools? Since President Bush and Congress will depend on national tests to identify weak schools and then on intervention by states to improve these weak schools or face the cutoff of federal funding, has state intervention worked?

Has state intervention in state after state led to technically training teachers who can work with weak readers, as John Goodlad advocates? Has state intervention led to new authority for teachers to provide materials, as Samuel Bacharach urges in his studies of school resources and the deprofessionalization of teachers? We will examine the effects of state intervention in the next chapter.

NOTES

1. John Goodlad, "Producing Teachers Who Understand, Believe, and Care," *Education Week*, February 5, 1997, 48.
2. Goodlad, "Producing Teachers," 36.
3. Goodlad, "Producing Teachers," 36.
4. For information on testing in Texas, see Stephen P. Klein, Laura S. Hamilton, et al., *What Do Test Scores in Texas Tell Us?* (Santa Monica, Calif.: RAND Corporation, 2000), which includes a long bibliography on the topic. Another article skeptical about success in Texas is John Mintz, "An Education Miracle or Mirage?" *Washington Post*, April 21, 2000, p. A1. Two writers who believe that the Texas success in fourth-grade math on the NAEP is an extremely important indicator of overall quality are William J. Bennett and Chester E. Finn Jr. in "The Real Improvement in Texas Schools," *New York Times*, October 27, 2000.
5. In an interview, Kelley Wilmuth of Brooklyn, New York, described how she took a course on exercise walking for credit at Kingsborough Community College as part of her sabbatical year.

Chapter Nineteen

Is State Intervention Effective?

Failed Schools and State Intervention in New York, New Jersey, Maryland, and California

As mentioned in the last chapter, states' ability to intervene in the schools that they have identified as being weak is at the heart of the Bush education plan. These state interventions are now routine business in education; they are a regular feature of the education landscape. The New Jersey Department of Education saw the weak achievement in Camden, Patterson, and Newark, pushed aside the local boards of education in these cities, and appointed new leadership. The Ohio Department of Education took over the administration of the Cleveland schools. The state of Maryland used the weak results in a number of Baltimore schools to seize control of these schools.

Are these state interventions a major part of the school reform process? Can parents count on state interventions to help local schools build more literate teenagers ready for success in higher education or the workplace? Or are these interventions just paper tigers, part of an accountability movement that has not strengthened classrooms and given teachers and students new tools and new resources?

New York has perhaps the longest history with this process of identifying weak schools. Looking at the long history of school intervention in New York may give us some indication of the ability of state intervention to make radical improvements in literacy.

The school improvement process—called *school registration review*—began in the early 1980s when a state education official realized that education was failing at his alma mater in Brooklyn, and he ordered state investigators to visit the school and report.[1]

From this failed high school in Brooklyn grew a statewide program in which investigators visited each school in the state on a four-year cycle and compared achievement and indicators such as attendance against state standards. Schools failing to meet state standards had to file improvement programs or close their doors.

Fifteen years later, this intervention process was evaluated. What were the results of having the state education department intervene in local schools across New York State? The two authors, Robert Berne, now a vice president at New York University, and Dolores M. Fernandez, then a professor of education at Hunter College and now the president of Hostos Community College in New York City, used language rarely seen in state reports. In the transmittal letter in figure 19.1, their conclusions are clear. Outrage at the failure of the intervention process to provide educational opportunity is the first conclusion.

The second conclusion is that the school intervention process did not make adequate resources available to teachers. "Unfortunately, despite the best of intentions, the resources that are available are unfocused and dispersed. Not only the quantity of resources and the inequity of their distribution, but the way resources are used must be significantly different than current practices. The report includes numerous examples of effective resource use that draw on the experiences of successful schools and communities."[2]

Finally, Berne and Fernandez report that failure is so widespread after fifteen years of state interventions that "radical changes in rules and regulations" are necessary:

> Our outrage goes well beyond resource issues. We believe that in some cases the failure is so harmful and deep-seated that the time is past for marginal changes and tinkering within the current system. Action that some of us would not have advocated under ordinary circumstances—new forms of school leadership, radical changes in rules and regulations, and even school closings and reorganizations—must be part of the response to these extraordinary conditions.

As state inspectors visited schools throughout the 1980s and into the 1990s, they wrote up reports on the deficiencies they discovered. It is these reports and the failure of the state to remedy these conditions that led Berne and Fernandez to use words like *outrage*.

What did the state discover as it inspected schools around New York state? Each school in the following sample follows failed state standards

Dear Members of the Board of Regents:

We are pleased to present the report and recommendations of the Regents Subcommittee on Low Performing Schools Advisory Council. The members of this Council have drawn on their extensive knowledge and experience and formulated strategies to improve educational conditions and outcomes for students in Schools Under Registration Review (SURR).

Three words can be used to characterize the detailed findings and recommendations of the Council: OUTRAGE, RESOURCES, and ACTION.

All members of the Council are outraged that so many thousands of students are denied educational opportunity for year after year in schools that everyone knows are failing. The sheer numbers of students, the long periods of failure, and the fact that this news surprises no one is a tragedy that cannot be tolerated. The challenge for us, and for you, is to channel that outrage in productive ways, before it is too late for these children and the next generation.

One response to this failure is to marshal the array of available resources to right this incredible wrong. Unfortunately, despite the best of intentions, the resources that are available are unfocused and dispersed. Not only the quantity of resources and the inequity of their distribution, but the way resources are used must be significantly different than current practices. The report includes numerous examples of effective resource use that draw on the experiences of successful schools and communities.

Our outrage goes well beyond resource issues. We believe that in some cases the failure is so harmful and deep-seated that the time is past for marginal changes and tinkering within the current system. Action that some of us would not have advocated under ordinary circumstances—new forms of school leadership, radical changes in rules and regulations, and even school closings and reorganizations—must be part of the response to these extraordinary conditions.

The reaction to this report cannot be limited to the Regents and State Education Department. School personnel, superintendents, district staff, Chancellors, and school boards have the responsibility, authority and opportunity to address the problems of failing schools under their jurisdiction. We do not want this report to remove the responsibility from school districts; however, it is the responsibility of the Regents to ensure *A New Compact for Learning* is fulfilled with equity and equality for every child in the State. If you do less, then as a society we all fail.

For the
Council,

Robert Berne and Dolores Fernandez
Co Chairs, Subcommittee Advisory
Council

Figure 19.1. Letter of Transmittal.

in a variety of indicators, usually beginning with reading tests. In addition to failing scores on state tests, state inspectors discovered many details about how schools fail to educate youngsters.

The first school in this sample is well known because of its size. With an enrollment that varies from four to five thousand students, Lane has long been the largest public high school in New York City, but size is not what attracted the attention of state inspectors. Even though the Board of Education tried to reduce the effect of the total size of Lane by enrolling teenagers in eleven separate houses, attempts to change the climate of the schools were not enough. The state believed that literacy also mattered. State inspectors found a school where there was a lack of reading and writing activities in English and social studies.

NO READING IN CONTENT AREAS: "NOT A PRINT-RICH ENVIRONMENT"

According to a 1996 report:

> Franklin K. Lane High School is a very large inner city school, built during the 1930s, that presently houses over 4,500 students. This five story structure contains over 100 instructional areas and accommodates almost 300 professional and support personnel within its walls. As a Project Achieve School, the school is presently divided into 11 houses.
>
> Franklin K. Lane High School is situated in a working class neighborhood where there has been an ongoing change during the last 20 years. The neighborhood, once inhabited by families of German, Italian, Irish and Polish heritage, is now home to many residents from the Caribbean and the southern hemisphere. . . .
>
> Student work is not evident in the classrooms or in the halls. Classrooms lack displays of appropriate material that would stimulate student discussions. The school does not provide a "print-rich" environment.
>
> Not all classes require students to spend sufficient time on task. Much classroom lateness was observed. Classroom management techniques and instructional practices were not consistent within various departments.
>
> Instruction in most classes is very traditional. Few classes actively engaged students in active learning activities or cooperative learning. Only a few students were observed to be engaged participants, when encouraged to

do so. Most classes provided few opportunities for students to utilize higher level thinking skills.

There is no standard core curriculum uniformly followed in the English classes across grade levels. Most reading and writing instruction observed appeared not to be sufficiently planned, focused or appropriate enough to result in improved student outcomes. In most cases students were observed to be writing in the 22 English classes that were observed, but direct instruction on the writing process, necessary to pass the RCTs (Regents Competency Tests), was not consistently observed. Foreign language, ESL and NLA classes were generally teacher dominated and did not provide sufficient opportunities for student interaction.

And the teenagers at this school had little opportunity to read or write in subject areas such as social studies: "Academic area classroom did not appear to provide reading or writing activities across curriculum areas in order to ensure improvements in reading and writing skills."[3]

INOPERATIVE LIBRARY

School libraries are, of course, an important pillar of any plan to develop literacy of teenagers. But first these libraries have to exist. At one intermediate school in Brooklyn in 1995, the State Education Department found an "inoperative library" in addition to weak sixth-grade test scores.

The State Education Department has identified IS 291 as a school under registration review as a result of declining scores in the area of 6th grade reading. As a result the Department assembled a team of individuals from both the State and the City, to visit the school and provide the school, the District and the New York City Board of Education with a comprehensive report concerning what it observed.

Concerns:

It was generally observed by the Team that there is little or no supervision of the instructional process at the school.

The team observed a propensity to rely on outdated educational practices in classroom instruction.

A significant percentage of the student population was of Dominican Republican origin. However, the team observed very little evidence of this culture in student work; bulletin boards or national emblems in the school.

The library is effectively inoperative in that there is no comprehensive schedule, materials are scant and outdated and the facility had no apparent formal connection to any of the instructional programs of the school.

The current Chapter I scheduling model is not prepared to address the instructional needs of students when reimbursable staff is absent.[4]

INSTRUCTION IS COPYING
ASSIGNMENTS FROM THE BLACKBOARD

The next situation reinforces Goodlad's idea that teacher training is essential and that teachers need to carefully examine their instructional practices. Phrases such as "instructional practices" sometimes numb parents. What does this jargon mean? In the case of the next school, it means your child spends forty-five or fifty minutes straight copying assignments off the board in the front of the room. Rather than critique a writing assignment, or discuss sentence structure, or preview a reading assignment, or hold a classroom debate or discussion, this class just sat and copied from the board. And the practice was so prevalent that the state said, "Instruction in some general education classes consists mostly of children copying from the chalkboard with little teacher-guided instruction." The following report was written in 1997, more than fifteen years after the beginning of the state intervention process in New York state.

Community and School Background

P.S./I.S. 73, now known as the Thomas S. Boyland Landmark School, is located at 241 Macdougal Street in the Ocean Hill/Brownsville section of Brooklyn, New York. This educational institution was built 108 years ago and has rightfully taken its place among the landmarks of New York City.

Presently, the school serves some 578 students in grades pre-k through eighth. Approximately 18% of this population receives special education services. The school is organized into two divisions: an elementary school (pre-k through fourth grade) and a middle school (fifth through eighth grade). In 1995–96, the percentage of pupils eligible for free lunch was 93.5%, and the percentage of limited English proficient pupils was 10.6%.

Many general education classrooms look sparse. With the exception of the primary grades mentioned above, the classroom environment at P.S. 73

is not sufficiently stimulating to motivate student achievement. Supplies and materials (i.e., manipulatives, science equipment, etc.) are minimal. Displays, where they exist, often do not contain examples of creative student work.

Whole-class instruction predominates in most classrooms. There is a lack of attention to children's diverse learning styles and the varied instructional strategies required to accommodate them. Instruction in some general education classes consists mostly of children copying material from the chalkboard, with little teacher-guided instruction. Classrooms are teacher-dominated, with little structured opportunity for student interaction. Students in many classrooms were not engaged in the lesson being taught. On the whole, classroom instruction is not sufficiently challenging. This indicates that, generally, teachers have low expectations for student achievement and/or that the lesson has not been properly prepared.

Evidence of lesson planning is not consistent throughout the school. Some teachers had very well developed lesson plans, while others were sketchy and lacked definition. In addition, it was observed that some teachers did not always teach what had been planned.

Based on classroom observations, instructional principles related to literacy development are not universally practiced within the school.

The math program is outdated (from 1992). It does not reflect the new National Council of the Teachers of Mathematics standards and does not emphasize higher order thinking skills.[5]

ONLY ONE ROOM WITH
FUNCTIONING WATER FOUNTAINS

Sunset Park in Brooklyn has been a neighborhood in flux for the last thirty years. As white ethnics—predominantly Italian and Irish—age out, they have been replaced by Latinos from a number of countries in the apartment buildings along Fifth Avenue and by professionals of all ethnic groups who buy the brownstones on the numbered streets. And as the entrepreneurs in new Chinatown in Brooklyn expand west and open more restaurants, garment factories, and other small businesses, more and more of Sunset Park may become Asian.

Has all of the commercial activity in the surrounding community also revitalized the neighborhood's public schools? The middle school in the next report serves this ever-changing neighborhood of Sunset Park; it also feeds John Jay High School, the subject of chapters 3 and 4. In 1995, the state found a school unable to teach reading effectively and unable even to provide drinking water on each floor.

Middle School 136 in Community School District #15 has been identified as a School Under Registration Review (SURR) in the area of reading. There has been a three-year decline in sixth grade reading scores on the PEP Reading Test [a state reading test].

Both the school's library and computer laboratories appear to be under-utilized.

Recommendation: Ways should be considered to make the utilization of the library and computer laboratories greater. Some of these include: making the library the intellectual center of the school by scheduling the librarian to perform no greater number of coverages than other staff members, thus allowing greater numbers of classes to receive regular library instruction; the infusion of a greater breadth and depth of relevant bilingual materials to the library and the coordination of the library with other computer-assisted instructional capabilities already extant in the building.

Concern: The science laboratory at the site is underutilized. Few "handson" laboratory experiences exist for children.

Recommendation: The school should consider the use of a laboratory assistant to increase the level of science laboratory experiences for children. Utilization of science skills which already exist on the staff should be optimally exploited.

Concern: The gymnasium appeared to be the only room throughout the building with working drinking fountains; the school was generally overheated and water damage from a leaking roof was evident throughout most of the building.

Some chemicals are poorly stored.[6]

"FEW [TEXTBOOKS] ARE ALLOWED TO GO HOME WITH STUDENTS"

Bushwick in Brooklyn is far from the prosperous western edge of the borough where lawyers, journalists, and Wall Street brokers live in neighborhoods such as Brooklyn Heights, Park Slope, and Bay Ridge. There is no fear of dislocation due to gentrification in Bushwick. Poverty is endemic, and the end of this poverty is not in sight. The City University of New York is not planning to open a campus nearby; IBM is not planning a new fabrication plant in Bushwick. Certainly, one would expect that in this high-poverty neighborhood, where success in school could be a ticket to middle-class prosperity, the New York City Board of Education would provide print-rich environments, with books to take home and other standard features of a well-organized school.

Here is a report from 1996 about an elementary school in Bushwick—P.S. 106—where the majority of teachers are officially well trained. They hold city and state teaching certificates. The teachers mentioned in these reports were not temps; they were not substitute teachers; they were not temporary per diem teachers or TPDs working on emergency licenses. These were adults whose competence had been certified by the city or the state.

> In a few classrooms there was evidence of learning occurring in an orderly and moderately stimulating environment. In a few others the environment appeared out of control and unsafe, and the students appeared to be engaged in little or no learning. The review team's holistic assessment of P.S. 106 [in Brooklyn] was of a school that lacked a coherent and pedagogical focus. The school was seen as generally dysfunctional educationally and lacking in instructional leadership.[7]

The state report found that teachers were not developing students' language skills:

> There was no evidence that curriculum delivery was consistent with any understanding of the students' developmental capacities. Nor was an understanding of language acquisition reflected in the instruction observed. There was only scant evidence that instructional delivery was based on an understanding of the relationship among reading, writing, speaking and listening. There was no evidence of formative and summative assessment systems in place. Of the meager assessments used, evidence of item and test analysis for strategic instructional planning was not apparent.

The state report found that the teachers were poorly trained:

> Many observed teaching strategies were inconsistent with current research about the teaching and learning process. For the most part, observed instruction

was teacher centered and text or handout driven. In a number of cases, the instructional material and teaching methodology were so inappropriate that most of the students were incapable of doing independently the work that was given to them. The pedagogical staff does not make sufficient use of a variety of models to deliver instruction. Too frequently teachers demonstrated a pronounced lack of understanding of essential elements of effective instruction. Yet, this was a staff that universally worked energetically and diligently with their classes. They cared about their students. However, too much of their talent and energy was misdirected and spent engaged in ineffective practices—in some cases practices which inhibit learning, including the verbal and written use of incorrect English.

The state report found that school was chaotic:

Evidence of classroom chaos was commented upon by nearly every reviewer. The evidence ranged from the inability of teachers to engage students and the absence of student management systems to the extremes of students in early childhood classrooms physically attacking each other. Where teachers had thoughtful and consistent management procedures there was more learning evident. Despite the persistent suggestion that more paraprofessionals would improve the school, the team's observation of paraprofessional's roles in the classroom did not support this assertion. While there was evidence of paraprofessionals who were in tune with the teacher and the instructional delivery strategy and who functioned well to assist with management and instruction, there were also too many instances where the paraprofessionals' interventions were disrupting learning.

In addition, the state report found that the teachers were not equipped. Like so many high schools, and junior high schools, this elementary school was

not print rich . . . textbooks were distributed during lessons and few were allowed to go home.

Available texts were often outdated, of insufficient number, and lacking in instructional congruence across the grades. Classrooms had meager or non-existent libraries. As a result, the environment was not print rich. Materials and supplies were stock piled in a supply room and in the staff developer's office. Textbooks were distributed during lessons and few were allowed to go home with students.

These are state- and city-certified teachers—and members of a powerful teachers' union—who think so little of their children that they continue teaching without adequate books.

The state report found that art, music, and physical education also were missing from the daily lives of these children in this school: "A school based curriculum was not present. Without the availability of an auditorium and gymnasium, and without assigned art, music, and physical education teachers, these required subjects became the responsibility of the classroom teacher. Yet such subject area instruction was not evident during our visit."

According to the state inspectors, the final result of all these deficiencies was

> an academic tone in the classrooms that communicates low expectations for student achievement. Beginning in the second grade, the school essentially tracks students. The skills of too many primary teachers did not demonstrate they understood the approaches and techniques needed to teach reading to all students. Rarely was there evidence of instruction in higher level thinking skills.

Not surprisingly, the inspectors from the New York State Department of Education wanted many changes at this school and many others in Brooklyn. They called for extensive staff development at P.S. 106. They also called for the "creation of a school wide curriculum in literacy" at P.S. 106.

NO CONSEQUENCES

There was no timetable for these actions, however. There were no consequences spelled out if improvements were not made. In fact, there may not be possible to have any remediation. According to the state, "the vast majority of staff at P.S. 106 are certified."[8] In other words, the state has made a political decision that these teachers have received all the training they need for an entire career in the schools. And retraining is difficult when teachers are expected by their union contract to spend only an hour a month in meetings learning new pedagogy or learning what they never learned in the first place. (The New York City Board of Education has expanded the school day in its most recent contract with its teachers' union, but the new time will be used on instruction rather than teacher training.[9]) So while the state can cite deficiencies, it can't do much more. Failure of state standards does not add even a week of retraining for teachers in failing schools.

When teachers in New York State now fail to teach successfully, school improvement plans now must be filed with the state. But teachers are not touched. Principals are not fired. Neither teachers nor principals at low-performing schools receive significant retraining or significant new equipment. Both principals and teachers have already received certification for life as "professionals" from New York state so as licensed "professionals," they cannot be pushed into retraining during summer vacations.

Year after year, teachers and principals in low-performing schools receive their salaries, their health benefits, their dental plans, their prescription plans, the city's contributions to their pensions, and other benefits, in spite of state reports showing that they are incompetent. Their rights as "professionals" are not touched. By providing state education licenses, the state has created an occupation shaped by licensure rather than performance. When state inspections subsequently find that education has failed, the state has little recourse. The licenses have already been granted for life.

VIEWS AND RECOMMENDATIONS

This is my main question: What can we as a nation do with tens of thousands of classrooms with underequipped and undertrained teachers? We know that powerful political forces in state capitals chain both parties to the status quo. Neither party in the state capital in Albany has mentioned adding a month to the school year in New York to retrain weak teachers or the entire faculties of schools and local superintendents. We know that strong political forces are at work in state capitals to protect the credentials of these ineffective teachers. Where can we go?

To date, no state has been able to use its intervention process to radically improve achievement in urban education. New York has failed in New York City and the other large cities of the state, as the Berne–Fernandez report cited earlier in this chapter shows. Maryland has failed in its intervention in Baltimore and in the Washington suburbs of Prince George's County.[10] New Jersey has failed in Patterson, Camden, and Newark.[11] It is too soon to evaluate California's new round of efforts at state intervention, but the first report out is not promising. Literacy in secondary schools does not seem to be a topic of great interest among the education planners in Sacramento. This report does not provide any data about new resources being available to teachers. Key phrases such as *volume of reading, reading lists, habit of reading, literacy sponsors,* and *summer reading* are not present[12] (copies are available at www.cde.ca.gov/iiusp/).

For the most part, in the last twenty years state intervention has not led to more resources, more training, and new incentives for effective teaching. Yet, given the history of these failures in state intervention since the early 1980s, our national leaders are asking us in the current school reform bill proposed by President George W. Bush and Congress once again to trust state education officials to intervene in local schools. Have they read the evaluations of these state interventions, or are they just looking for any program which looks new and promising to the public? Chapter 22 looks at the national school reform program proposed by President Bush in more detail. The next chapter looks at another well-known politician and his efforts to improve high schools in his home state.

NOTES

1. Interviews in 1988 with Louis Yavner, a former member of the Board of Regents, the group of trustees that oversees public and private education and the professions in New York state. In addition to his years on the powerful Board of Regents, Yavner had previously served New York City in a variety of other civic roles.

2. Robert Berne and Dolores Fernandez, *Perform or Perish: Recommendations of the Advisory Council to the New York State Board of Regents Subcommittee on Low-Performing Schools,* Interim Report (Albany: New York State Education Department, 1994).

3. State Education Department of the State of New York, "Registration Review Report on Franklin K. Lane High School," April 15, 1996.

4. State Education Department of the State of New York, "Registration Review Report on Intermediate School 292," January 19, 1995.

5. State Education Department of the State of New York, "Registration Review Report on P.S. 73," April 25, 1997.

6. State Education Department of the State of New York, "Registration Review Report on Middle School 136," January 25–27, 1995.

7. New York State Education Department, "Registration Review Report for P.S. 106," March 5, 1996, 3–9. The next several quotes are from this source as well.

8. New York State Education Department, "Registration Review Report for P.S. 106," 7.

9. Abby Goodnough, "Teachers Agree to a New Plan for 100 Extra Minutes a Week," *New York Times,* October 1, 2002.

10. A report describing Maryland's failure to intervene effectively in Baltimore's school system, *Making Accountability Work: An Initial Assessment of Maryland's School Reconstitution Program,* is available through Advocates for Children and Youth, 34 Market Place, 5th Floor, Baltimore, Maryland 21202, (410) 547-9200.

11. For reports describing New Jersey's takeover of two city school systems, see Arthur Anderson and Company, *Patterson Public Schools: Evaluation of State Takeover* (November 1994), (201) 403-6100; and New Jersey State Department of Education, *Newark Public Schools: Level III External Review* (April 16, 1993).

12. California is just beginning its statewide school intervention process, but a preliminary report on this intervention is troubling. It looks like California is adopting a completely top-down reform scheme that forces schools to choose from "research-based models" rather than concentrating on improving the literacy practices of individual teachers. See a preliminary report available at www.cde.ca.gov/iiusp/. The next chapter shows one result from a top-down model of reform.

Chapter Twenty

The Lure of Investing New Money into Old Environments

The New York State Experience of 1984 to the Present

Elected governor of New York in 1981, Mario Cuomo was different. Citizens who desired better government services had high expectations when they voted for him that fall. He wasn't the usual favor-trading, backslapping, elbow-grabbing, cross-endorsing veteran of the political clubs of Brooklyn, Queens, and the Bronx. He had not moved up the usual career ladder of a New York City politician: first a district leader (which is an elected post in a political party), then an assembly or city council member, then a congressman, and then the governor. Instead, Mario Cuomo was a man of reason. He had gained prominence as a mediator in a dispute over the siting of low-income housing in a middle-class neighborhood called Forest Hills in Queens. Cuomo presented himself first to the voters of New York and later in national speeches as a man who could bring the diverse groups of New York together and make democracy work.

Twelve years and three terms later, Governor Cuomo was defeated in a reelection bid, and his record in education may have been a factor in his defeat. What happened?

During the Cuomo era, the attempts at better schools were numerous and involved the spending of hundreds of millions of new money. Mario Cuomo sent a laundry list of new education programs from the state capitol in Albany to local schools of New York City, Buffalo, Rochester, and the other smaller school districts of the state. What did these programs achieve?

Perhaps Governor Cuomo's education policies were driven by the media. The dropout horror story was—and is—a staple of the education beat.

Each year the city's newspapers report the annual dropout rate. Numbers such as a 45 percent dropout rate in New York City shocked the public and the press.[1]

So it looks like Governor Cuomo went to an area that the media had selected: toward an attempt to reduce the number of dropouts.

Governor Cuomo and Assembly Member Jose Serrano, then chair of the Assembly Education Committee, created the Attendance-Improvement Dropout Prevention Program (AIDP), known informally during the decade as "Serrano Dollars." They began dropout prevention programs that continue to this very day. But the state did not send a blank check to local schools.

Taxpayers might expect that these efforts were aimed at a general improvement in each local school receiving funds. They might expect that if the roof was leaking, these new state funds could be used to fix the roof. Or if books or paper were short, the new state monies could be used to buy books for all the students in the building. But the program didn't work this way. Instead, after the first year, all the funds were spent on a narrowly targeted group of students. Most of the students in the New York City high schools received no benefits from Serrano Dollars at all.

This new state program was explicit in its requirements. Local efforts must include but not be limited to:

> [t]he services of additional staff and support personnel including attendance, counseling, and social work personnel; the institution of new or additional programs for in-school suspension programs, work-experience, diagnostic screening, computerized telephone contact systems, alternative education programs and other services designed to improve student attendance and retention rates. Such services may be provided by contract with non-school based organizations.[2]

Local schools did what they were told since they wanted the new money. The state believed that giving at-risk teenagers more personal attention would help hold them in schools. High schools hired more counselors and more social workers. They purchased computerized telephone machines that could tell parents when a son or daughter had been truant. And they paid teachers to stay after school and direct the extracurricular activities. But few students in each building received these services. These state programs targeted only the most vulnerable students, only the most at-risk students.

FEW STUDENTS RECEIVE SERVICES

A typical number of students served was 150 in a school of 2,500 to 3,000. In other words, 3.5 to 4.0 percent of high school students received AIDP services in most high schools. The actual percentage of students in the high schools receiving AIDP services ranged from a low of 1.9 percent at Bronx Regional to a high of 9.0 percent at Dewitt Clinton.[3]

LIMITED IMPACT: ENROLLING THE MOST DISCOURAGED STUDENTS

What happened? Did the major attempt of Mario Cuomo and Jose Serrano to improve the New York City schools and reduce the dropout rate work?

"One reason that AIDP received such negative evaluations is the standard we set," said Bernard Wolinez, who supervised the AIDP program for the New York City Board of Education. "We took the most vulnerable kids, the ones with the worst attendance records and we said that 50 percent would go onto the next grade. We didn't achieve that standard."

The reports from the advocacy groups and the State Comptroller's Office never made any accusations about the administration of the program, Wolinez said. "The administration was flawless. But was the program a good use of the state's resources? Were we saving enough kids?"

The problem was that many of the students that AIDP tried to help in the high schools were overage, Wolinez said. "Age is the most important indicator of failure. If a seventeen-year old has only two or three credits and needs forty credits to graduate, he or she is highly vulnerable. AIDP enrolled many such students; the mandate was to enroll the students who had had the worst attendance problems. Even if we could keep them in school, they weren't on track to graduate."

Also, for some students, as Wolinez explained, AIDP was too late. Many of the students enrolled in AIDP programs were very short of academic credits and were not likely to graduate from high school with or without AIDP. That these students became discouraged and stopped coming to high school and to their AIDP programs is not surprising.

THE SAME OLD MOVIE

AIDP encountered the obstacles that make many of the city's secondary schools failures in the first place. In other words, was it wise to add yet another program to the city's large, impersonal, chaotic high schools? The report from the Public Education Association (PEA) on the program showed how difficult dropout prevention is in New York City. This PEA report suggests that adding new programs to overcrowded high schools may actually worsen conditions in these schools.

> *School-wide conditions.* The difficulty of the task of dropout prevention is aggravated by several school-wide conditions. The immense size of the schools, the large proportions of below-grade students, and the bewildering array of academic programs which flow from these were cited by school staff as significant obstacles to dropout prevention. Ironically, the introduction of dropout prevention programs into the schools worsens these conditions. Furthermore, the glaring inadequacy of space for programs in school buildings was frequently identified as delaying implementation and slowing the rate of service delivery.[4]

In other words, putting more programs into already-crowded schools doesn't work. The space for these programs doesn't exist. And, of course, the dislike of many students for large anonymous environments is never addressed.

"These problems haven't gone away," said Wolinez. "When you have a school with a population of four thousand, it's tough. The physical factors are very important. The ambiance of the school and the comfort the students experience are very important. No one wants to be stepping all over others in the halls or classrooms at school.

"All the counseling in the world isn't enough, if the kids go back to the same milieu. The kids will still see the same old movie at school," Wolinez added.

The at-risk students who attended an after-school activity paid for by AIDP still returned to junior or senior high school the next day to be one of 150 or 160 students that his or her English teacher faced that day. The state AIDP program never considered how to increase "personal contact" for all teenagers within the existing large middle schools and high schools in New York City and within the contract between the Board of Education and the UFT.

WHY DID THE CUOMO–SERRANO INTERVENTIONS FAIL?

Essentially, the Cuomo–Serrano dropout prevention program was thirty years out-of-date. Education policy in the Cuomo era was based on the assumption that the children of New York City could be effectively educated in the largest secondary schools in the United States. What Cuomo and Serrano missed was the last thirty years of research about school design that question the wisdom of the large-city high school or junior high school.

The first researchers to question the value of large schools were Roger G. Barker and Paul V. Gump (1964). The research of James S. Coleman (1973), James Garbarino (1979), and Ernest Boyer (1984) also showed that small environments work better for at-risk students.

Barker and Gump's main point is that the size of the school determines if students will feel needed in the school building. In very small schools, they note, each student is needed to staff the school's extracurricular activities: the yearbook, the newspaper, the athletic teams. Even students with average or below-average athletic or musical skills are pressured to participate. This participation bonds students to the schools. What these activities bring, of course, is attention from peers and teachers that may not be available during the school day. A student who finds trigonometry difficult may find satisfaction writing for the school newspaper or acting in the school play or playing on the school basketball team.

At larger high schools, of course, all students are not needed in the school's extracurricular activities. Only the very talented need apply for the athletic teams in big city high schools. The attention and the recognition that extracurricular activities would have provided in a smaller school are not available for a majority of students.

Are the questions of bonding and allegiance to institutions that Barker and Gump raise important in New York City? James Garbarino, a child psychologist with the Erickson Institute in Chicago, told me in a June 1986 interview that as schools try to educate all children, the relevance of school size grows. According to Garbarino, children from poor families, who may have been left out of school previously, are now enrolled. As you move down the socioeconomic ladder, you enroll children with special needs, Garbarino said. These children need more nurture and encouragement and they can receive this encouragement in small schools. We need very small schools to draw them in and encourage them. "Our studies in the 1960s and 1970s showed that there were lower dropout rates in smaller schools."

Diana Oxley, a psychologist at Temple University, believes that cities shouldn't design schools just to be able to offer advanced placement calculus in every building. Some children especially the poor simply can't cope with large buildings, Oxley said in a February 1988 interview. They need the personal attention and recognition available in smaller buildings.

The question of school size has been plagued with too much sloppy research, Oxley added. "There have been studies that looked just at middle-class schools, and then judgments were made about all schools. Middle-class kids can cope better with large schools, so when researchers include small schools in their studies the factor of school size may not stand out."

Oxley also said that in some research the range of schools studied was not sufficient to see the school size factor. "There may not be much difference between a school of 2,000 and one of 2,500." Researchers need to look at schools as small as five hundred to see the effects of size, she said.

NEW YORK CITY IN THE 1990s:
THE ECOLOGY CRISIS CONTINUES

But Garbarino's studies and the work of other researchers did not reach New York's legislative leaders. Governor Mario Cuomo and Assembly Education Chair Jose Serrano did not try to overcome any of the conditions that make New York City's high schools "the same old movie" in the eyes of students. AIDP was an add-on program; it added new resources such as counseling to existing schools; the state's politicians did not force any changes in existing local high schools.

For twelve years, Mario Cuomo and his advisers missed opportunities to change New York City's factory schools. Rather than demand that New York City replace its factory schools with smaller environments for students—as state law allowed—Cuomo and the legislature poured millions of taxpayer dollars with little benefit into the old factory schools. The entire decade of the 1980s was wasted. Cuomo and the state legislature seemed to have missed all the literature on school reform that appeared in the 1970s and 1980s. They missed James S. Coleman's warning that in schools with over five hundred students, principals would no longer know the names of each student and be able to encourage each student individually. He missed Theodore Sizer's warning that assigning each high school teacher 160 students damages both students and teachers. Sizer's suggestion that a single humanities teacher could do both history and English and thus have only eighty students never received attention from Governor Cuomo and his state education department.

Only in the early nineties, with the help of grants from the Annenberg Foundation, did New York City begin creating a large number of smaller high schools for teenagers. But these New Vision high schools may not be enough. Even as the smaller Annenberg high schools are being formed, new large elementary and junior high and high schools are still being built. Can a teenager spend junior high school with 1,800 classmates in an environment of chaos and then be saved in a smaller Annenberg high school? Where will his or her identity be formed in junior high or later in a large high school?

For twelve years, Governor Cuomo and the state legislature missed opportunities to professionalize teaching. Large increases in state aid to education led to salary increases for teachers during the Cuomo era, but no efforts were made to improve other aspects of teaching. Teachers in cities across the state still suffered chronic shortages of books at the end of the Cuomo era. Even after three small increases in state textbook aid from Governor Cuomo, state textbook funds were still only $35 per student per year in 1994, merely enough to purchase one textbook and a fraction of the $300 to $400 spent per student annually on books in private schools.

For twelve years, Governor Cuomo did not improve the training of teachers. At the end of twelve years of promised improvements in education, the training of teachers was still limited to a few afternoons and half-day sessions a year. Even as state inspectors discovered failing schools, they did not mandate new training of teachers during the Cuomo era or subsequently.

Finally, for twelve years, Governor Cuomo did not confront the back-door deals that have weakened the ability of local superintendents to remove weak administrators.

THE BACK-DOOR DEALS OF GOVERNOR HUGH L. CAREY

How have the professionals—the teachers and the principals—gained privileges and job protection even when their schools have failed? For example, how can the same principals stay in power year after year in schools operating with achievement levels below the twenty-fifth percentile—with many of the children in the building reading years below grade level?

One case shows how it works. In New York, as in other states, endorsements from unions are currency. Endorsements are investments. Because with an endorsement from a union, a politician knows that union campaign contributions will follow, and the union phone banks and union volunteers will follow. Now voters can be called or canvassed before the election and ones who have responded favorably will then be called several times on Election Day until they have promised they have voted. When the installation of a single phone can cost a campaign hundreds of dollars, access to rooms full of union phones is a powerful inducement to cooperation—to listening when a union official says "our people need tenure."

Hugh Carey, who preceded Mario Cuomo as governor of New York, knew how to listen. In exchange for an endorsement from the principals' union, he gave the principals of New York City a protection previously unknown in the entire United States. Before Carey, principals had enjoyed the benefit of job tenure for life in a school system. Carey extended this protection. He saved low-performing principals from the inconvenience of being transferred from a building even if the school was low performing. This is how the *New York Times* explained Carey's payoff of the principals' union:

> The union's most stunning achievement was in the spring of 1975, when the Legislature was considering a measure to restore tenure for principals. Gov. Hugh L. Carey, who was grateful for the union's help in his election the previous fall, supported the bill strongly.

When it was being considered in the rush before adjournment, a last minute touch was added. Not only would principals be protected against dismissals unless formal charges were brought, but they could also not be transferred to other schools against their will.

The feature, known as tenure to a building, is singular to New York and has annoyed a succession of chancellors, who complained they were hampered in efforts to improve the system because they could not move around administrators.[5]

Hugh Carey's legacy in education was providing the children of New York with no-fault principals who could not be transferred. No matter how little leadership a principal provided, he or she could not be fired and not even moved to another building. Politicians since Carey from both parties have protested against tenure for life. Twenty years later, however, the protection for principals is weaker, but it is still difficult to dismiss a principal. Now in New York City, weak principals with tenure can be transferred from their buildings, but they can't be dismissed without years of appeals. Some makeshift job has to be found for them in a local district office at a cost to the taxpayers of around $80,000 each while they appeal. (This does not include benefits.) This cost of transferring principals out of schools while still having to pay their salaries for years as principals appeal their dismissals is a major burden for local schools. Today in New York City, principals essentially work without being accountable; only three of the more than one thousand principals have been fired since 1988, according to an article in the *New York Post*. Eleven more resigned rather than face charges.[6] At the very end of his first term as mayor and on the eve of an election, Republican mayor Rudolph Giuliani proposed eliminating tenure for principals, a move that would take the approval of the state legislature.[7]

Not surprisingly, with much larger and wealthier unions, teachers enjoy similar protections. New York City manages to fire about ten tenured teachers a year for incompetence out of a teaching corps of about fifty-five thousand. School board members estimate the cost in legal fees for dismissing a tenured teacher is about $100,000 in New York state.[8] So far, the politicians now in office, Mayor Michael Bloomberg and Governor George Pataki, have made no more progress on teacher and principal tenure than their predecessors.

SENIORITY RATHER THAN PERFORMANCE

This relationship of politicians to the well-organized professionals and their unions in the states is, of course, a central part of the politics of education. Neither party, as we will see in subsequent chapters, is rushing to challenge the protection of unionized education workers. The training of teachers received little attention in the media; an issue that receives even less attention in the media is the automatic salary increases local teachers receive. Teachers talk about colleagues who could be doing much better work but have no incentives to improve. These teachers receive annual raises based on seniority without any improvements in their work in the classroom and without any additional education or retraining. What if teachers' salaries depended on annual performance reviews rather than seniority? What if teachers were encouraged to bring evidence of their own growth as professionals to these performance evaluations? What if teachers had to bring in their written responses to twenty scholarly articles at annual review time? Rather than receiving automatic increases in salaries, we might see teachers reading articles about language development from the *Reading Research Quarterly,* the *Journal of Reading, Developmental Psychology,* and other journals that study cognitive development.

But by sending seniority-based salary increases to faculty, politicians do not encourage intellectual growth in teachers. They keep teachers as an undifferentiated mass—separated for salary purposes only by degrees obtained years ago. These salary differentials are published in the union contracts. The teacher with a master's degree and ten years' experience receives *x* more dollars than a teacher with a bachelor's degree with the same ten years. If neither teacher wants to mentor the new teachers in the building, that is fine. If neither teacher ever reads an article about cognitive psychology on his or her own time, this is fine. If neither teacher is willing to stay after school and coach the debate team, this is fine. The principal cannot punish them for their sloth. Performance-based salary reviews might lead to more cooperation in school buildings.

Of course, many factors influence literacy practices in secondary schools. In past chapters, we have looked at state curricula and the practice of a single textbook in such subjects as social studies to prepare for state exit tests, the authority and lack of authority of teachers, the schedule of teachers, the balkanization of teachers into subject areas, and the seniority clauses in the union contracts that may influence the technical expertise of teachers. But one more factor exists: Presumably policymakers in state education departments and local school districts have looked at the research on the practice of reading. Does adding time to the school day to sit and read silently—as the teacher does the same and thereby models reading—improve the reading skills of teenagers?

NOTES

1. Since the 1980s, New York City has reduced its dropout rate sharply through a new accounting procedure. Each teenager who leaves a high school to attend a GED program is not counted as a dropout regardless of whether this student finishes the GED program, passes the GED, or even attends the GED program for the second day. One day of attendance in the GED program is enough for the Board of Education to classify the student as a transfer rather than a dropout for accounting purposes. A similar sleight of hand now exists at the federal level. The federal government counts GED holders as high school graduates in its surveys of educational attainment in spite of data showing that GED holders do very poorly in four-year colleges as compared to young adults with four years of high school and a high school diploma.

2. See *McKinney's Consolidated Laws of New York Annotated,* 326, Section 3602.25 s.47 c.

3. Office of Educational Assessment, *High School Attendance Improvement Dropout Prevention (A.I.D.P.) Program, 1986–1987: End of Year Report* (New York: New York City Board of Education, 1987), 110.

4. Public Education Association, *Effective Dropout Prevention: An Analysis of the 1985–86 Program in New York City* (New York: Author, 1986), 7.

5. Neil A. Lewis, "Union Warns Fernandez on Proposals," *New York Times,* September 29, 1989, p. B3.

6. Angela Mosconi and Lawrence Goodman, "Crew Shapes Up for Tenure Battle with Principals," *New York Post,* April 27, 1996, p. 4.

7. Paul H. B. Shin, Jon Sorensen, and Laura Williams, "Rudy Seeks to Ax Principal Tenure," *Daily News,* September 16, 1997, p. 10.

8. Interview with Joyce Zaritskey, a former school board member in Dobbs Ferry, Westchester County, New York.

Chapter Twenty-One

Measuring Reading Programs

What Should the Researchers Be Doing?

Has poorly designed research become an additional barrier to improving the literacy of teenagers? Are university scholars capable of hit-and-run research where they arrive, looking for change in two or three months after the implementation of a new program and they write up their findings? Roger J. Pritzke, who has studied the evaluation of reading programs, doesn't use impolite phrases like "hit and run," but he thinks that each reading program should be given at least a year to prove itself rather than the eight- or nine- or ten-week measurement periods some researchers use. He says that the "length of study should be at least one school year."[1] (See table 21.1 for the length of the evaluations Pritzke studied.)

We would have to look at each study to see what was being done in the name of silent reading. For example, did teachers sit in front of their classes and model reading in each study, or did they spend the silent reading period grading papers or gabbing in the hall?

It is also possible that, as already mentioned, few of the studies took the time needed to measure changes in habits. For example, at Jefferson Junior High, described in chapter 14, a school recognized by President Ronald Reagan in the Federal Blue Ribbon School program, the principal reported that it took three years before the silent reading program led to changes in reading scores. It may be that silent reading in school eventually leads to more reading at home but that this change in reading habits takes far more time than researchers are willing to spend.

This same measurement error—making conclusions about silent reading programs after very brief studies—appeared in a recent federal study on reading from the National Reading Panel. Stephen Krashen, a professor of

Table 21.1.   Pritzke's Studies of Reading Evaluations

Evaluation Team	Length of Study	Length of Silent Reading Period	Result of Silent Reading Period
Mikulecky and Wolf	Nine weeks		No effect on comprehension
Evans and Towner	Ten weeks		No effect on comprehension
Farrell	One year	42 minutes	Positive effect on comprehension

Source: Roger J. Pritzke, "The Research on Uninterrupted Sustained Silent Reading," *Research on Reading in Secondary Schools*, Fifth Monograph (Tucson: Reading Department, College of Education, University of Arizona, Spring 1980).

education at the University of Southern California, believes that this federal study contained three major flaws: In addition to including very brief studies, the federal panel did not understand the research on ceiling effects in silent reading programs; that is, while silent reading may help weak reading improve, it may not help very strong readers do better on comprehension tests. If a study includes only strong readers, silent reading may not be influential. These readers may be close to the top of the tests to start with. Krashen also charged that the federal study also missed a number of important studies.

Krashen's arguments are detailed:

> In Davis (1988), according to the NRP, SSR helped medium level readers but not better readers. This is exactly what one would expect. SSR is designed to help less mature readers get better; those who are already excellent readers will not show dramatic gains. It is doubtful, for example, that readers of this note will improve if they add an extra ten minutes per day of reading for 180 days (one school year).[2]

He mentioned that some of the studies the panel included were very short term.

"Eight of the studies they list are very short term. I concluded that short term programs, less than one year, do not show consistent results, but longer term programs do. Some of the studies listed by the NRP lasted one or two months. It takes that long for children to settle down and get involved in a book. It is surprising that this was not pointed out, as the NRP listed Power of Reading as one of its sources for finding studies."

Finally, Krashen argues that the National Reading Panel simply missed a number of studies which show that silent reading is effective:

> The NRP did not include many long term studies that show SSR and similar programs to be effective, such as Elley and Mangubhai (1983), Elley (1991), Aronow (1961), Bohnhorst and Sellars (1959), Jenkins (1957), Bader, Veatch and Eldridge (1987), Mason and Krashen (1997), Hafiz and Tudor (1989), Greaney and Clarke (1973), and Johnson (1965). The omission of Warwick Elley's studies is especially mysterious, as they appeared in very prominent journals. In addition, some successful short term programs were not mentioned (see Krashen, 2000 for references).

Since growth as readers depends on the volume of reading being accomplished, it is difficult to see how teenagers who do not read much at home will become better readers without reading a great deal at school. Educators seeking to close the reading gap need to look closely at the studies Krashen cites. One reason for the success of Jefferson Junior High was that Principal Vera White had a vision based on research of what was necessary to develop more literate teenagers in her school. But it is difficult to imagine how school systems can immerse teachers and administrators in this research while still maintaining seniority-based reward systems.

What plans have our politicians of the last ten years had to move public schools away from current conditions to more productive organizations where both teachers and students will work more efficiently and effectively? The next section looks at the responses of Presidents Bill Clinton and George W. Bush.

NOTES

1. Joseph L. Vaughan Jr. and Patricia L. Anders, *Research on Reading in Secondary Schools,* Monograph Number 5 (Tempe: University of Arizona, 1980), 63.

2. See Stephen Krashen, "Comments on the National Reading Panel—Errors and Omissions," *Education Week,* May 20, 2000; available at www.languagebooks.com/education/2.0/articles/TheNational12.31PM.html.

Chapter Twenty-Two

Clinton to the Rescue?

> If it's true that New York City spends $8,000 a student on education but only $44 goes to books and other materials, that's a disgrace, that's wrong. And that's true in a lot of other school districts.
>
> —President Bill Clinton, March 27, 1996, speaking before the
> National Governors Association Education Summit[1]

Some of the tools that President Clinton used in his attempts to repair American schools are well known. To give youngsters a solid beginning with reading in elementary schools, he asked Congress to spend to reduce class size in the early years of elementary school. Congress agreed and money was spent. Twenty-nine thousand new teachers were hired under the initiative to reduce class size, according to a Clinton White House press release. An army of tutors were needed to help youngsters in danger of falling behind, President Clinton thought, and he persuaded Congress to create AmeriCorps, which hired young adults to provide a variety of social services, including tutoring. A third initiative to begin national testing of schools was controversial. Congress resisted voluntary national tests during the Clinton years only to adopt the mandatory national tests at the very beginning of the presidency of George W. Bush.

But what about literacy in the years after elementary schools? What about the issues of missing books and print-poor schools, and what about the ecology issues in high schools where teachers are expected to take 150 or 160 writing assignments home to grade each weekend? What exactly did President Clinton do for the students and teachers who live in American high schools, which Richard Elmore of Harvard has called "probably

either a close third or tied for second as the most pathological social institutions in our society after public health hospitals and prisons."[2]

President Clinton noticed a least one barrier to the literacy of teenagers
during his presidential campaign of 1996. In a speech at the National Governors Association in March 1996, he ripped a local school system, which
had not been buying many books. "If it's true that New York City spends
$8,000 a student on education but only $44 goes to books and other materials, that's a disgrace, that's wrong. And that's true in a lot of other
school districts," Clinton said.[3]

As Clinton continued talking about education in his reelection year,
things got worse: Clinton showed a fundamental misunderstanding of
how American children learn. Most of Clinton's policies and Bush's policies since then are based on the assumption that if only schools can produce effective readers in third grade, these youngsters will prosper for the
rest of their school careers.

On his campaign stops throughout the summer, Clinton told about the
dangers children face who fall behind in reading. He told audience after
audience about the worlds that would be closed to children who were not
fluent readers. On a campaign stop in Michigan, he proposed hiring teachers and paying them for the after-school tutoring of weak readers:

> We know—look at what we know—we know that students who can't read
> as well as they should by third grade are much less likely even to graduate
> from high school. We know that without reading, the history books are
> closed, the Internet is turned off, the promise of America is much harder to
> reach. We know the children who can read can learn from our founding fa-
> thers, explore the limits of the universe and build the future of their dreams.
> If we're going to ensure that those are the children of America's future, they
> need not only the best possible teaching in school, they need individualized
> tutoring, help with their homework before school, after school and over the
> summer, and they need more parents involved in helping them to learn to
> read and keep reading.
>
> To meet this challenge we need one million tutors ready and able to give
> our children the personal attention they need to catch up and get ahead. Today
> I propose a national literacy campaign to help our children learn to read by the
> third grade—a plan that offers 30,000 reading specialists and volunteer coor-
> dinators to communities that are willing to do their part. People who will mo-
> bilize the citizen army of volunteer tutors we need, America's reading corps.

We will only succeed, however, if the 30,000 are joined by legions of volunteers—seniors and teenagers, business and civic groups, libraries and religious institutions and, above all, parents. We have to build on the groundwork we have been laying by AmeriCorps, our nation's national service program. Today I am giving AmeriCorps a new charge: Make reading central to your mission.[4]

The president continued and talked about the success of AmeriCorps tutors in a county in Kentucky: "Let me tell you what they have done already. Let's just take one place—in Simpson County, Kentucky, a county in rural Kentucky, 25 of our young AmeriCorps volunteers helped 128 second-grade students make up almost three years of reading progress in just one school year. We can do that. We can do that."

Much of his speech is appealing. Reading as a link to our history and the founding fathers. Reminding us of the need to read to our children. But what about the heart of President Clinton's message: Will intervention in third grade be enough to keep youngsters on the road to be fluent readers and writers? James McPartland, a professor of sociology and the director of the Center for Social Organization of Schools (CSOS) at Johns Hopkins University, argues that this inoculation assumption is based on faulty interpretation of research.

He writes that third-grade reading skills and high school graduation rates may be associated, but if poverty is also considered, the correlation may not be strong enough to offset the problems of poverty for youngsters from high-poverty backgrounds:

> One assumption is that concentrating compensatory programs in high-poverty elementary schools to produce competent readers by an early (third) grade will set the foundation for students to successfully move through good programs in the middle and high school grades without any further extra help. By this reasoning, early intervention to prevent reading problems is the "inoculation" that poor students need to avoid failure in later grades. The competing view is that "booster shots" of compensatory support will be needed by many poor students to help them capitalize on early reading skills and prosper at high standards learning goals in the middle and high school years.
>
> Evaluations of early childhood and elementary grade interventions have frequently found that early achievement gains tend to fade away as students move on to later grades. Students from disadvantaged backgrounds who

moved ahead of comparable students that had not participated in early compensatory education programs often become indistinguishable from them in
following years if the extra help is not continued. . . .

The correlation between students' early reading scores and probabilities
of dropping out is frequently cited as evidence for concentrating extra educational resources in the early grades for students from high-poverty neighborhoods. Studies used to argue for early intervention have reported a high
correlation between third grade reading scores and high school dropout
rates. . . . But, instead of assuming a direct causal connection that a major
increase in early reading scores will be sufficient to produce major de-
creases in later dropout rates, the continuing role of another variable that is
strongly related to early test scores and dropout rates—student poverty—
should be fully acknowledged. We would expect the high poverty levels of
some students' homes and neighborhoods that contributed to low elementary grade achievement that calls for extra school resources to offset problems of poverty, will continue to weaken students' chances to achieve well
at later grades and require compensatory assistance for success at the more
advanced middle and high school learning goals.[5]

As the inoculation thesis—the belief that if students can read well in
third grade, they are more likely to finish high school—is now the cornerstone of federal educational policy, it is worth examining the support
for this thesis. For the two articles that McPartland cites as he discusses
inoculation, only the research by Dee Norman Lloyd addresses the pre-
dictive power of student characteristics in third grade. Lloyd studied a cohort or group of students from third grade through high school. He found
that a number of factors or variables including parents' educational levels,
occupation of father, IQ, marks in third grade, and scores in reading, arith-
metic and language on standardized tests would predict approximately 70
percent of the future dropouts. "Approximately three out of four students
were correctly predicted either to drop out or to graduate. The classifica-
tion was more accurate for graduates than for dropouts; however, approximately 7 of every 10 dropouts were correctly classified by the third-grade
measures," Lloyd writes.[6]

Third grade was chosen for a number of reasons, according to Lloyd:

The third grade was chosen as a point for comparison because standardized
tests were given in that grade. It also stands out as an important point in the

educational process both in the design of educational curriculum and in studies of achievement. As the last of the primary grades, the third grade is the point at which basic reading skills have been "taught (and hopefully learned), as well as the grade in which it has been estimated that 50% of future achievement patterns have been set.[7]

There are a number of reasons why this study, as well-designed as it looks, should not be the sole basis of the Clinton–Bush education policy.

First, the study says nothing about the skills of the teenagers who do graduate from high school; it only says that reading skills in third grade are associated with high school graduation. We have two educational crises in the United States, the low level of high school graduation—71 percent—and the fact that too many high school graduates lack the skills for success in college and the workplace. Lloyd's study was not designed to help understand the skills crisis, and does not contribute any information toward the skills crisis, yet the idea that third grade inoculation is enough has led to expensive investments in reducing class size in the early grades, and to no new federal investment in literacy in secondary schools that might influence skills.

Second, as McPartland pointed out, the effects of poverty are not clear in Lloyd's research. The study was small—1,552 students—and gathered from one school district. Were there sizeable numbers of poor people in the study? Readers don't know. Today a sample might be built to reflect demographics of the nation, rather than to use children from one school district.

The Lloyd study also faces the problem of more recent research. Subsequent studies have raised questions that inoculation in third or fourth grade will last until high school. Policymakers who believe inoculation is enough should also look at research conducted after New York City's attempts to inoculate its youngsters in the early 1980s.

When a new leader, Frank Machiarola, took over the New York City school system, he decided that social promotion was no longer acceptable. Beginning in the 1980–1981 school year, students were to meet standards in reading to be promoted after fourth grade and seventh grade. Fourth graders had to read within one year of grade level. Seventh graders had to read within one year and a half of grade level. Youngsters who failed to meet these criteria repeated fourth or seventh grade in special Gates classes receiving intensive instruction.

Fourth grade was selected as a gate because of the belief it is a "point at which the transition from reading readiness to reading comprehension is completed. Grade seven was selected to serve as a check point prior to entry into higher grades and high school."[8]

Richard Gampert, a researcher with the Office of Educational Assessment (OEA) in New York City, tracked a cohort for five years, and his results can cast doubt on the inoculation assumption — at least for at-risk students.

The Gates program provided intensive instruction in the year that the students were retained in fourth or seventh grade due to weak reading or mathematics scores, but what happened after the Gates year? Gampert explains, "Students who failed to meet their promotional criteria were retained and became eligible for placement in promotional Gates classes. The Gates classes provided intensive instruction to the students, particularly in the areas of reading and mathematics."[9]

To evaluate Gates, Gampert looked at the achievement of students selected for Gates classes five years later. He looked at their achievement on both reading and mathematics achievement tests.

Gampert concluded that the Gates program had succeeded in raising achievement in the year that students spend in Gates classes, but after students left Gates classes this progress failed to stick. "The initial gains in reading achievement were substantial; following the Gates year, however, students returned to a lower level of achievement and made only minimal gains thereafter."[10]

This failure to make progress after the Gates year was especially significant to the lives of youngsters who had repeated seventh grade in a Gates class. Five years after Gates, many who had been retained in Gates had already dropped out of high school. "By the 1986–1986 school year, approximately 40 percent of the seventh-grade Gates population had dropped out of school compared to 25 percent of the grade-comparison students."[11]

Gampert concluded that the early success of the Gates program for the retained students washed out because of the lack of services Gates students received after returning to regular classrooms:

> These results indicate that the majority of the Gates students made significant gains during the Gates year, particularly in reading achievement. The Promotional Policy, therefore, did produce initial increases in student achievement. Unfortunately, after the Gates year, students received few, if any, educational

or social services to assist them in building on those gains and they failed to continue to make adequate progress. These findings indicated that the school system has not provided the educational and social services necessary to ensure that the Gates students complete their educational on a timely basis.[12]

Prudence Opperman, also of the Office of Educational Assessment, wrote of the obstacles such as a lack of materials that existed even in the Gates classrooms. In other words, new intervention programs don't erase local obstacles.

INADEQUATE RESOURCES, INADEQUATE TRAINING

When Opperman and her research team evaluated Gates classrooms, they found that only 53 percent of Gates classroom had sufficient reading materials.[13] And these were special classrooms designed to provide intensive remediation in reading.

It would also be nice if the teachers had received adequate training before new money poured in. Raymond Domanico's evaluation of the teachers involved in the Gates program will shake the belief that spending more money is enough. He writes, "Some Gates teachers have no experience teaching reading and/or mathematics, a problem more prevalent in junior high schools than in elementary schools. Furthermore, some Gates teachers received no program training prior to teaching Gates classes."[14]

Will we see this situation again? Will federal money fund local programs where the local teachers are not well trained and where they do not have adequate resources? Is it time to nationalize the training of teachers in low-performing schools and to nationalize the supply of resources to these schools?

VIEWS AND RECOMMENDATIONS

Set a Benchmark—A Threshold

If the median reading score of youngsters in a school is more than one year below grade level, July needs to be the time to retrain the teachers in that school, public school, or charter school. Make a guarantee to these retrained teachers that when they return to school in the fall, resources will follow them. For once, the national government will send them books and paper. They will not need to organize bake sales or dip into their own wallets for the materials they need to be effective.

We need to hear this from our politicians. We need to nationalize these questions of the training of our teachers. Tell our teachers in low-performing schools that from now on they will need to spend July in training to become more effective teachers.

President Bush should ask Congress for the authority to abrogate the provisions of local contracts that limit the training of teachers already at work with our children. And move the training of teachers away from the local schools of education that have produced failures. If the FBI can provide a national training center at Quantico, why not create regional teacher training centers in our top schools of education? Use the new technologies of distance-based learning to create a consistent skill set for teachers if these technologies are effective. We need to create videos of successful teaching so that teachers can see that putting notes on a board for teenagers to copy is not a day's work.

After you have added training, add materials so that the national government will provide materials for schools, as Japan does. Then add time so that each below grade level reader will receive extra help for the duration of his or her school career.

Continue the programs for years for students who have read below grade level, not just a one-year approach. The literature makes it clear that a one-year tutoring program is not a serious attempt to improve the literacy of American youngsters. Reading is a developmental process. To grow as a reader, to develop as a reader, you have to keep reading more books each year. If you help in third grade and you want these results to stick, you have to keep helping. You have to keep providing books and encouragement to read and time to read during the school day and at home and over summers and holidays.

Is either political party ready to make an investment in struggling readers?

Training, changes in teachers' schedules, authority, authorship—the belief that your teaching matters—all are missing in too many American secondary schools. Is help on the way?

The Democrats do not seem to be engaged with the question of training teachers to be more effective in developing literacy. If school districts have to pay teachers with local funds for another month of training in the summer, this is a budget buster. New training will not occur. And the unions compete so aggressively for any scarce resources, that the monies needed for books, magazines and newspapers, and other classroom supplies are never adequate. Localism has failed in high-poverty schools, but the Democrats let the education show continue in the cities they control: poorly trained teachers working with inadequate resources in school after school. What do the Republicans think about these issues of training and adequate resources? What would intervention in high schools look like from Washington? While rejecting the inoculation thesis, McPartland is still optimistic about intervention in general. He writes:

> [T]here is growing evidence that extra help for low-performing high school students can produce significant learning gains that open the doors to enrollment and success in higher level high school courses in English, mathematics, and science. Effective extra help usually entails both additional time in basic academic courses in the early high school grades and new approaches to motivate students, build their confidence in basic subjects, and provide them with the skills they need to move on to advanced courses in the major subjects.[15]

Are the Republicans planning to deliver this help through No Child Left Behind, the cornerstone of President George W. Bush's plan for the nation's schools?

NOTES

1. Russell Ben-Ali and Corky Siemaszko, "Bill Lectures Govs on Ed," *Daily News*, March 28, 1996, p. 18. For the full text of the president's statement, see "Remarks by the President at the National Governors Association Education Summit," White House, Office of the Press Secretary, March 27, 1996.

2. Richard F. Elmore, "The Limits of 'Change,'" *Harvard Education Letter Research Online* (January/February 2002); available at www.edletter.org/current/limitsofchange.shtml.

3. Ben-Ali and Siemaszko, "Bill Lectures Govs on Ed."

4. See "Remarks by the President to the People of the Wyandotte Area, Bacon Memorial Public Library, Wyandotte, Michigan, August 27, 1996." President Clinton made similar remarks about helping third graders at the Congressional Hispanic Caucus Institute Dinner on September 25, 1996, and at other speaking engagements during the fall of 1996.

5. James McPartland, "Older Students Also Need Major Federal Compensatory Education Resources," paper presented at the Title I: Seizing the Opportunity Conference Sponsored by the Civil Rights Project, Harvard University and Citizens' Commission on Civil Rights, Washington, D.C., September 18, 1998; available at www.law.harvard.edu/civilrights/conferences/title/drafts/mcpartland.html.

6. Dee Norman Lloyd, "Prediction of School Failure from Third-Grade Data," *Educational and Psychological Measurement* 38 (1978): 1,194.

7. Lloyd, "Prediction of School Failure," 1,197.

8. Richard D. Gampert, *A Follow-Up Study of the 1982–83 Promotional Gates Students*, Office of Educational Assessment Evaluation (New York: New York City Board of Education, 1983), 10 (ERIC Document 303 556).

9. Gampert, *A Follow-Up Study*, 10.

10. Gampert, *A Follow-Up Study*, 7.

11. Gampert, *A Follow-Up Study*, 7.

12. Gampert, *A Follow-Up Study*, 7.

13. Prudence Opperman et al., *The 1982–83 Promotional Gates Program: Mid-Year Assessment and Analysis of August, 1982 and January, 1983 Test Results* (New York: New York City Board of Education, 1983), 29–30 (ERIC ED 237 597).

14. Opperman et al., "The 1982–83 Promotional Gates Program," 57.

15. McPartland, "Older Students."

Chapter Twenty-Three

What about the Republicans?

The Republican Party was once closely associated with American nationalism. Newcomers to the United States may not know that it was the Republicans who defended the nation during the American Civil War. It was a Republican president, Abraham Lincoln, who kept the nation together during the Civil War. It was a Republican, Theodore Roosevelt, who built a system of national parks and extended American military might into the Caribbean and Asia. More recently, it was the Republican Dwight Eisenhower who used our national government to help rebuilt Europe and Asia after World War II. While President Truman may be associated with the Marshall Plan to rebuild Europe in the 1940s, it was Eisenhower who worked to build political stability in Asia with new military alliances with Australia, Britain, France, New Zealand, Pakistan (until 1973), the Philippines, and Thailand through the South East Asia Treaty Organization (SEATO). The goal was to contain communism through the economic development of south Asia. And as Eisenhower used American foreign aid in Asia to train police officers, agronomists, and other scientists in Asia, he expanded the reach and influence of the federal government in Washington.

His successor, Richard M. Nixon, expanded the reach of the federal government at home. Nixon used the national government to add new protections to the environment through the Clean Water Act and the creation of the Department of Environmental Protection (EPA). He believed that the states were not going to be able to clean up the nation's air and water on their own. He believed that federal standards for air and water pollution were needed, and "sent Congress a thirty-seven point program for a 'total mobilization' on environmental issues."[1]

Are today's Republican leaders as willing to act in the national interest as Presidents Eisenhower and Nixon and expand the federal government in situations when only federal power and resources can influence the problem? Why, for example, has education not received the same attention from Republicans as Eisenhower paid to the political stability in South Asia or Nixon paid to the environment?

Why is Congress resisting more federal involvement and more control over local education? So why is there so much reverence in Washington for solving problems in education "at the local level"?

The answer as we will see may be that some local schools just don't need it. Their children can read well—at least by American standards. Their children score well on the college boards and graduate from college in large numbers. In some areas, the politics of education still work. Local school boards actually give teachers enough books and paper and chalk to work with. These local school boards are also able to identify incompetent teachers and remove them before they receive tenure. New York City's affluent suburbs of Westchester County are a case in point. The tradition in Westchester County is extreme localism. Each town, no matter how small, maintains its own elementary schools—sometimes combining efforts at the high school level. The small school systems in Westchester show how it is not just more money but also the size and scale of the system that matter. School board members in the small towns talk of conversations with citizens over the lettuce in the grocery story.[2] "You know, Joyce, that new third-grade teacher just isn't working out." After hearing a few more complaints, Joyce, the school board member, calls the superintendent who then observes the teacher's class. And if the superintendent ignores the school board's complaints, there is a solution for this also. Westchester County school boards are not afraid—in fact, some say they are even eager—to replace superintendents who retain ineffective teachers. These school board members in small towns and villages know the faculties of their schools teacher by teacher. Energetic school boards can force superintendents to maintain the quality of teaching or be replaced themselves.

Not surprisingly, there is no outcry from these suburbs to bring in the bureaucrats of the Department of Education. But a strong case can still be made for federal involvement. The success of these suburban schools in wealthy school districts does not in any way reduce the urgency of intervention in areas where the politics of education are not working. The federal government could still pick its spots, based on student achievement. I suggest that without federal intervention, education in the largest city school districts and in low-income states such as those in parts of the South will continue to be a sham. Given the number of students attending these schools, the lack of achievement matters to the entire country. Big cities will continue to operate what are now called "attendance centers," where the ritual of counting students is observed, but the substance of teaching English and mathematics is neglected. This national problem of low-achieving schools is not limited to big cities.

In the South, educational levels in some large states dropped during the 1980s. According to a recent report, "three of the region's most important states, however, Virginia, Georgia and Florida, *dropped* in the rankings in the seven year period, with all three showing discouraging declines in the actual graduation rates. . . . Georgia and Florida with [high school completion] rates of 61% and 58% respectively, have what appears to be an educational crisis on their hands."[3]

Is localism working in states such as Florida or Georgia or Louisiana, where an entire third of the population doesn't even finish high school and where high school completion rates declined during the 1980s? Table 23.1 shows the decline in graduation rates in the 1980s and that conditions have not improved in these states since then.[4]

In the United States, the national government continues to avoiding one of the responsibilities of a modern state—that is, responsibility for the literacy of its citizens. Local schools, no matter how bad, are allowed to remain in operation. On this issue, there is consensus. Our three branches of national

Table 23.1. High School Graduation Rates in Selected States, 1982–2000

	High School Graduation Rate (%)		
State	*1982*	*1988*	*2000*
Florida	65.4	58.0	55
Georgia	65.9	61.0	56
Louisiana	64.0	61.0	66
South Carolina	64.3	64.6	59
North Carolina	68.4	66.7	63
U.S. average	72.8%	71.1%	71%

Sources: Data for 1982–1988: Gary W. Tapp, *Southern Exposure: The South's Achilles Heel: Education Must Improve to Sustain Economic Growth* (Atlanta: Robinson-Humphrey, 1990), (404) 266-6000; data for 2000 are from the Manhattan Institute for Policy Research, available at www.manhattan-institute.org/html/cr_31_table_1.htm.

government so celebrated in civics books all agree. Don't interfere. If children don't have books to take home for homework, don't interfere. If cities continue to build schools so large that students literally get lost, don't interfere. If local boards of education still assign 150 or a 160 students a day to English teachers—as happens across the United States—don't interfere.

That's local business. Of course, these bizarre local practices are especially damaging to the literacy of the poor, who cannot learn a middle-class vocabulary at the dinner table. What can be done?

In other words, can there be a middle ground between today's federal policy of nihilism—no involvement in providing resources, no involvement in providing training, no demands for improved skills from individual teachers each year, and the invasions of busloads of GS-14s from the Department of Education ready to take over each and every local school at the other extreme? What would this involvement look like?

VIEWS AND RECOMMENDATIONS

If improving the literacy of American teenagers is the goal, and President Bush has said that closing the achievement gap is his goal, then make the materials needed to build the habit of reading accessible. We cannot as a nation compete with television and headphones by providing our youngsters with ditto sheets and textbooks. We need biographies, autobiographies, and novels and historical fiction in the hands of teachers.

Research on reading shows that accessibility to books is the factor most closely associated with the development of reading, but towns and cities across the nation have not responded to this research about accessibility.

Based on the experiences of the public school students whom I have interviewed, it's time to do something. Ditto sheets are not enough. A lumpish six-hundred-page textbook is not enough. Classroom discussions are not enough. Waiting years or even generations for the results of experiments with vouchers and charter schools is not necessary.

We know and we have known for years that to be a better reader, you need to have access to more books and do more reading. Local government has not responded to this research. In other nations, it is the national government that guarantees access to books. Access to books is not an issue in these nations. The central government is involved. Japan is an example of a nation where the central government ensures that each child has books. Japan moved from providing textbooks for youngsters with "financial difficulties" in the 1950s to free textbooks for all students beginning in 1963.[5] "This free distribution, in conjunction with national financial measures, was gradually introduced on a yearly basis from 1963, and the free distribution of textbooks to all grades in compulsory education was completed in 1969."[6] Currently in Japan, the national government pays half the cost of these free textbooks, with prefectures and municipalities paying the rest.[7]

Thomas Rohlen, who studies Japanese high schools, writes that Japan has a "willingness to make resource allocations [for books] automatic."[8] At one period in our history, Republicans wanted to do what Japan is doing now: make sure that all children had sufficient books. There was a time when Republicans thought of providing books for all American children.

The historians David Tyack, Robert Lowe, and Elisabeth Hansot write about the efforts of Republicans to use the federal government to intervene in the states:

> During the 1870s and 1880s, however, Republican congressmen from New England advocated granting federal aid for public schools under different plans of federal accountability. In 1870 George Hoar introduced a bill into the House that would not only have given the federal government authority to set standards and inspect schools, supervise production of textbooks, and even run schools where states were delinquent. It went too far even for most of his Yankee Republican colleagues and was condemned by the NEA as well.
>
> Later bills concentrated on allocating aid to states with a minimum of federal control and proposed grants in proportion to illiteracy in the states. Several of these passed either the House or the Senate, but none passed both; Gordon Lee attributes this defeat to Democratic legislators responsive to southern and Catholic opposition to federal aid.[9]

The Republicans of the nineteenth century wanted more centralization and more power in the federal government. They believed that the states could not be trusted to deliver effective education. Whereas Democrats had platform planks attacking Republican policies in education as undue centralization, Republicans repeatedly called for federal aid, arguing that "the free school is the promoter of that intelligence which is to preserve us as a free nation."[10]

Taxpayers may want to ask how much sense has it made for local governments to operate schools without adequate books for generations. How much sense has it made for the national government to ignore these fundamental deficiencies in local schools? How much sense does it make for the federal government to allow local school systems to provide seniority based wage increases rather than wage increases based on the acquisition of new skills?

In the end, these questions of rational government may not matter to Republican legislators. Just as Democratic legislators play it safe and do not disturb teachers' unions by calling for retraining of ineffective teachers, Republican legislators have stayed with Reagan's antinationalism during the 1990s. Antinationalism is a safe song; it is a song the party faithful want to hear. It is a song that helps keep their taxes as low as possible.

National education policy is still dominated by the beliefs of Ronald Reagan and his tax cuts. Newcomers to the United States may not know the full extent to which Reagan cut taxes and thus made any new expenditures by the federal government impossible.

So Reagan's legacy has two parts for his true believers to follow: The first part is never spend any money on government as new expenditures will sooner or later lead to tax increases on the rich. The second part is leave the states alone for generation after generation no matter how incompetent these states have proven to be.

Ironically, the Republicans are the ultimate statists. In state after state where both the governors and legislatures are Republicans, the Republicans continue to employ thousands of individuals who are often poorly equipped or poorly trained, but with teaching certificates from the states, these individuals have jobs for life.

STATES' RIGHTS

The Republicans would have the public believe that all problems with education can be attributed to weak federal programs, but federal spending on education is only 7 or 8 percent of total national education spending. It is states that provide credentials for life to teachers who are ineffective. And it is the states that protect these teachers. Congress could end state certification for life in low-performing schools. Lifetime certification is an assault against both common sense and a special assault on the lives of the poor who work with teachers who hand out ditto sheets rather than books or spend an entire period having students copy notes from the board, as the state inspections in New York City showed in chapter 19. There are alternatives to the lifetime certification which Republican governors continue to offer teachers. Provide the same requirements for teachers that other professionals face: lifelong continuing education. Nationalize these courses so that these credits mean something.

New York state, under a Republican governor, George Pataki, and Republican mayor, Rudolph Giuliani, allowed teachers to take exercise walking for academic credit during their sabbatical years as mentioned earlier. (See table 23.2 for a list of acceptable sabbatical courses.) This is not what taxpayers expect of tax-payer supported sabbaticals. But this course and empty courses are acceptable to Republican leaders such as Governor Pataki and Mayor Giuliani and to the previous Democrats in the same positions. Leaders of both parties rarely denounce teachers or the training teachers receive. They conveniently overlook how the weak standards they set for the teachers contribute to the low achievement of students.

There is no connection between what a teacher is allowed to take and the teacher's job. For example, the guidance counselor who alerted me to this waste took the course on exercise walking. How exercise walking made her a more effective guidance counselor is difficult to see.

And the courses listed in table 23.2 are only part of the scandal. If a teacher is able to complete fifteen credit hours of independent study in swimming

Table 23.2.   Spring 2001 Course Descriptions at the Kingsborough Community College, City University of New York

Course Title	Course	Credits
Walk, Jog, Run	PEC00200	1
Stress Management	HE03300	2
Intro to Television	MCB04500	3
Golden Ages of Radio and Television	MCB04500	3
Independent Study in Swimming	PEC081B4	1
Beginning Tennis	PEC1100	1
Exploring Leisure	REC07200	2
Skills in Arts and Crafts	REC03300	2
Deep Water Exercise for Fitness	PEC03300	1

Source: Lawrence Feigenbaum, director, Office of Teacher Studies, Kingsborough Community College, (718) 934-5946.

and beginning tennis during a sabbatical year, he or she is then eligible for a salary increase. Each level of education beyond a bachelor's degree leads to more salary—regardless of the quality of the courses. A course in "Exploring Leisure" counts for just as much as a course in "Language Development" in an applied linguistics program. The teachers' unions and the higher education industry—so eager to sell credits of any quality in any area—have conspired to deskill teaching and to deny children the presence of teachers whose training is appropriate to the situations they face.

But our Republican states' rights advocates will defend the rights of states to provide such taxpayer supported training in leisure and exercise walking. Rather than provide a national accreditation of all courses granting credits to teachers, they play the token solution game.

Providing two or three token charter schools in political jurisdictions will not help the majority of students who work with teachers who have taken exercise walking rather than cognitive development for academic credit.

Also in state after state, the Republicans impose curricula from state education departments on local schools. As the interviews show in chapters 7 through 10, these state curricula put boring and unchallenging materials on children's desks. When will Republicans rescue teachers from state curricula and move toward the obvious solution of syllabi with reading and writing assignments created by teachers and parents? When will our political leaders separate teachers from the bureaucracy that limits them and makes teachers invisible, inaccessible, and ineffective? A nation could decide that on every Wednesday a teacher's expectations for reading and writing for the following week are mailed out and posted on a web page. Teachers do not have to be invisible; it is our choice to hide teachers behind local and state bureaucracies.

When will the Republicans with their philosophy of deregulation rescue teachers from the century old tradition of control from above and ensure that teachers enjoy the same opportunities to be effective as other professionals?

VIEWS AND RECOMMENDATIONS

Teachers' Rights and Responsibilities

What rights should teachers have? If the New York state curriculum calls for memorization of the names of long-dead Indian emperors in a global history class, should a teacher be able to ignore this curriculum and assign a biography of Malcolm X, or Bill Gates, or Susan B. Anthony? When the goals of the state curricula and the development of reading skills conflict, which takes precedence?

While there are places in the curriculum where subjects need to be closely tied, the humanities are not such a place. Of course, teenagers need algebra in high school before they can succeed in statistics in college or graduate school, but they do not need endless survey history from sixth grade through freshman year in college. One can read and enjoy *Thurgood Marshall: Warrior at the Bar, Rebel on the Bench* without having studied the Reconstruction. In fact, just jumping into an era may motivate teenagers to want to learn more history—to go back into the past to see how the deal that ended Reconstruction led to the Jim Crow era—a major tragedy of the twentieth-century United States. History and English teachers need the freedom to develop reading lists from texts they are committed to, rather than the survey textbooks that now control the humanities in American secondary schools.

So far, Republicans have avoided these questions of the rights and responsibilities of teachers. They prefer their tried and true scapegoats in the 1990s. "Look at how bad bilingual education is," they cried, as if American schools were teaching the poor effectively before bilingual education began.

When will our political leaders from both parties decide what teachers need to be effective? When will they listen to survey after survey that discovered that teachers do not have adequate materials? (See appendix A for news stories about missing and inadequate materials.)

Since it is possible that voters may grow skeptical of the Republicans' reliance on local standards as the only tool of education reform and force a turn to new initiatives in education and literacy, the next chapter has some suggestions for providing more books for American parents and children. It also looks at the education proposals of President George W. Bush and No Child Left Behind, the bipartisan education bill. Are the new national tests he proposes capable of making public education far more productive? Students in cities such as New York already face state and local tests each year from grade 3 to grade 12.[11] They have faced these tests for the last twenty years, and these tests have not lead to a renaissance in public education in New York City. Why will his proposals succeed where past accountability efforts based on testing have failed?

NOTES

1. Timothy J. Conlan, *New Federalism: Intergovernmental Reform from Nixon to Reagan* (Washington, D.C.: Brookings Institution, 1988), 86–88.

2. Interviews from 1985 to 1987 with Joyce Zaritsky, a former school board member, Dobbs Ferry, Westchester County, New York.

3. Gary W. Tapp, *Southern Exposure: The South's Achilles Heel: Education Must Improve to Sustain Economic Growth* (Atlanta: Robinson-Humphrey, September 1990), 3.

4. Jay P. Greene and Marcus A. Winters, "Public School Graduation Rates in the United States," Civic Report 31, Manhattan Institute for Policy Research, November 2002; available at www.manhattan-institute.org/html/cr_31.htm.

5. National Institute for Educational Research of Japan, *The School Textbook System in Japan* (Tokyo: Author, May 1984), 3–4.

6. National Institute for Educational Research of Japan, *The School Textbook System in Japan.*

7. National Institute for Educational Research of Japan, *The Teaching Materials System in Japan* (Tokyo: Author, May 1984), 9.

8. Thomas Rohlen, "Differences That Make a Difference: Explaining Japan's Success," *Educational Policy* 9 (June 1, 1995): 103; available at www.elibrary.com. Rohlen's book, *Japanese High Schools* (Berkeley: University of California Press, 1983), is an excellent study of secondary schools in Japan.

9. David Tyack, Robert Lowe, and Elisabeth Hansot, *Public Schools in Hard Times: The Great Depression and Recent Years* (Cambridge, Mass.: Harvard University Press, 1984).

10. Tyack et al., *Public Schools in Hard Times.*

11. See a calendar of tests for New York City public school students at www.nycenet.edu/daa/schedule/index.html.

Chapter Twenty-Four

Why Postpone Literacy?

The Plans of President George W. Bush and the 107th Congress

Tragically, over the last seven and a half years of the Clinton–Gore Administration, our nation has experienced an education recession — decline and stagnation in student achievement. Too many schools are not teaching our children basic skills, such as reading and writing. Too many schools are plagued by violence and disorder that hinder learning and development. And children who want to excel in subjects like math and science are not given enough opportunities to realize their potential.

America must undertake education reforms to recover from this education recession. It is time for a change and a President who will challenge our schools, restore local control, empower parents, and help lead our students to success. To do so, our nation must have the courage to confront decline and stagnation in the following areas: Reading, Math and Science, School Safety, Character and Discipline, Closing the Achievement Gap.

> —From "America's Education Recession," George W. Bush's
> campaign promise to reform American
> education and close the achievement gap

Now that George W. Bush has been elected president, how will he fulfill the promises made in this quoted passage? What are his strategies for closing the achievement gap? What exactly is in the school reform toolbox that President Bush and the 107th Congress offered to the American people through the legislation known as "No Child Left Behind"?

The core provisions of the bill are easily presented. Notice the assumption throughout No Child Left Behind that localism—local control of schools—can still be made to work:

On Jan. 8, 2002, President Bush signed into law the *No Child Left Behind* Act of 2001 (NCLB). This new law represents his education reform plan and contains the most sweeping changes to the Elementary and Secondary Education Act (ESEA) since it was enacted in 1965. It changes the federal government's role in kindergarten-through-grade-12 education by asking America's schools to describe their success in terms of what each student accomplishes. The act contains the President's four basic education reform principles: stronger accountability for results, increased flexibility and local control, expanded options for parents, and an emphasis on teaching methods that have been proven to work.

An "accountable" education system involves several critical steps:

- States create their own standards for what a child should know and learn for all grades. Standards must be developed in math and reading immediately. Standards must also be developed for science by the 2005–06 school year.
- With standards in place, states must test every student's progress toward those standards by using tests that are aligned with the standards. Beginning in the 2002–03 school year, schools must administer tests in each of three grade spans: grades 3–5, grades 6–9, and grades 10–12 in all schools. Beginning in the 2005–06 school year, tests must be administered every year in grades 3 through 8 in math and reading. Beginning in the 2007–08 school year, science achievement must also be tested.
- Each state, school district, and school will be expected to make adequate yearly progress toward meeting state standards. This progress will be measured for all students by sorting test results for students who are economically disadvantaged, from racial or ethnic minority groups, have disabilities, or have limited English proficiency.
- School and district performance will be publicly reported in district and state report cards. Individual school results will be on the district report cards.
- If the district or school continually fails to make adequate progress toward the standards, then they will be held accountable.[1]

Will this new emphasis on state standards and accountability in No Child Left Behind lead American schools out of the educational recession, as President Bush has promised?

As noted in chapter 10, Samuel Bacharach, a professor of organizational behavior, stated that based on his survey research teachers will become more effective if working conditions change in five areas:

- Authority
- Time and space
- Human support
- Equipment, supplies, and materials
- Knowledge, skills, and information

How will No Child Left Behind influence these five conditions?

SUPPLIES, MATERIALS, AND VOLUME OF READING

Since an argument could be made that a shortage of books would be the easiest obstacle to remove, let's consider materials first. With more money to spend on materials, teachers will no longer be limited to the lumpish textbook that treats each topic in a paragraph or two and then races on to the next topic. Lynne Cheney called these textbooks "flea-markets of disconnected ideas" in chapter 8. Alternatives to these history textbooks that could now exist. And as teachers with bigger budgets for books could now assign biographies, historical novels, and other exciting materials, the volume of reading accomplished by teenagers will increase.

Some states have paid at least lip service to this idea that the volume of reading accomplished in high school needs to increase. California now expects its teenagers to read voraciously but completely on their own, without teachers providing books, without teachers recommending books, without teachers being able to make reading a central part of the curriculum. Here is an excerpt from the *English–Language Arts Content Standards for California Public Schools*: "In addition, by grade twelve, students read two million words annually on their own, including a wide variety of classic and contemporary literature, magazines, newspapers, and online information."[2] Two million words is an ambitious goal. With each book at fifty thousand words, students in California are now being asked to read forty books a year on their own.

Will the new education bill provide teachers of twelfth graders with any of these required forty books? Will there be a new program of direct federal aid to classroom teachers in high schools so that teachers can avoid the book shortages chronic in American classrooms?

The new bill, No Child Left Behind, does not provide a dollar of direct federal aid to classroom teachers in American public high schools. A change in the tax law later in the spring of 2002 provided a very small tax deduction for out of pocket purchases by teachers. "Teachers and other educators in public, private and religious elementary and secondary schools will now be able to take an above-the-line deduction for classroom expenses they incur of up to $250 per year."[3] But is a $250 tax deduction adequate? Is if fair to ask moderate income teachers to buy supplies out of their own pockets year after year? Here is what the *New York Times* discovered in September 2002, in the full first school year after the passage of No Child Left Behind: Nothing had changed in American classrooms.

In the two years since she gave up a business career to become a New York City teacher, Leslie Fiske has become a relentless bargain hunter. She combs the newspaper ads in August for hot deals on crayons and glue sticks. She has discount cards for Staples and Barnes & Noble, and has enlisted friends in the corporate world to donate stickers, pencils and award certificates.

Yet Ms. Fiske, a second-grade teacher at Public School 195 in the Soundview section of the Bronx, has still spent about $4,000 of her own money on books and supplies for her classroom, including $400 in the last few weeks. In other words, Ms. Fiske has funneled roughly 5 percent of her total earnings from her new career back into a school system that has long scrimped on everything from writing paper to paper towels. She is among legions of public school teachers around the country who dig deep into their own pockets to pay for the ever-larger list of supplies that schools insist they cannot afford.[4]

"What other job expects you, even subtly pressures you, to spend all your own money?" said Fiske, who has started her third year of teaching and adds more items to her list of needed supplies every day. "The expectation is that out of the goodness of our hearts, teachers should want to provide this stuff for our students, and frankly, that is what many of us end up doing."

Moreover, the situation that the *New York Times* noticed was national rather than local:

> While it is hardly a new phenomenon, the expectation that teachers should pay for their own supplies becomes more ingrained in the national mind-set every year. In March, President Bush signed into law a measure that allows teachers in both public and private schools a federal tax deduction of up to $250 annually for classroom expenses—perhaps the bluntest acknowledgment yet that such spending has become a job requirement. (Previously, teachers could only deduct work-related expenses, including the cost of classroom supplies, that exceeded 2 percent of their adjusted gross incomes, and only if they filed itemized tax returns.)
>
> And though teachers are hardly rich—the average national salary was $43,230 in 2001, according to the American Federation of Teachers—they do not cut corners. Elementary and middle school teachers spent an average of $521 of their own money on supplies in 2001, according to a survey by Quality Education Data Inc., a market research firm in Denver. A 1999 survey by the same firm found that those teaching kindergarten through 12th grade spent an average of $448.
>
> The 2001 survey of 4,618 teachers found that first-year teachers spent even more, about $700. It estimated that teachers' out-of-pocket expenses totaled more than $1 billion a year, on top of $700 million in discretionary funds provided by their school or district.[5]

How could this crisis of classroom materials be solved? Certainly the current plans of the Bush administration and Congress will not do it. If each high school teacher spent the entire tax-deductible amount of $250, this would provide only $1.56 for each of this teacher's 160 high school students.

Imagine a different scenario.

Imagine a history teacher at John Jay or Prospect Heights or another of the high schools in Brooklyn discussed in chapters 2 through 4 with 160 students—a typical high school teaching load. With $100 per student for ten new biographies and other trade books purchased at school discounts, this teacher could provide a print-rich environment where teenagers who entered high school reading below grade level could make progress in high school. As city high school students read more in grades 6 through 12, they also reduce the skill gap with their more affluent suburban peers.

How much would $100 per secondary school student available for each history teacher cost the federal treasury? With about twenty-four million secondary school students in grades 6 through 12, providing them with $100 of new books would cost about $2.4 billion.

But sending books without providing training is not efficient. Social studies teachers could provide half the opportunities to acquire reading and writing skills in secondary schools, a responsibility that their schedules and resources do not allow today. But these teachers need to see models—they need to see how reading is encouraged and how reading and writing assignments are tied together. They need to read the literature. A month of training in July with a monthly stipend of $4,000 each to make up for lost wages as camp counselors, tutors, grocery store clerks, and other summer jobs teachers take would cost another $800 million if only two hundred thousand teachers in the most at-risk schools were recruited. So, for under $4 billion, the nation could begin to make use of all of its secondary school teachers in the struggle to close the achievement gap.

Increase the Visibility of Books

The nation could also use the prestige of the federal government to increase the visibility of books. Since some teachers are not readers themselves, according to the interviews in chapter 6, then we need to increase the visibility of books nationally. Build a program so visible and attractive that teachers will want to join in. For once, build a new program that will pour aid directly into their classrooms, make their lives more productive, and give them the capacity to become better teachers. Create a national book-of-the-month program in history across American secondary schools, since social studies classes seem to be an area where little is now being done to develop literacy in teenagers. Have the federal government distribute these books directly to the teachers who order them at the beginning of the school year—at no charge. And provide multiple selections: the book of the month and alternates. Let the teachers select the books from a book list for the first time in their professional lives. For many this will be a new experience. Show them that their commitment to having their students read more is now a national priority. Show them that radically increasing the amount of pages read by teenagers is a national priority so important that the federal government will pay for it.

The funding and distribution would be straightforward. Simply create an account funded at a vendor such as Amazon.com, Barnesandnoble.com, or buy.com. Fund this account so each teacher could buy a biography or autobiography or a new trade book on a topic in current events each month for each of his or her 160 students. Of course, buying at this scale would incur a discount of at least 40 percent from the list price to further spread teachers' dollars. And since a nation interested in literacy wants youngsters in the habit of reading before they arrive in secondary schools, additional funding in the same amount would provide a book of the month for each K–6 student.

The goal would not be to collect and reuse the books for next year's students but to build the libraries of individual teenagers as participants in a recent White House conference have advocated:

> At a White House conference in July (2001), Assistant Secretary of Education Susan Neumann lamented how few children's books were found in libraries and stores in low-income areas. Dr. Neumann's own researchers counted 12 children's book titles available for every child in a middle-class neighborhood, but a single title for every 353 children in a poor one.
>
> Little access to books, she said, leads to poor achievement: low-income areas need an "environment rich in print—children need books to view." And they need these books read aloud to develop a feel for the flow of words and stories.[6]

Of course, Congress could intervene and provide the books that Neumann says are necessary. Congress could build the collections of books at home that parents may need to stay involved with their children's educations. In study after study, researchers at Johns Hopkins University have shown that much of the gap between the poor and the well-to-do is a result of a lack of cognitive growth in the poor while school is closed.[7] Having more books at home might contribute to closing the gap in the acquisition of cognitive skills while school is closed.

As a nation we could pay for the books, newspapers, and magazines of the poor. Buy site licenses from publishers for the rights to duplicate millions and millions of copies of best-selling books for children and teenagers. Imitate the Book of the Month Club. Send the poor monthly postcards with lists of books for the following month. Have them choose what they would like to receive to read. Mandate reading as part of all summer jobs programs for low-income teenagers. If you don't bring a book and read during the forty-five-minute silent reading program, you don't keep the federally funded job. Make a commitment to books and reading a central part of all federally funded youth programs. Keep the public schools open all summer so that librarians can run reading clubs for children and adults. Mandate that each elementary school have a library and a librarian, and use federal funds to help pay for these advances.

But the White House and the 107th Congress have not followed through on Neumann's research and the research of many other scholars in educational psychology and applied linguistics that has shown that access to books leads to more practice of reading and then to more fluency in reading.

Authority—Release the Teachers from Lock-Step State Curricula in the Humanities

A second federal intervention aimed at improving literacy in secondary schools would be to release teachers from lock-step state curricula in the humanities in schools where reading and writing skills are not being developed.

While a strong case can be made that mathematics education is sequential, that a teenager needs algebra in high school to learn statistics in college, the case for sequence in the humanities is much more difficult to argue. The current sequential humanities curriculum developed by the experts in state education departments is putting too many teenagers to sleep. Give teachers the authority to select better reading materials than clunky six-hundred-page textbooks. Theodore Sizer, the author of *Horace's Compromise*, one of the early and most popular books on school reform, and a founder of the Coalition for Essential Schools, a national school reform group, has strong opinions that the authority of teachers influences life in public schools:

> Even though they are expected to be competent scholars, they are rarely trusted with the selection of the texts and teaching materials they use, a particularly galling insult. Teachers are rarely consulted, much less given significant authority, over the rules and regulations governing the life of

their school; these usually come from "downtown." Rarely do they have any influence over who their colleagues will be; again, "downtown" decides. One wonders how good a law firm would be if it were given manuals on how to apply the law, were told precisely how much time to spend on each case, were directed how to govern its internal affairs, and had no say whatever in who the partners were. Teaching often lacks a sense of ownership, a sense among the teachers working together that the school is theirs, and that its future and their reputation are indistinguishable. Hired hands own nothing, and are told what to do, and have little stake in their enterprises. Teachers are treated like hired hands. Not surprisingly, they often act like hired hands.[8]

This treatment of teachers needs to change but change is not coming from the White House or Congress. The rules and regulations in No Child Left Behind are designed to help state bureaucracies push teenagers through laundry lists of unrelated facts and concepts. The terms *accountability* and *state standards* appear on page after page of the act; other phrases such as *volume of reading, frequent writing assignments, adequate resources,* and *authority of teachers* are nowhere to be found. Not every teenager can absorb two or three centuries of ancient Chinese, Egyptian, or Indian history in a forty-five-minute period—and then face a new topic the next day and a new topic the day after that, all to prepare for a new state test based on a new state standard. Some would rather read about the same characters in a biography or a historical novel for a week or two. Some teenagers may need books that are closer to home, closer to the topics they care about rather than the abstract laundry lists of ancient European, Asian, and African history. Use the federal government to provide choice, not to continue the myth that one size school fits all children. Replace abstract state accountability standards with personal contracts with teachers, who, in exchange for new federal funding for materials and training, will work outside the union contracts and communicate much more aggressively with parents.

Where Is Your Reading List?

In schools designed to build fluency in reading and writing, each teacher would provide parents with a reading list at the beginning of each month so that parents could buy or borrow or be provided with—depending on their income level—books to read along with their children. The reading list could be a contract between teachers and students and parents. Keep the state curriculum experts in the state capitols out. They have done enough damage to the quality of reading assigned in our secondary schools in humanities classes. Parents need to know that teachers are assigning books rather than just leading discussions. A reading list can be an indication of this. To many teachers in the humanities, constructing a reading list is a major part of the job of a teacher; constructing a reading list should be the essence of being an English teacher or social studies teacher in a secondary school just as it is in higher education. If a teacher lacks the authority to construct a reading list because of a state mandate to cover material or because of budget shortages, he or she is not a professional. And the links between the deprofessionalization of city teachers and the lack of literacy in their students are obvious.

Parents, policymakers, and the media need to realize that teachers' expectations for reading depend on the books that they can find for their students to read. If teachers cannot order books year after year, their expectations shrink. Their enthusiasm declines.

Where Is the Funding Being Spent Now?

Unfortunately, in spite of large increases in federal spending, secondary schoolteachers should not look for help from Washington from the landmark bill No Child Left Behind. While the bill and the press release about the bill mention literacy repeatedly, Congress is targeting little new money on literacy except in the Reading First initiatives, which amounts to only $1.5 billion spread over the entire nation for fiscal year 2002, and these reading initiatives are available only for K–3 and earlier. Instead, Congress has decided once again to depend on the states, and the school districts in the states, called local education agencies (LEAs), to apply for federal grants to improve academic performance among low-income children, and these grants must be tightly connected to state content standards. The term *content standards* appears prominently in the federal government's instructions to the states and their school districts. Each state request for federal funding must meet the requirements stated here:

CHALLENGING ACADEMIC STANDARDS. Standards under this paragraph shall include—

(i) challenging academic content standards in academic subjects that—
  (I) specify what children are expected to know and be able to do;
  (II) contain coherent and rigorous content; and
  (III) encourage the teaching of advanced skills; and
(ii) challenging student academic achievement standards that—
  (I) are aligned with the State's academic content standards;
  (II) describe two levels of high achievement (proficient and advanced) that determine how well children are mastering the material in the State academic content standards; and
  (III) describe a third level of achievement (basic) to provide complete information about the progress of the lower-achieving children toward mastering the proficient and advanced levels of achievement.

Teachers are left out. Only school districts can apply for the $13.5 billion in federal funding for fiscal year 2002 that No Child Left Behind provides. Parents are left out. Low-income parents will not be choosing new books for their children through this bill. This act—passed with bipartisan support—does not move the nation's teenagers closer to the reading and writing skills they need to succeed in higher education and in the workplace. Trusting local teachers, giving them new resources, and strengthening the profession of teaching are not parts of No Child Left Behind. Rather than providing the "increased flexibility" and "expanded options for parents" it promises, this legislation reinforces the power of local bureaucrats and ignores the needs of local teachers.

When the federal government supports teachers and provides adequate resources in each classroom regardless of the local tax base or the customs of local bureaucracies, then we will see exciting books and engaging writing assignments. Then we will see teenagers who had to read widely and write frequently in high school rather than listen to lectures to prepare for state tests. Then, perhaps, more teenagers will arrive in college classrooms confident in their reading and writing skills with the belief that they belong in college. But the same localism that has produced shortages of books, factory schools where each teacher sees 160 students a day, teachers without authority, and high school graduates with weak skills will not be disturbed by No Child Left Behind. Congress and the White House could have done much better.

NOTES

1. A Department of Education introduction to No Child Left Behind is available at www.nochildleftbehind.gov/next/overview/index.html. Very readable summaries are available at other Washington public policy websites such as the Learning First Alliance at www.learningfirst.org/esea-related-resources.html.

2. California State Board of Education, *English–Language Arts Content Standards, Kindergarten through Grade Twelve*, adopted December 1997, p. 66; available at www.cde.ca.gov/board/pdf/reading.pdf or www.cde.ca.gov/standards/reading/grade1112.html.

3. See a press release from the Department of Education of April 15, 2002, at www.ed.gov/PressReleases/04-2002/04152002.html.

4. Abby Goodnough, "Teachers Dig Deeper to Fill Gap in Supplies," *New York Times*, September 21, 2002.

5. Goodnough, "Teachers Dig Deeper."

6. Richard Rothstein, "Both Sides Are Right in Reading Wars," *New York Times*, September 5, 2001, p. A-17.

7. Doris R. Entwisle, Karl L. Alexander, and Linda Steffel Olson, "Summer Learning and Home Environment," in *A Nation at Risk: Preserving Public Education as an Engine for Social Mobility*, ed. Richard D. Kahlenberg (New York: Century Foundation, 2000), 16.

8. Theodore Sizer, *Horace's Compromise: The Dilemma of the American High School* (Boston: Houghton Mifflin, 1984), 184.

Appendix A

National Press Clippings about Missing Books

CALIFORNIA

Straitjacketed Schools

Book shortages have plagued classrooms in both northern and southern California, according to reports from the *Los Angeles Times, San Francisco Chronicle,* and *New York Times.*
Source: Amy Pyle, "Book Shortage Plagues L.A. Unified; Education: High School Students Often Don't Have Texts for Classes, Despite States Law," *Los Angeles Times,* July 28, 1997.

Sophomore Angeles Herrera hurries down the halls of Fremont High School with a single slim notebook tucked under her arm. She carries no textbooks because she has none.

Textbooks remain the essential guide to education, second in importance only to competent teachers. But book shortages have become so common in big-city high schools that Angeles doesn't know she should expect more— that, in fact, state law guarantees her a text for every class. Ask when she last had a textbook of her own and Angeles looks puzzled. Was it French last semester? Yes, she thinks so. And maybe algebra last year.

In the absence of take-home books, she spends chunks of valuable classroom time reading and copying from a class set of 30 books shared by up to 150 students daily. Sometimes there are not even enough of those to go around.

Angeles senses the void most acutely when she digs into her homework at night. "You don't have the book for examples," she said. When she gets confused, she telephones a classmate and they try to muddle through together.

Her plight is education's tragic secret, one that threatens to undermine a generation's literacy: Across the nation, students routinely make do without textbooks in one or more classes. Those in urban areas fare worse than their suburban cousins. California's public school students are among the worst off, thanks to lower education funding, radically shifting education philosophies and a faster-growing, more transient public school population.

The problem remains hidden because it is rarely quantified. The 663-campus Los Angeles Unified School District can't take stock because it eliminated its centralized book purchasing department in 1990 to save money.

One of the few surveys on the subject, conducted last year by the Assn. of American Publishers in conjunction with the National Education Assn., found that 54% of California teachers did not have enough books to send home with their students, compared to 39% nationwide. A quarter of the California teachers said their students did not even have books to use in class.

Critical Situation in the High Schools

Source: "Straitjacketed Education: School District Needs Comprehensive Approach to Textbook Shortage" (editorial), *Los Angeles Times,* August 7, 1997.

The school board is expected to take up the textbook shortage Aug. 18, the next regularly scheduled meeting. Members should concentrate on solutions instead of reacting defensively to *Times* articles describing the shortage and quibbling over whether the district spends a woeful $26 per student on textbooks or a slightly less woeful $32. The district sets aside as much as $72 per student for instructional materials, but that must cover textbooks, workbooks, computer software, lab supplies and even paper and pencils. Finding new funds may prove easier than in past years because of a state revenue surge. That's in addition to Proposition BB bond money, which frees up general funds that previously were siphoned off for repairs. Private efforts like the one for Fremont High School, reported in the *Times* today, also can be part of the solution.

School board member Jeff Horton, a leader on the textbook issue, is expected to propose remedies that along with benefiting classrooms would restock school libraries, which suffered greatly during two decades of tight budgets. His colleague David Tokofsky would increase the textbook budget and also penalties on students who fail to turn in textbooks, a burden particularly at schools with high transiency.

Zacarias and the board need to take all these ideas and develop a comprehensive plan to restock classrooms now and keep them well-stocked.

The shortage is most critical in high schools. Too often textbooks may not be taken from the classrooms. Without take-home books, homework becomes guesswork and tests must be taken on material that could not be reviewed. The removal of this educational straitjacket seems very little to ask.

Missing Literature Books

Source: Lori Olszewski, "Shortages Plague Oakland Schools: Parents, Teachers Fuming over Lack of Books, Supplies," *San Francisco Chronicle*, October 10, 1997, p. A17.

A month after the start of school, some Oakland children still are without key textbooks in crowded classrooms, and teachers are being yanked from their students and reassigned.

Critics of the Oakland Unified School District say the continuing problems are indicative of a bureaucracy that is not doing its job despite its generous salaries.

Parents from Bret Harte Middle School said their children went without textbooks for four weeks as their principal worked to track them down. Many of the missing literature books finally found their way to school Wednesday.

THE SOUTH

Statewide Book Shortages

Source: Felton West, "Education Board Should Survey, Meet School Needs," *Houston Post,* September 22, 1992, p. A-21.

The basics needed for effective education are still missing in Texas. According to a survey organized by the Texas Federation of Teachers in 1992, "more than 72 percent of the teachers who responded to the survey said they lacked teaching materials, such as pens, pencils, mimeograph paper, construction paper, chalk, staples and computer paper . . . almost 30 percent of the survey respondents said their classes were short of textbooks . . . less than 8 percent of the respondents said they had all the teaching tools they needed."

No Reading Books to Take Home

Source: Diane Loupe, "Parents Criticize DeKalb Schools; Book Short-ages, Dirty Facilities and Unfair Treatment on List of Complaints," *Atlanta Constitution,* October 21, 1998, p. 01B.

Almost 200 parents complained to the DeKalb school board Tuesday night about a broad agenda of problems, from inequities between black and white schools, to textbook shortages, dirty schools and a lack of respect for Muslim students during religious holidays.

Tuesday's hearing at Tucker High School on the results of a scathing critique of the 93,000-student school system will be followed Thursday by a similar hearing at Towers High School at 7 p.m., which promises to be more explosive.

A team from Phi Delta Kappa, an international education fraternity, was paid by the school system to evaluate the system. It reported that the system's curriculum is inadequate, many teachers use ineffective teaching strategies, and there are unequal resources between affluent schools and poor, majority black schools.

"I stayed up all night reading the whole thing. It made me cry, some of the things I read," said Martha Hutchins, who complained about filthy conditions at McNair Junior and Senior High schools. "What happened before this audit? Did you not know all these things were going on?

"I'm here to say I'm not going to take it anymore. I want accountability," Hutchins said.

Several parents complained about textbook shortages. Parents told of fifth-grade reading books that were not allowed to be sent home; middle-school algebra textbooks returned because the word algebra was misspelled on the spine; and an elementary math textbook so confusing that teachers abandoned the text for their own supplementary materials.

Children Prevented from Taking Books Home

Source: Kent Fischer, "Textbook Shortage Not a Concern," *St. Petersburg Times,* October 10, 1998, p. 1.

Textbooks have become a hot-button education issue as many parents and lawmakers have begun to question why some children have to share books or are prevented from taking their books home.

Last legislative session, state Sen. Anna Cowin, R-Leesburg, slipped some fine print into the Senate's education budget that would have required schools to buy enough books for every child in every class. The proposal was killed, although the Legislature did increase textbook funding 17 percent, to $ 181.9-million, this year.

NEW ENGLAND

Boston Schools Short of Books

Source: Lauren Robinson, "Boston Schools Short of Books Despite Vows — Availability to Students Is Varied," *Boston Globe,* October 20, 1992, p. 1+.

The *Boston Globe* in the 1990s talked about kids who leave school each day "empty-handed" without the books needed for homework. It talked about classrooms where books must be shared in class:

> Nearly a year after Boston officials promised adequate supplies of text-books for the beleaguered system, thousands of students still go home empty-handed from school.
>
> In some classrooms, there are so few books that students must share them in class, while parents who believe that homework is not possible without textbooks express fears that their children will only lag further behind their contemporaries in other school systems.

The *Boston Globe* showed that public schools and private schools have different attitudes toward what classrooms and youngsters need.

> One parent, Hetty Mitchell of Mattapan, watched one day last week as her daughter Elizabeth, with three hours of homework already under her belt, flipped past the page she was assigned to work up to in her French textbook, determined to learn more.
>
> But Elizabeth attends private school, while two of her sisters who attend Boston public schools can only bring worksheets home from school.
>
> Mitchell said when Amanda, 11, and Andrea, 7, do homework from work sheets it usually takes no more than an hour per evening. She does not believe the work she has seen is enough to reinforce what has been taught in class or to encourage family involvement in education.

"I think that by fifth grade they should have books—for the classroom and for homework," Mitchell said. "I want to see the books so that I know what my children are being taught."

To avoid this nightmare, the *Globe* shows that some parents stretch and pay for private schools in cities like Boston. These parents believe that children should leave school with books in their hands.

Edward L. Bullock, a sales support specialist from Mattapan who attended Boston public schools, said he is "broke" from sending his children, Jarod, 9, and twins, 5, to private schools but that he will keep them there. Bullock said he is appalled when he sees public school children stepping off school buses at the end of the day with "nothing in their hands."

"It's unconscionable to me because homework is an extension of the classroom. It means that learning does not end in school and it's a chance to find out if the teacher was understood," Bullock said. "These kids need every opportunity to get an early start and I just don't see that happening."

Little School Aid in New Hampshire

Source: Fox Butterfield, "In New Hampshire, Needy Schools Test a Tradition: Little School Aid," *New York Times,* January 2, 1992, p. A-1+.

The school system had to lay off its librarians and art teachers, and last spring it ran out of paper for students. Pupils in the sixth, seventh and eighth grades must share textbooks, so that, Mrs. Viar said, "if you have a test on Monday and it isn't your weekend to have the book, you are out of luck."

Lack of Books and Funds in New York City

Sources: Gene I. Maeroff, "Overcoming Obstacles in a Student's Home," *New York Times,* March 5, 1985, p. C-1; Raphael Sugarman, "Kids Burned on Books—Crisis Has Them Going Home Empty-Handed," *Daily News,* June 12, 1994, p. 3; and Josh Barbanel, "$7,512 Per Pupil: Where Does It Go?" *New York Times,* January 23, 1994, p. 1+.

In the mid-1980s, the *New York Times* discovered an entire school district in Brooklyn with twenty thousand students where books were not allowed to be taken home. According to the *Times,* "schools in District 16 have for the most part stopped giving work that calls for taking the books home." As the *Times* explained, "the books are kept in school and assignments are on mimeographed papers because the district cannot afford to replace the textbooks that were regularly lost when pupils took them home.

Shortages of books continued in the late 1990s, as the *Daily News* and the *New York Times* report:

> Meager textbook allocations and threats of still more budget cuts make it unthinkable for many teachers and principals to let precious books leave their classrooms. "If a child loses a book, we might not be able to replace it for two or three years," said Gloria Guzman, principal of PS in Sunnyside, who admitted the effect of children not taking their books home is "devastating."

The *Daily News* noted, "'New York City public schools receive less than $35 a student in textbook money,' said Max Messer, president of the New York City Superintendents' Association. 'Roughly $30 a year comes from the state, the remainder from discretionary funds of individual schools,' he said."

In 1994, the *New York Times* reported that "across the city, a half penny of every dollar went for library books and textbooks." In this story, the *Times* noted that the average amount being spent on textbooks was $32.50, and the citywide average for library books was $4.79.

Appendix B

Student and Teacher Interview Guides

STUDENT INTERVIEW GUIDE COVER SHEET

Date:_____

Student Name:_____ Date of Birth:_____

Age:_____ Sex: M F Name of School:_____

Borough:_____Year in School:_____

Residence: What neighborhood_____

Junior High School Attended:_____Elementary School:_____

Type of Secondary School: Public or Catholic

If Public High School: **If Public School:**

Neighborhood   Regents Classes

Vocational   Non-Regents Classes

Educational-Option

Science

Usual arrival time:_____   Usual departure time:_____

Are you enrolled in a special program such as a magnet or educational

option in this school:_____

Do you work after school?_____

Do you work on the weekends:_____Total hours of work per week:_____

STUDENT INTERVIEW GUIDE

(Responses were written in after the questions during the original interviews.)

1. Please tell me what happens in your school during the school week. What classes do you take? What labs or special programs do you go to?
2. Do you have a different teacher for each subject? *Probe:* Which subjects are combined?
3. Are there any special programs after school or before school that you go to?
4. Does this school give you a list of books that your teachers want you to read for each course such as English?
5. Did this school give you a list of books to read during the summer before school started?

(Skip question 6 for high school students.)

6. In your school, do you go to a separate English and a separate Language Arts class, or are the two classes combined?
7. Are you enrolled in a separate reading class? Is it a Chapter I class?
8. In this school, do you have a time to read to yourself during the school day? *Probe:* What is this reading period like?
9. How long does this reading period last?
10. How many times a week do you have this reading period?
11. Do you choose what you read during this silent reading period? What do you usually read during this silent reading period?
12. What does your teacher do during this reading period?
13. In this school, do you buy your books or do you borrow them from the school?
14. What kinds of things do you work on in your English class?
15. Does your English class that you are taking now have a particular name, like English I or English II?
16. Tell me about the books that you use in your English class. If little response, then *probe:* Do you have a textbook? What else do you read in your English class?
17. What are these books like that your teacher asks you to read for your English class?
18. How much of the books do you really read?
19. Does your English teacher or reading teacher or language arts teacher take you to the library each week?
20. Do you go to the library on your own each week?
21. When was the last time that you went to the library?

22. About how many books have you taken out of the school library this year?
23. Which book was the best one?
24. Getting back to the books, are you allowed to take all of your English books home? *Probe:* Which of your English books are you allowed to take home?
25. How many books have you read this year for your English class?
26. Which of the books that you have read this year in English would you recommend to a friend to read?
27. Are there other good books that you read this year in English class?
28. Which was the worst book assigned so far this year in English class?
29. What kind of shape are your English books in?
30. How many times a week do you take books home in order to do English homework?
31. We talked about buying books before, and you said that you buy _____books in this school. *Probe if appropriate:* Does this ever change? Do any of your teachers ever ask you to buy paperback books? (The next three questions will then only be asked of students who have ever bought books.)
32. Which books have you bought so far this year?
33. Where do you get the money to buy these books?
34. Where do you buy these books?

If the student has a social studies class, then the next thirteen questions will be asked.

35. What have you worked on so far this year in your social studies class? What kinds of things are you studying now in social studies?
36. Does your social studies class that you are taking now have a particular name, like Social Studies I or Social Studies II or Global History?
37. Tell me about the books that you use in your social studies class. If little response, then *probe:* Do you have a textbook? What else do you read in your social studies class?
38. What are these books like that your social studies teacher asks you to read?
39. Does your social studies teacher take you to the library each week?

40. Getting back to the books, are you allowed to take all of your social studies books home? If not, which social studies books are you allowed to take home? Which social studies books are you not allowed to take home?
41. How many times a week do you take books from your social studies class home in order to do homework?
42. How many books have you read this year for your social studies class?
43. Which of the books that you have read this year in social studies would you recommend a friend to read?
44. Are there other good books that you read this year in social studies class?
45. Which was the worst book assigned so far this year in social studies class?
46. If appropriate—that is, affirmative in 13 or 31: Does your social studies teacher have you buy any of the books you read for social studies class?
47. Which social studies books have you bought so far this year?

The next thirteen questions will only be asked of students who take reading or language arts in addition to English and social studies. Skip to 61 if student has a Chapter I class, but not a language arts class. Skip to 73 if student doesn't have a separate language arts class or Chapter I class.

48. What do you work on in your language arts class?
49. Does your language arts class that you are now taking have a particular name, like Language Arts I or Language Arts II?
50. Tell me about the books that you use in your language arts class. If little response, then *probe:* Do you have a textbook? What else do you read in your language arts class? What are the books in language arts class like?
51. Does your language arts teacher or reading teacher take you to the library each week?
52. Getting back to the books, are you allowed to take all of your language arts books home? *Probe if appropriate:* Which books are you allowed to take home? Which books aren't you allowed to take home?

53. How many books have you read this year for your language arts class?
54. Which of the books that you have read this year in language arts would you recommend a friend to read?
55. Are there other good books that you read this year in language arts class?
56. Which was the worst book assigned so far this year in language arts class?

The next three questions will only be asked if the student has previously said that he or she has bought books:

57. Does your language arts teacher have you buy any of the books you read for language arts class?
58. Which books have you bought so far this year?
59. Where do you get the money to buy these books?
60. Where do you buy these books?
61. Some schools have special programs for reading. Some of these programs are called Reading Enrichment, or Chapter I or PSEN. I would like to ask you if you are in any of these special programs. Do you go to a special reading program at any time during the week? What is it called?
62. Tell me about the books that you use in your special reading class. If little response, then *probe:* Do you have a textbook? Do you have workbooks? What do you read in your reading class? What are the books in your reading class like?
63. Does your reading teacher take you to the library each week?
64. Getting back to the books, are you allowed to take all of your reading books home? *Probe if appropriate:* Which books are you allowed to take home? Which books aren't you allowed to take home?
65. How many books have you read this year for your reading class?
66. Which of the books that you have read this year in reading class would you recommend a friend to read?
67. Are there other good books that you read this year in reading class?
68. Which was the worst book assigned so far this year in reading class?

The next three questions will only be asked if the student has previously said that he or she has bought books:

69. Does your reading teacher have you buy any of the books you read for reading class?
70. Which books have you bought so far this year?
71. Where do you get the money to buy these books?
72. Where do you buy these books?
73. In total, in all of your classes, how many books have your teachers had you read this year?
74. How do the teachers know that you read the books?
75. Do you like writing book reports?
76. How many book reports have you written so far this year?
77. Do you like taking tests on books?
78. About how many tests on books have you taken so far this year?
79. In general, what are the textbooks like that you have used this year?
80. What about any other books that the school has assigned, what are they like?

TEACHER INTERVIEW GUIDE

Teacher Cover Sheet

Name:_____ Date:_____

School:_____ Department:_____

Years at This School:_____ Years in Teaching:_____

State Licenses Held:_____

Highest Level of Education:_____

Any Administrative Duties:_____

_____

Any Duties in Extracurricular Programs:_____

_____

Any Duties in Staff Development:_____

_____

Public School Teacher Interview Guide

These are the questions composed February 11, 1996; questions 2–4 and 34–39 were added on March 1, 1996, after the first interview. Responses were taped and then transcribed.

1. How has the school year been so far?
2. What are the students like in your school? Could you describe them, please?
3. What neighborhoods do the students come from?
4. Do students in your school choose your classes or are they scheduled into them?
5. What classes are you teaching this year? How many minutes does each class last? Are the sections together for the entire year or only one semester?
6. What kind of homework do you give your students in these classes this year?
7. What are your tests based on? In other words, what do your students need to study for your tests?
8. There has been talk about giving teachers more influence over budgeting? Who makes decisions about such items as buying new books for your classes?
9. Which new books were you able to order this year?
10. If applicable, how many copies of each title?
11. How many students do you have? In other words, does each student have a copy of each book? Can they take the books home or do the books stay in school?
12. We have talked about new books. Now, I'd like to look at all the reading available to the students? Which textbooks, paperbacks, magazines, newspapers are your students reading for your class this year? What are all the titles?
13. Do you have your students read in class? Out loud or silently? How many times a week, for how long?
14. Do you hand out a booklist or a syllabus with reading assignments each semester? May I have a copy of your syllabus?
15. How do you like the books you are using this year?
16. About how many pages a week do they read in their textbook or paperback for homework for your class?
17. How do you know that they have done this reading?
18. Now I would like to ask some questions about how the students feel about the books they are reading. What do you think your students think of the books they are reading for your class? Any comments which really stick out in your mind?

19. Which books do you think your students have especially enjoyed this year?

20. Does your school or department have a procedure to evaluate what students think of the books they have been given?

21. Can you have the students buy paperbacks for your class? Is there a school policy about asking students to buy books beyond what the school provides? Or is this decision left up to individual teachers?

22. If applicable, which paperbacks did you ask them to buy this year?

23. In some schools—I.S. 51, for example—the PTA provides some funds for additional books? Any help from the PTA here?

24. What do you think of the books your students have?

25. How effective is your school in building the habit of reading in students?

26. Some teachers say that they see students who don't like to read. These students actively resist reading and may try to turn the class against reading assignments. Do you see resistance to reading assignments in your classes? If applicable, how do you deal with it?

27. How do you think students developed this resistance to reading?

28. What is the library in the school like in terms of books that you would like for your students to read?

29. About how many books have your students taken out of the library and read for your class this year?

30. Who are your favorite writers? Did you use any of these writers in school this year?

31. About how much does your school spent on books per student each year?

32. What do you think of this level of spending?

33. What changes, if any, would you like to see in terms of how your school obtains books?

34. What else should I ask you about books and reading and homework in your school? What additional questions could I ask to find out more about how your school deals with reading?

35. *For veteran teachers with more than two years at a school:* You have probably had more than one principal at this school. How many principals have you worked with? How effective have they been in improving the reading skills of students in this high school?

36. In your years at this school, what has the union done to improve education in the classrooms?

37. What has the teachers' choice program done for your classes? How does it work in your building? What have you been able to buy with it? Do you know the exact amount it provides?
38. What has the training been like this year? What has the training been like in general over your career?
39. Are teachers treated as professionals in your school? If applicable, what changes would you like to see in how teachers are treated in your school?
40. What else should I ask you about your school?

Summer Reading for St. Albans Upper School, Washington, D.C.*

In the Upper School at St. Albans some years ago summer reading was required. For many years all boys were expected to read the same books from a small list for each form. That system had the virtue of imposing upon an entire class a common background; English classes could then draw upon that background during the school year. On the other hand, the system had defects; a list small enough for an English syllabus excluded worthy books, and clever student could evade the annoyance of assigned reading with ease.

We no longer require summer reading; instead, we appeal to good sense when we suggest that a summer spent without good reading is a summer partly wasted. Summers out of school provide a leisure to read that later years too often deny. Too much genius and beauty reside in the literature of this age and of past ages to be left unread and unemployed.

Any lover of books scanning any short reading list will be astonished at the breadth of its omissions and the eccentricity of its selections. To defend the list that follows, we can only state our principles of inclusion and ask pardon for sins of omission and commission. Our principles are these: the books must stand a good chance of surviving an encounter with the tastes of today's students; the list must offer enough variety to serve the broad-minded and the eclectic; and finally, the books must have generally recognized merit.

While we rejoice in their relevance, we do not seek to propagate the classics during the summer, trusting to winters and to time. We do not use

---

*Reprinted with permission of St. Albans Upper School, Washington, D.C.

summer reading to provide background for forthcoming courses or to transmit the common cultural heritage, the vital texts of which are seldom agreed upon.

These books are set forth in the hope that students will find them stimulating and enjoyable, that students will, through even casual reading, draw closer to a sense of place, of time, of history, of balance, closer to the life of the imagination. We require no set number. "The more the better" seems a sound enough principle.

FORMS III AND IV

Agee, James. *A Death in the Family*. The bittersweet tale of a family coping with the untimely death of a husband and father.

*Angelou, Maya. *I Know Why the Caged Bird Sings*. An autobiography of a young girl—black, poor, and gifted—growing up in segregated America.

*Baker, Russell. *Growing Up*. Chronicles the writer's beginnings in the Depression, his family life and early career as a journalist.

Baldwin, James, *The Fire Next Time*. The personal story of James Baldwin growing up in Harlem and an examination of race relations in America.

Beagle, Peter. *A Fine and Private Place*. A sweet fantasy about life and love after death.

Conrad, Joseph. *Victory*. Written in an atypically lucid style, a terrific adventure story set in the Dutch East Indies. Evil eventually invades an idyll.

Dixon, Steven. *Garbage*. Kafka and pulp fiction meet in the story of a small-time bar owner threatened by mobsters—or is he?

Eco, Umberto. *The Name of the Rose*. A medieval murder mystery that follows the conventions of detective fiction; the story raises contemporary moral and intellectual questions and gives a provocative look at a historical period.

*Feinstein, John. *A Civil War*. A top sports journalist vividly recounts one year (1995) of the Army–Navy football rivalry,

*Frank, Anne. *The Diary of Anne Frank*. An account of a young girl and her family hiding from the Nazis in Amsterdam during World War II.

Gaines, Ernest. *A Lesson before Dying*. An award-winning coming-of-age story set in the segregated South.

Greene, Graham. *The Human Factor*. A well-designed spy/espionage novel set in England during the height of the Cold War.

---

*Nonfiction

*Gunther, John. *Death Be Not Proud*. A father's powerful story of his son's courageous battle against cancer.

*Herrigel, Eugen. *Zen in the Art of Archery*. A Western philosopher studies archery in Japan as a way of seeking Zen enlightenment.

Hersey, John. *Hiroshima*. Eyewitness accounts of Hiroshima's destruction by the atomic bomb.

Johnson, Charles. *Middle Passage*. A classic sea saga about a newly freed slave who attempts to escape his Louisiana debts by stowing away on the first available ship.

*Junger, Sebastian. *The Perfect Storm*. A true account of a terrible storm in 1991, which wrecked a commercial fishing boat and killed its crew.

Klllins, John Oliver. *Youngblood*. Chronicles the lives of an African-American family and their friends in Crossroads, Georgia, from the turn of the century to the Great Depression.

*Kingston, Maxine Hong. *China Men*. Patriarchal forebears and succeeding generations journey from homelands to the Gold Mountain, examining the relationship between China and the United States, as well as between men and women.

*Kingston, Maxine Hong. *The Woman Warrior*. An account of growing up Chinese-American in California.

*Krakauer, John. *Into Thin Air*. A suspenseful first-person account of the 1996 ascent of Mt. Everest that left ten dead.

Lee, Harper. *To Kill a Mockingbird*. Classic coming-of-age novel.

*Malcolm X. *The Autobiography of Malcolm X*. A modern classic that traces the struggle for black Identity, as told to Alex Haley.

Martin, Valerie. *Mary Reilly*. The story of Dr. Jekyll and Mr. Hyde, told by a young housemaid in Dr. Jekyll's house; terrific companion piece to the original.

*McPhee, John. *Levels of the Game*. A great non-fiction writer, profiles tennis players Arthur Ashe and Clark Graebner, whose backgrounds, styles, and personalities embody very different levels of play and understanding.

Miller, Walter. *Canticle for Lebowitz*. Many would argue that this post-Armageddon novel is the best science fiction work of the twentieth century.

Moore, Lorrie. *Who Will Run the Frog Hospital*. A middle-aged woman reflects on the summer of her fifteenth year.

Morrison, Toni. *Song of Solomon*. A young man strikes out alone, drawn away from his home in the South by the promise of buried gold, adventure, and the truth of his own family's buried heritage.

Orwell, George. *Animal Farm*. An allegorical satire of totalitarianism, in this instance, communism.

Paton, Alan. *Cry, the Beloved Country*. A lyrical novel, which explores the complications and intricacies of race and personal relations in apartheid-era South Africa.

Preston, Richard. *The Hot Zone*. The nation's capital threatened by a potentially catastrophic biological accident.

Rosengarten, Theodore. *All God's Dangers: The Life of Nate* Shaw. A heroic African-American sharecropper's tale of his eighty-eight-year saga of surviving all God's dangers—from the wrath of nature to the wrath of prejudice.

*Saltzman, Mark. *Iron and Silk*. An American college grad journeys to mainland China to teach English and learn martial arts.

Shaara, Michael. *The Killer Angels*. A Civil War narrative that focuses on the turning point of the war—Gettysburg.

Steinbeck, John. *Travels with Charley*. Steinbeck on the road with dog Charley, traveling across America.

Taylor, Robert Lewis. *The Travels of Jamie McPheeters*. A tale full of humor and adventure, narrated by a fourteen-year-old boy crossing the U. S. with his father in a wagon train during the Gold Rush.

Theroux, Paul. *The Mosquito Coast*. Dark and often funny adventure story narrated by the fifteen-year-old son of a counter-culture father who takes his family to live in the jungle of an unnamed Central American country.

Tolkien, J. R. R. *The Lord of the Rings*. Any part of the classic fantasy series deserves a read.

Wiesel, Elie. *The Accident* or *Dawn*. Two gripping novellas about the Holocaust.

White, T. H. *The Once and Future King*. A wonderful retelling of the King Arthur legend by a writer whose awareness of the totalitarian threat posed by Hitler adds a dimension to the story of how idealistic heroes are eventually brought to grief by evil; four volumes, best read separately.

Wright, Richard. *Native Son*. The fierce story of Bigger Thomas, in the privileged white world of Chicago, and the brutal murder of a white woman.

FORMS V AND VI

*Albom, Mitch. *Tuesdays with Morrie*. A poignant chronicle of a college professor's slow struggle with his terminal illness, narrated by his former student.

*Allende, Isabel. *Paula*. The story of the death of the author's daughter, told in an unsentimental and transforming fashion.

Benet, Stephen Vincent. *The Devil and Daniel Webster*. Marvelous American legend of folk hero Daniel Webster and his contest with the devil. Makes New Hampshire more famous than do the primaries.

*Besieger, H. G. *Friday Night Lights*. A non-fiction account of high-school football in pigskin-crazed Texas that examines class, race, and gender.

Boulle, Pierre. *The Bridge over River Kwai.* Superb characterizations and themes in the clash between a perfectionist British colonel and the Japanese commandant of a World War II prisoner-of-war camp.

Calvino, Italo. *Invisible Cities.* A fanciful collection: After his return, Marco Polo is invited by Kublai Khan to describe the cities Polo has visited; in the exchange, each discovers a way of creating "something perfect out of chaos."

Chappell, Fred. *I Am One of You Forever.* The coming-of-age story of a young boy who creates and populates a vivid imaginative world in western North Carolina.

Chesnutt, Charles. *The Colonel's Dream.* A novel critically exploring the convict lease system in the South of the early twentieth century.

Chesnutt, Charles. *The Conjure Woman.* A story about the terrible anti-Negro riot that occurred in Wilmington, North Carolina, in 1901.

Clemens, Samuel (Mark Twain). *Huckleberry Finn.* A marvelous collection of humor, narrative, theme, and characterizations as Huck and Jim, the escaped slave, travel down the river with or without the rogues and fools of the period; a novel to be read and reread at different ages.

Conrad, Joseph. *The Secret Agent.* Humor and irony make for an enjoyable narrative about incompetent anarchists in Victorian England.

Conroy, Pat. *Lords of Discipline.* An exploration of friendship and masculinity in the South.

Cooper, James Fenimore. *The Last of the Mohicans.* Nineteenth-century American novel with romantic narration and characterization, set in New York State.

Davies, Robertson. *Fifth Business.* A funny, well-crafted bildungsroman by Canada's most prominent contemporary novelist.

Doctorow, E. L. *Ragtime.* A vandalized automobile is the catalyst for a fictional account of early twentieth-century America and one man's insistence on social justice.

Duncan, David. *The Brothers K.* A big, entertaining novel about baseball, religious faith, and the conflicts that challenge the four Chance brothers.

Endo, Shusaku. *Silence.* An intense historical novel about a Jesuit's missionary efforts in Japan.

*Epstein, Joseph. *A Line out for a Walk: Familiar Essays.* Witty and memorable observations from the best informal essayist in America today.

Exley, Frederick. *A Fan's Notes.* Hilarious and moving novel about a man's acceptance that he is a fan, not a star.

Fast, Howard. *April Morning.* The morning and the day of the Battle of Lexington and the effect on a boy of his encounter with war and death.

Fitzgerald, F. Scott. *This Side of Paradise.* Thinly veiled autobiographical novel of growing up, college at Princeton, and beyond.

Gaines, Ernest. *A Gathering of Old Men*. Perhaps the author's finest book, a work that gives voice to a group of old Southern black men and their response to racially motivated violence.

Greene, Graham. *A Burnt-Out Case*. Superb study of a successful architect whose interest in life has burned out but who regains part of himself in an African leprosy mission.

Hammett, Dashiell. *The Maltese Falcon*. The most famous hard-boiled detective novel. Also a must-see movie.

Heller, Joseph. *Catch-22*. World War II classic that wickedly satirizes military life, war, government policies, and a wide range of human follies.

Hemingway, Ernest. *A Farewell to Arms*. World War I novel about a disillusioned American ambulance lieutenant, who falls in love with an English nurse taking care of him while he is wounded, and they are happy—for a while.

Hemingway, Ernest. *In Our Time*. Terse, hard short stories whose style revolutionized American literature.

Hersey, John. *A Single Pebble*. Sensitive story of the education of a young engineer who comes to understand the values of Chinese life on his trip up the Yangtse River.

Hoban, Russell. *Riddley Walker*. Set in a dark, treacherous future, this novel, described by its author as "difficult, dangerous and harrowing," is also experimental, ambitious, and memorable, one of the great novels of the post–WWII period.

Hunt, Irene. *Across Five Aprils*. A Civil War story about the relationship between brothers and those fighting on opposing sides.

Jones, Madison. *A Cry of Absence*. After a racially charged and particularly violent crime stuns a small Southern town, a mother and brother cope with the knowledge that they harbor one of the murderers.

Kerouac, Jack. *On the Road*. The most famous of the literary efforts left to posterity by the "beat generation."

Keyes, Daniel. *Flowers for Algernon*. A moving novel about a gentle, retarded man who is given a superior intelligence for a short time before he lapses into his original state.

Kundera, Milan. *The Unbearable Lightness of Being*. A love story, but much more than that, set in Prague in the days of the Cold War.

Malamud, Bernard. *The Assistant*. An aimless young man of Catholic upbringing confronts and learns from a poor Jewish grocer in this poignant tale of transgression and redemption.

Maugham, Somerset. *Of Human Bondage*. About the growth of a young man who overcomes many problems, reevaluates his aims, and becomes a country doctor.

*McCourt, Frank. *Angela's Ashes*. Memoir of growing up poor in Limerick, Ireland; funny and heartbreaking, awful and inspiring.

McPhee, John. *A Sense of Where You Are*. A splendid account of Bill Bradley's final year at Princeton and his exploits on the basketball court and in the classroom.

Moore, Lorrie. *Who Will Run the Frog Hospital*. A middle-aged woman reflects on the summer of her fifteenth year.

Morrison, Toni. *Beloved*. A searing tale about the ghost of a young black girl who is killed to protect her from the cruelty of slavery—a novel by America's most recent Nobel Prize winner.

Morrison, Toni. *Sula*. Two African-American women travel different paths in their search for self-identity.

*Murray, K. M. Elisabeth. *Caught in the Web of Words*. An absorbing biography of James Murray, the first editor of the Oxford English Dictionary.

O'Brien, Tim. *The Things They Carried*. A semi-autobiographical novel that tells, through a variety of distinct voices, the story of a platoon in Vietnam.

*Parks, Gordon. *Voices in the Mirror*. Captivating autobiography of this Renaissance man, a photographer, playwright, musician, author, and Civil Rights leader.

Percy, Walker. *The Moviegoer*. This novel, against a background of New Orleans in Mardi Gras, follows the progress of a twenty-nine-year-old New Orleans stockbroker, addicted to movies, in his search for what is valuable in life, and the help he provides to a saddened, anxious young woman.

Rushdie, Salman. *The Satanic Verses*. Set in modern London, a book that abounds in Joycean richness and magic realism.

*Sacks, Oliver. *Awakenings*. A heart-wrenching story about patients who recover from years of sleeping sickness.

Salinger, J. D. *Nine Stories*. Entertaining, well-written stories by a modern master.

*Sobel, Dava. *Longitude*. One man saves thousands of lives by solving naval navigation's "longitude problem."

Steinbeck, John. *The Grapes of Wrath*. Steinbeck's greatest and perhaps the greatest novel of America in the Thirties, a chronicle of a family of displaced Oakies traveling from Oklahoma to California. Also an Academy Award winning film.

Updike, John. *Rabbit Run*. Harry "Rabbit" Angstrom strives in vain to recapture his former basketball glory.

Updike, John. *The Centaur*. The story of a small-town Pennsylvania boy's relationship with his father, with parallels drawn from Greek myth.

Vonnegut, Kurt, Jr. *Slaughterhouse-Five*. An unconventional anti-war novel using the experiences of an American soldier who survived the fire bombing of Dresden.

Warren, Robert Penn. *All the King's Men*. A masterpiece about politics, corruption, infidelity, and much more, set in Huey Long's Louisiana.

Waugh, Evelyn. *Brideshead Revisited*. Waugh's lyrical chronicle of grace, redemption, and damnation within a decaying aristocracy in fractured, post-war England.

*Wiesel, Elie. *Night*. A terrifying account of the death camp the author survived as a child.

Welty, Eudora. *Delta Wedding*. Covers the activities of a large Southern family on their Mississippi plantation, waiting for the wedding of one of their members—evocative of the mood and pace of Southern life.

*Wolfe, Tom. *The Right Stuff*. A highly fictionalized and very entertaining account of America's first astronauts.

Wolfe, Thomas. *Look Homeward, Angel*. An autobiographical novel about a young man whose capacity to love is smothered by family and environment.

Selected Bibliography

Apple, Michael W. "Whose Knowledge Do We Teach?" *Focus in Change,* no. 6. Madison, Wisc.: National Center for Effective Schools Research and Development, 1992.

Aronowitz, Stanley. *False Promises: The Shaping of Working Class Consciousness.* Durham, N.C.: Duke University Press, 1992.

Anderson, Richard C., et al. *Becoming a Nation of Readers: The Report of the Commission on Reading.* Washington, D.C.: National Institute of Education, U.S. Department of Education, 1984.

Bacharach, Samuel B., Scott C. Bauer, and Joseph B. Shedd. *The Learning Workplace: The Conditions and Resources of Teaching.* Ithaca, N.Y.: OAP, 1986 (ERIC ED 279-614).

Barker, Roger G., and Paul V. Gump. *Big School, Small School: High School Size and Student Behavior.* Boulder, Colo.: Westview, 1990.

Bennett, William J., and Chester E. Finn Jr. "The Real Improvement in Texas Schools." *New York Times*, October 27, 2000.

Berger, Allen, and H. Alan Robinson. *Secondary School Reading.* Urbana: ERIC Clearinghouse on Reading and Communication,1982.

Berne, Robert, and Dolores Fernandez. *Perform or Perish: Recommendations of the Advisory Council to the New York State Board of Regents Subcommittee on Low-Performing Schools,* Interim Report. Albany: New York State Education Department, 1994.

Board of Education of the City of New York. "Agreement between the Board of Education of the City of New York and United Federation of Teachers—Local 2, American Federation of Teachers, AFL-CIO, Covering Teachers, October 16, 1995–November 15, 2000."

Boyer, Ernest. *High School: A Report on Secondary Education in America.* New York: Harper & Row, 1983.

281

Brandt, Deborah. *The Sponsors of Literacy*. Albany, N.Y.: National Research Center on English Learning and Achievement, 1997. (ERIC 412 537) Also available online: http://cela.albany.edu/sponsor/sponsor.html.

Burr, Elizabeth, et al. *Crucial Issues in California Education 2000: Are Reform Pieces Fitting Together?* Berkeley: Policy Analysis for California Education, 2000.

Carlson, Dennis. *Teachers and Crisis: Urban School Reform and Teachers' Work Culture*. New York: Routledge, 1992.

Carroll, John B., and Jeanne S. Chall. *Toward a Literate Society: The Report of the Committee on Reading of the National Academy of Education*. New York: McGraw-Hill, 1975.

Chall, Jeanne S. *Learning to Read: The Great Debate*. New York: McGraw-Hill, 1967.

Chall, Jeanne S., Vicki A. Jacobs, and Luke E. Baldwin. *The Reading Crisis: Why Poor Children Fall Behind*. Cambridge, Mass.: Harvard University Press, 1990.

Chicago Tribune. *Chicago Schools: Worst in America*. Chicago: Author, 1988.

Chubb, John E., and Terry M. Moe. *Politics, Markets and America's Schools*. Washington, D.C.: Brookings Institution, 1990.

Cline, Ruth K. J., and George L. Kretke. "An Evaluation of Long-term SSR in the Junior High School." *Journal of Reading* 23, no. 6 (March 1980).

Coalition of Essential Schools. "Prospectus" (October 1988), 6.

Coleman, James S., et al. *Equality of Educational Opportunity*. Washington, D.C.: U.S. Government Printing Office, 1966.

Conlan, Timothy J. *New Federalism: Inter Governmental Reform from Nixon to Reagan*. Washington, D.C.: Brookings Institution, 1988.

Cookson, Peter, Jr., and Caroline Hodges Persell. *Preparing for Power: America's Elite Boarding Schools*. New York: Basic Books, 1985.

Corcoran, Thomas B., Lisa J. Walker, and J. Lynne White. *Working in Urban Schools*. Washington, D.C.: Institute for Educational Leadership, 1988.

Csikszentmihalyi, Mihaly. "Literacy and Intrinsic Motivation." *Daedulus* (Spring 1990).

Cunningham, Annie E., and Keith E. Stanovich. "What Reading Does for the Mind." *American Educator* (Spring/Summer 1998).

Damon, William. "Reconciling the Literacies of Generations." *Daedalus* 119, no. 2 (Spring 1990): 15–32.

Educational Policy Research Center. *Patterns in ESEA Title I Reading Achievement*. Research Report EPRC 4537-12. Menlo Park, Calif.: Stanford Research Institute, 1976.

Educational Priorities Panel. *School Libraries . . . No Reading Allowed.* New York: Author, May 1985.

Elmore, Richard F. "The Limits of 'Change.'" *Harvard Education Letter Research Online* (January/February 2002). Available at www.edletter.org/current/limitsofchange.shtml.

———. "Unwarranted Intrusion." *Education Next* (Spring 2002). Available at www.educationnext.org/20021/30.html.

Entwisle, Doris R., and Karl L. Alexander. "Winter Setback: The Racial Composition of Schools and Learning to Read." *American Sociological Review* 59, no. 3 (June 1994).

Entwisle, Doris R., Karl L. Alexander, and Linda Steffel Olson. "Summer Learning and Home Environment." In *A Nation at Risk: Preserving Public Education as an Engine for Social Mobility,* ed. Richard D. Kahlenberg. New York: Century Foundation, 2000.

Fader, Daniel N. *Hooked on Books.* New York: Berkeley, 1966.

———. *The Naked Children.* New York: Macmillan, 1971.

Feur, Alan. "Prosecutor Heads Inquiry into Politics of Court Post." *New York Times,* February 1, 2000.

Finn, Chester E., Jr., et al., eds. *Against Mediocrity: The Humanities in America's High Schools.* New York: Holmes & Meier, 1984.

Fitzgerald, Frances. *America Revisited.* Boston: Little, Brown, 1979.

Foertsch, Mary A. *Reading In and Out of School: Factors Influencing the Literacy Achievement of American Students in Grades 4, 8, and 12 in 1988 and 1990.* Washington, D.C.: Office of Educational Research and Improvement, 1992.

Fruchter, Norman. "Needed: A New Exchange Relationship between Students and Schools." *Social Policy* (Summer 1988): 5–8.

Gagnon, Paul. *Democracy's Half Told Story: What American Textbooks Should Add.* Washington, D.C.: American Federation of Teachers, 1989.

Gampert, Richard D. *A Follow-Up Study of the 1982–83 Promotional Gates Students.* Office of Educational Assessment Evaluation. New York: New York City Board of Education, 1983 (ERIC Document 303 556).

Gardner, John. *The Art of Fiction.* New York: Vintage, 1985.

Goodlad, John I. *A Place Called School: Prospects for the Future.* New York: McGraw-Hill, 1984.

———. "Producing Teachers Who Understand, Believe, and Care." *Education Week,* February 5, 1997, p. 48.

Goodman, K. S. "Behind the Eye: What Happens in Reading." In *Theoretical Models and Processes of Reading,* ed. Harry Singer and Robert B. Ruddell. Newark, Del.: International Reading Association, 1971.

———. "Reading: A Psycholinguistic Guessing Game." In *Theoretical Models and Processes of Reading*, ed. Harry Singer and Robert B. Ruddell. Newark, Del.: International Reading Association, 1971.

Goodnough, Abby. "Teachers Agree to a New Plan for 100 Extra Minutes a Week." *New York Times,* October 1, 2002.

Harding, Vincent. *Hope and History: Why We Must Share the Story of the Movement.* Maryknoll, N.Y.: Orbis, 1991.

Hargreaves, Andy. *Changing Teachers, Changing Times: Teachers' Work and Culture in the Postmodern Age.* New York: Teachers College Press, 1994.

Hess, G. Alfred, Jr., and James L. Greer. *Bending the Twig: The Elementary Years and Dropout Rates in the Chicago Public Schools.* Chicago: Chicago Panel on Public School Policy and Finance, July 30, 1987.

Hirschman, Albert O. *Exit, Voice, and Loyalty.* Cambridge, Mass.: Harvard University Press, 1970.

Institute for Educational Leadership. *Supporting Leaders for Tomorrow—Working in the D.C. Public Schools: A Survey of Teacher Working Conditions in the District of Columbia Public Schools.* Washington, D.C.: Author, 1989.

Jencks, Christopher, and Meredith Phillips, eds. *The Black–White Test Score Gap.* Washington, D.C: Brookings Institution, 1998.

Kahlenberg, Richard D., ed. *A Notion at Risk-Preserving Public Education as an Engine for Social Mobility.* New York: Century Foundation Press, 2000.

Katznelson, Ira. *City Trenches: Urban Politics and Patterning of Class in the United States.* New York: Pantheon, 1981.

King, Caryn M. "Creating a Literate Environment for Learning Social Studies Content" (ERIC ED 348654).

Klein, Stephen P., Laura S. Hamilton, et al. *What Do Test Scores in Texas Tell Us?* Santa Monica, Calif.: RAND Corporation, 2000.

Lapp, M. S., W. S. Grigg, and B. S.-H. Tay-Lim. *The Nation's Report Card: U.S. History 2001.* NCES 2002-483. Washington, D.C.: U.S. Department of Education, National Center for Educational Statistics, 2002.

Lewis, Neil A. "Union Warns Fernandez on Proposals." *New York Times*, September 29, 1989, p. B3.

Lloyd, Dee Norman. "Prediction of School Failure from Third-Grade Data." *Educational and Psychological Measurement* 38 (1978).

Lortie, Dan C. *Schoolteacher: A Sociological Study.* Chicago: University of Chicago Press, 1975.

Manning-Dowd, Alice. "The Effectiveness of SSR: A Review of the Research" ERIC document ED 276-970. 1985.

Marshall, Ray, and Marc Tucker. *Thinking for a Living: Education and the Wealth of Nations.* New York: Basic Books, 1992.

McCracken, Robert A. "Initiating Sustained Silent Reading." *Journal of Reading* 14, no. 8 (May 1971).

McPartland, James. "Older Students Also Need Major Federal Compensatory Education Resources." Paper presented at the Title I: Seizing the Opportunity Conference Sponsored by the Civil Rights Project, Harvard University and Citizens' Commission on Civil Rights, Washington, D.C., September 18, 1998. Available at www.law.harvard.edu/civilrights/conferences/title/drafts/mcpartland.html.

Meek, Margaret. *On Being Literate*. Portsmouth, N.H.: Heinemann, 1992.

Meier, Deborah. *The Power of Their Ideas*. Boston: Beacon, 1995.

Mintz, John. "An Education Miracle or Mirage?" *Washington Post*, April 21, 2000, p. A1.

Mork, Theodore. "Sustained Silent Reading in the Classroom." *Reading Teacher* 25, no. 5 (February 1972): 438–40.

Mosconi, Angela, and Lawrence Goodman, "Crew Shapes Up for Tenure Battle with Principals." *New York Post*, April 27, 1996, p. 4.

Mosteller, Frederick, and Daniel P. Moynihan, eds. *On Equality of Educational Opportunity: Papers Deriving from the Harvard University Faculty Seminar on the Coleman Report*. New York: Vintage, 1972.

National Association of State Boards of Education. *Rethinking Curriculum: A Call for Fundamental Reform*. Washington, D.C.: Author, 1988.

National Center for Educational Statistics. *NAEP 1992 Reading Report Card for the Nation and the States*. Washington, D.C.: U.S. Department of Education, 1993.

———. *National Assessment of Educational Progress. Learning to Read in Our Nation's Schools: Instruction and Achievement in 1988 at Grades 4, 8, and 12*. Washington, D.C.: U.S. Department of Education, 1990.

National Center for Effective Schools Research Development. *Textbooks: What's at Stake*. Madison, Wisc.: National Center for Effective Schools, 1992.

National Institute for Educational Research of Japan. *The Teaching Materials System in Japan*. Tokyo: Author, May 1984.

New York State Education Department. The reports of this agency are one of the largest windows into the school lives, and to some extent, the intellectual lives of teenagers in cities such as New York. Write Office of New York City Field Services at 55 Hanson Place, Brooklyn, N.Y. 11217.

Newfield, Jack, and Paul Du Brul. *The Permanent Government: Who Really Rules New York?* New York: Pilgrim, 1981.

Newfield, Jack, et al. "Kings County Princes, Party Faithful Find Favor in Surrogate's Court." *New York Post*, November 9, 1997.

Office of Educational Assessment. *High School Attendance Improvement Dropout Prevention (A.I.D.P.) Program, 1986–1987: End of Year Report*. New York: New York City Board of Education, 1987.

Ogbu, John U. "Minority Status and Literacy in Comparative Perspective." *Daedulus* (Spring 1990).

Pate-Bain, Helen, et al. *The Student/Teacher Achievement Ratio (STAR) Project: STAR Follow-up Studies, 1996–1997.* Lebanon, Tenn.: Health and Education Research Operative Services, 1997.

Public Education Association. *Effective Dropout Prevention: An Analysis of the 1985–86 Program in New York City.* New York: Author, 1986.

Ralph, John, and James Crouse. *Reading and Mathematics Achievement: Growth in High School, Issue Brief.* Washington, D.C.: National Center for Education Statistics, 1997 (ERIC ED-415-275).

Resnick, Daniel P. "Historical Perspectives on Literacy and Schooling." *Daedalus* 119, no. 2 (Spring 1990): 15–32.

Riddle, Wayne Clifton. *Expenditures in Pubic School Districts: Why Do They Differ?* Washington, D.C.: Congressional Research Service, Library of Congress, 1990.

Rivlin, Alice M. *Systematic Thinking for Social Action.* Washington, D.C.: Brookings Institution, 1971.

Rohlen, Thomas P. *Japan's High Schools.* Berkeley: University of California Press, 1983.

Rosenholtz, Susan J., and Carl Simpson. "Workplace Conditions and the Rise and Fall of Teachers' Commitment." *Sociology of Education* 63, issue 4 (October 1990): 241–57.

Rothman, Robert. "Carnegie 'Units' Should Go, Says Study by Boards, Views Curriculum as Schools' 'Fatal Flaw.'" *Education Week*, November, 2, 1988, p. 18.

Rothstein, Richard. "Both Sides Are Right in Reading Wars." *New York Times*, September 5, 2001, p. A-17.

Sachar, Emily. *Shut Up and Let the Lady Teach: A Teacher's Year in a Public School.* New York: Poseidon, 1991.

Salaman, Shelley K. "The Effectiveness of Sustained Silent Reading at the Secondary Level." In *Research on Reading in Secondary Schools: A Semi-Annual Report,* ed. Patricia L. Anders. Monograph no. 6. Tucson: Reading Department, College of Education, University of Arizona, 1980.

Schlesinger, Arthur M. *The Disuniting of America: Reflections on a Multicultural Society.* New York: Norton, 1992.

Shin, Paul H. B., Jon Sorensen, and Laura Williams, "Rudy Seeks to Ax Principal Tenure." *Daily News*, September 16, 1997, p. 10.

Sizer, Theodore. *Horace's Compromise: The Dilemma of the American High School.* Boston: Houghton Mifflin, 1984.

Stanovich, Keith E., and Anne E. Cunningham. "Where Does Knowledge Come From? Specific Associations between Print Exposure and Information Acquisition." *Journal of Educational Psychology* 85, no. 2 (June 1993): 224.

———. "Studying the Consequences of Literacy within a Literate Society: The Cognitive Correlates of Print Exposure." *Memory and Cognition* 20 (1992): 51–68.

Singer, Harry, and Robert B. Ruddell, eds. *Theoretical Models and Processes of Reading.* Newark, Del.: International Reading Association, 1976.

Smith, Frank. *Psycholinguistics and Reading.* New York: Holt, Rinehart & Winston, 1973.

———. *Understanding Reading: A Psycholinguistic Analysis of Reading and Learning to Read.* New York: Holt, Rinehart & Winston, 1971.

Strauss, Anselm, and Juliet Corbin. *Basics of Qualitative Research.* Newbury Park, Calif.: Sage, 1991.

Taylor, Dianne L., and Ira E. Bogotch. "Teacher Working Conditions and School Reform: A Descriptive Analysis." Paper presented at the annual meeting of the Southwest Educational Research Association, January 19, 1992 (ERIC document ED357473).

Tapp, Gary W. *Southern Exposure: The South's Achilles Heel: Education Must Improve to Sustain Economic Growth.* Atlanta: Robinson-Humphrey, 1990.

Thomas, Thomas C., and Sol H. Pelavin. *Patterns in ESEA Title I Reading Achievement.* Palo Alto Educational Policy Research Center, SRI Project 4537. Menlo Park, Calif.: Stanford Research Institute, 1976.

Tyack, David, Robert Lowe, and Elisabeth Hansot. *Public Schools in Hard Times: The Great Depression and Recent Years.* Cambridge, Mass.: Harvard University Press, 1984.

U.S. Department of Education. *Prospects: The Congressionally Mandated Study of Educational Growth and Opportunity—The Interim Report.* Washington, D.C.: Author, 1993.

———. *Reinventing Chapter 1: The Current Chapter 1 Program and New Directions—Final Report to the National Assessment of the Chapter 1 Program.* Washington, D.C.: Author, 1993.

Useem, Elizabeth L. *Low Tech Education in a High Tech World: Corporations and Classrooms in the New Information Society.* New York: Free Press, 1986.

Vaughan, Joseph L., Jr., and Patricia L. Anders, *Research on Reading in Secondary Schools.* Monograph Number 5. Tempe: University of Arizona, 1980.

Viadero, Debra. "Students' Reading Skills Fall Short, NAEP Data Find—Achievement Gap for Blacks Remains Wide." *Education Week,* September 22, 1993.

Worthy, Jo, Megan Moorman, and Margo Turner. "What Johnny Likes to Read Is Hard to Find in School." *Reading Research Quarterly* 34, no. 1 (1999).

Index

About the Author

As a writing instructor in New York City, Jim McCabe saw the damage done when teenagers arrived in college classrooms unprepared for higher education and without much enthusiasm for books and reading. He now lives with his wife and three daughters outside Washington, D.C., and works as a consultant in faculty development in the Center for Teaching Excellence at American University.